FINALLY, FOREVER FREE

FINALLY, FOREVER FREE

Tammy Thies

Founder and Executive Director

Compiled and Edited by Verena Rose

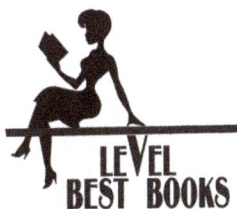

LEVEL
BEST BOOKS

First published by Level Best Books 2020

Copyright © 2020 by Tammy Thies

Tammy Thies asserts the moral right to be identified as the author of this work.

Author Photo Credit: The Wildcat Sanctuary

Editor Photo Credit: Iden Ford

First edition

ISBN: 978-1-953789-00-6

Cover art by Level Best Productions

Dedication

*To the animals who sacrificed their wild lives
to teach us the most important lesson of all,
compassion,
I dedicate this book.*

TABLE OF CONTENTS

Introduction

Over 20 years ago, I rescued my first wild cat. My mission to take in and rescue any wild cat in need, to provide them a better life, began.

But I never planned for all the losses I would experience. At the time, I did not understand the impact saying goodbye would have on me personally, our staff, and our supporters.

I once read the loss you feel today is only mirrored by the love you felt when they were here. I would never trade loving each and every one of my rescued friends. Over the years, writing their memorials has helped me cope with the difficulty of losing them, one by one.

I did not want each of these rescued cats' lives to have been in vain. Many came from abusive and neglectful situations. Others were exploited and some given up because they did not act like a household pet.

I wanted their stories to live on. Not only to honor them, but also so people would care enough to prevent their stories from happening to other animals.

As you read the memorials, you'll notice I do not focus only on the difficult histories they had. I also share their amazing capacity for forgiveness, and their gift of resiliency. Every part of their story needs to be shared and each part has a lesson.

Just as they are each individuals with unique personalities, they also share a common bond. They are all part of the big cat crisis. The big cat crisis contributes to the surplus of wild cats in captivity, often in substandard conditions, while also negatively impacting their ancestors in the wild.

It's a profit-driven industry where big cats are used for entertainment, cub petting and selfies, kept as pets, bred for the color of their coat, or hybridized to create a new designer pet. All of this is to the benefit of the human, to the detriment of the animals.

Through their stories, I invite you to help create a world where wild animals are respected and there is an end to the big cat crisis.

Evolution of The Wildcat Sanctuary—How the Sanctuary Began

"If I only make a fraction of the impact that Sampson and the other cats have made on me, then I am very blessed."

Days like this are when I realize how fast time flies and how special each moment is. Today, I'm spending a few of the last days with Sampson, the caracal.

At 17, he's spent his entire life here at The Wildcat Sanctuary. He was our second resident and I remember him being a little ball of red fur and fire, hissing non-stop.

Over the years, we became very close and he was the most easygoing caracal anyone had ever met. His best friend, Cleo, the serval, was the first resident to call TWS home.

Caracal Sampson with Serval Cleo

Seventeen years has gone fast. I feel like it's the end of an era. The original cats have been here from the beginning, since I had the first crazy notion that I wanted to make a difference in the lives of animals, but had no idea how I was going to do that.

A day doesn't go by that I'm not asked "How did you start the Sanctuary?" Some of you have been on this journey from our inception in Atlanta. Others have joined the cause once you heard about our first tigress Meme. Others recently joined. Thank you to each and every one of you who has made mine and so many cats' rescues possible.

As a young girl, I was always eager—eager to do as much as I could in as little time as possible. Some would say I haven't changed much. In high school, I started attending college when I was just 16.

After high school, I double majored in marketing and advertising, graduating in 3-1/2 years while holding down a job. I knew I wanted to work my way up the corporate ladder as fast as possible in a creative advertising agency.

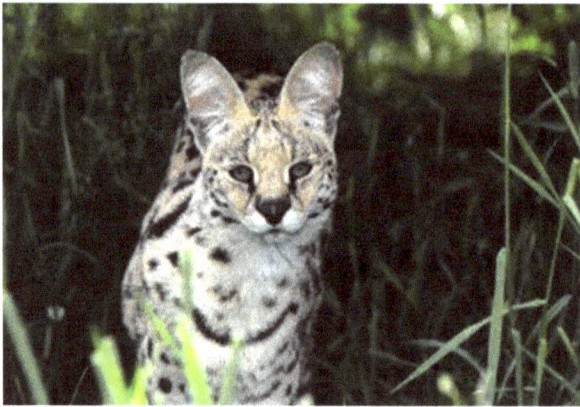

I worked for a few smaller agencies before being recruited to The Coca-Cola Company in Atlanta. I was the youngest in their marketing department and the first to be hired without a Masters Degree.

Later in my career, I worked for many international, high profile companies, too.

Cleo, the serval

I was introduced to exotic cats during my work in advertising and on photo shoots. On one particular shoot, there were two young Bengal tiger cubs named Titan and Tango. At first I was smitten, like everyone else. How cute and adorable they were. The cubs were on leashes, being pulled in many directions. They started screaming when they got tired, but their job was not over, so the trainer kept redirecting them to stay on cue.

After that, I decided to volunteer for a few organizations only to find out they were breeding and selling. **Each time I volunteered, a favorite animal would be gone and a new one would appear.** I never got straight answers. Once, an owner wanted to prove to me he did nothing wrong and asked me to accompany him to pick up a baby cougar.

What I saw that day, I'll never forget. Metal corn cribs cut in half, turned on their side to create an 8 x 12 space no higher than 5 feet at the tallest point. On one side was a severely scarred leopard with fur missing and flattened feet due to a declaw. The owner said the leopard had been in the house when she was younger and been burned by boiling water.

I looked to the right and tears welled up in my eyes. There was the male lion I'd loved so much, that I'd volunteered to care for at the other facility. He'd been traded for the cougar kitten we were picking up today. He could barely turn around in the small space, his face was bloody from scraping the fence and his paws were raw from the hard surface he paced on. He was a shell of the cat I'd met before.

But that wasn't the worst. We went into a pole building that had dozens of small galvanized boxes with round holes. They were no bigger than a copy paper box. The only thing you could see were small eyes peering back from the round air holes. The sound coming from those boxes was deafening—the screaming and hissing, I can still hear it today. I was told they were all bobcats that would be electrocuted for their pelts.

I was physically ill. Incredibly, the owner thought it would somehow bring me peace to see the lion I'd loved so much. To him, this was just a regular business transaction. **That was one of many days I vowed to make a change, but I had no idea how.**

In 1999, I was contacted by a volunteer who was still helping one of the facilities I had volunteered with. She told me one of the adult Bengal tigers would no longer work on a leash and the trainer deemed him dangerous. The tiger's reward for years of service and profit to the trainer was to be killed and taxidermied.

I didn't know how I could help from so far away, but I had to do something. My mom had given me a *Parade* magazine featuring actress **Tippi Hedren** and her big cat preserve. I dialed the number in the article and, to my surprise, Tippi answered the phone.

She committed to finding a sanctuary for the tiger if the trainer would relinquish custody. It had only been hours since the first phone call, but when I called back, the tiger had already been killed and put on dry ice.

Tippi and I were outraged and quickly became friends. She mentored me and introduced me into the sanctuary world for big cats. I incorporated in 1999 to do advocacy and education with wild cats, but quickly learned more sanctuaries were needed.

Tippi told me *"You have to quit thinking you are saving big cats by getting them surrendered and sending them to other sanctuaries, you need to become your own sanctuary."*

So, I did.

It began on two small acres in a suburb of Atlanta, then moved to five acres in the country. In the beginning, we purchased some cats, trying to save them. But soon realized giving the "bad guys" any money at all was only contributing to the problem.

Running a nonprofit was harder than I thought, so I moved back to my roots in Minnesota, bringing our 10 cats to 10 new acres.

After a zoning dispute over a geriatric tiger I rescued named Meme, we moved north to 40 plush acres in Sandstone, MN where we reside today.

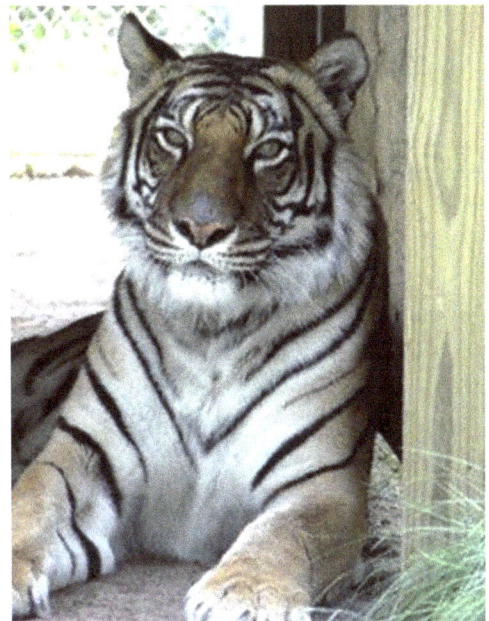

Meme, our first tiger rescue

For the first several years, I worked both a full-time job and also ran the sanctuary. I received no salary from the sanctuary and invested tens of thousands of dollars of my own money to build habitats and care for the animals. This is because it was, and still is, a labor of love.

Over the years, I've acted as Executive Director, animal care director, keeper, construction manager, fundraiser, financial manager, and overnight caretaker of the facility. Often all at the same time. Anybody who has started a business understands the commitment and sacrifice it takes. Starting a sanctuary is no different, except there are 100+ animals whose lives depend on us.

I have made my share of mistakes, but never wavered from the mission. **Life came full circle as it often does.** Just weeks after moving to our property in Sandstone, MN, we were contacted by authorities that Cynthia Gamble had been killed by one of her performing tigers just five miles down the road.

I knew that property all too well. It had been years since I'd been there.

My heart sank when I heard it was Titan and Tango—the two cubs that I'd met years earlier on the photo shoot. They'd been through so much over the years. Another tiger, Lilly, was also on the property and had her own troubled past. All had experienced starvation multiple times. Titan and Tango survived when 30 other cats perished in the barn from dehydration and starvation just a few years earlier.

Tango's fate was sealed by authorities who euthanized him after Gamble's death. Thankfully, The Wildcat Sanctuary was able to offer survivors Lilly and Titan a home. Over a decade had gone by since I first met Tango and Titan.

I made a new vow that no cat should ever have to withstand a decade of abuse and neglect before being rescued. And we would dedicate ourselves to inspiring change to decrease the number of cats needing sanctuary.

Lilly and her love Titan at TWS

Since 2006, with your help, we've:

- Built out 40 acres to provide natural habitats for rescued wild cats
- Added an onsite hospital to treat our ever-growing geriatric population
- Built a talented and compassionate team
- Become leaders for change nationally through our advocacy work and supporting legislation to stop the breeding and ownership of big cats as pets
- Grown our onsite internship program to help educate future animal advocates
- Mentored other sanctuaries to expand the number of homes available to rescued cats
- Acted as placement officers to coordinate national rescues with dozens of big cats needing placement at any given time

What you've helped us accomplish is amazing. I'm thankful for that daily. But still, on days like this, as I experience the last chapter in a very special cat's life, all goes silent. It's as if time stands still—or I just wish it to in order not to have to say goodbye.

I know that Sampson is one of the lucky ones. Arriving at a very young age, he has never known the abuse or neglect many of our other residents have. He has only known love and kindness. But more importantly, he changed our lives.

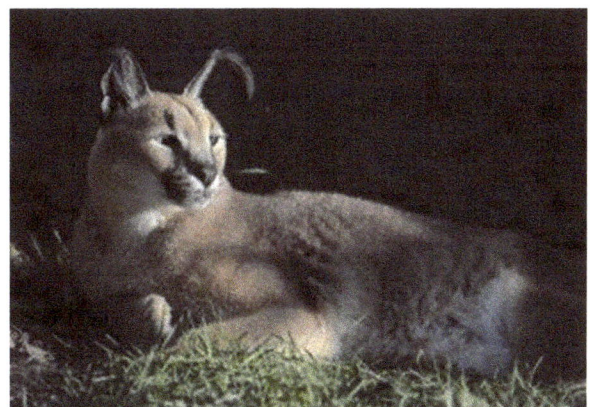

He was one of the first to teach us why wild cats should not be pets, why they need special care and deserve to live wild at heart.

People say I've built a legacy, but it is the cats' legacy. If I only make a fraction of the impact that Sampson and the other cats have made on me, then I'm very blessed. Because their legacy inspires change and only through their legacy can we end the captive wildlife crisis. It is the best way we can honor each and every one of them.

For now, I choose to celebrate the very special days and weeks ahead as Sampson and other founding cats move to the next chapter of life. And with your continued support, we will also start a new chapter here at The Wildcat Sanctuary by welcoming new cats that need refuge who will be just as special as the first to call TWS home.

Thank you for the past, present and future! You have truly made a difference in my life and all that call TWS home.

Tammy Thies, Founder & Executive Director

You can leave your own legacy for the cats:

You can continue to make a big difference in the lives of big cats by including a gift to benefit The Wildcat Sanctuary in your will or living trust. Learn more about this easy way to provide a bright future for wild cats in need at *wildcatsanctuary.org* by calling me at 320-245-6871.

Dealing with Loss— Good Grief

Dealing with Loss

Writing to you usually comes easily to me. I feel like I know each of you and the conversations are natural. So, I couldn't figure out why, when I decided to write an article about dealing with loss and grief, I couldn't get started.

Good Grief

I sat down several times to write, only to find anything else to do. I set timelines that I kept missing. And then I realized, I am in the midst of grieving myself and in the avoidance phase.

With so many losses the past few months, my head and heart hurt. I'm so tired of being sad. I mean really tired—exhausted. But at the same time, I feel guilty if I don't wallow in my feelings of loss for those animals I loved and miss so much.

Rationally, we know loss comes with the territory of rescue. Just as we know welcoming a furry friend into our family will eventually mean we have to one day say goodbye.

It's a cycle we as animal lovers face. It's the price of loving so much. And even though we wouldn't change it for the world, it can be quite a deep hole of despair when you're in it.

So, what is the right way to deal with the grief of losing our animal friends? I wish I had the answer.

The Emotional Roller Coaster

For me personally, it's a range of emotions. I feel saddened that I won't get to see their face once again as I walk through the sanctuary. I feel proud of who they were and that I was blessed to know them. I feel relieved that they're no longer in pain or have to live life in a cage.

But most of all, I often feel failure—like I let them down somehow. Intellectually, I know that's not true.

We have a dedicated and knowledgeable team observing them daily, providing first-rate care alongside our extended vet team.

But as their protector, I wanted to guard them from ever being sick or vulnerable again. And that I couldn't do, especially at the end of their lives.

Our losses at the sanctuary come in waves. And lately—tidal waves. Some we were providing comfort care and knew their end may be near. But others are unexpected and devastate us all. Each takes a piece of our heart.

Experiencing Loss After Loss

Sometimes, we don't get a moment to grieve because another animal or new rescue needs our focus. And other times, we're inconsolable. When we experience loss after loss, we sometimes question the work we do and if it's all worth it.

Some people think it should be easier since we've been in rescue for over 20 years. We've had to say goodbye countless times. But let me tell you, it

isn't. In fact, it can even be harder because all of the losses flood in all at once. And you replay each in your head and heart, over and over.

As you all know from loving one of your own, you get extremely close at the end of life. It's when the critical care happens, the quiet moments, the tears of love and thanks, and the tears of knowing the end is near.

You wrap your heart and soul around them ensuring you make the right decisions for them, while your own heart is breaking.

So as professionals, how do we deal with loss and grief? Just like you.

How Do I Cope?

I write memorials to provide some sense of closure. Caretakers are faced with cleaning out the cat's rooms and habitats—sometimes this is cathartic, and other times unbearable. We cremate our residents and hold a memorial ceremony twice a year. Their ashes are released as a symbol of finally being forever free.

You cry alongside us and show your love and support through their memorial plaques and rocks. We all feel the loss, and yet we all find strength to welcome another.

And loss is not only at the Sanctuary. Just like you, each of us also has furry ones at home. In the past few years alone,

I've had to say goodbye to four geriatric dogs and my first ever Bengal cat. I lose my Executive Director hat with my family pets. And just like you, I'm their mom/dad and guardian. And the losses cut a little deeper.

I wish I had an answer about how to make this all easier, but the truth is, I just don't. I think it needs to be this hard, because we gave our entire hearts to them.

And you know what? They deserved it. So, if we can't make it easier, how can we work through it to ensure we can provide another animal that same kind of love and compassion?

Seek Support

The first way is to remember, there's no right way to grieve and everyone grieves differently. And I've learned from personal experience, I don't always grieve the same for each loss. And that's okay.

We all try to cope and, if we can't, sometimes our physical body takes over to fill in the gaps. That may include sobbing or just the opposite, a feeling of numbness. And the roller coaster of emotion is normal—anger, sadness, denial.

But remember to be kind to yourself during this difficult time. Surround yourself with things you love—other animals, family, friends, nature. And reach out to those who understand how you're feeling. Sadly, we've all been there.

And if you need help, that's okay, too! Don't let the sadness overcome you. Feel it, sit with it for a while, but don't stay in it forever. There's still so much good out there—for you to give and receive. You don't want to miss out on it, and neither do the future animals that will benefit.
Thank you for loving and grieving as deeply as we do.

Tammy Thies, Founder & Executive Director

Five tips to help with loss:

1. Give yourself time to grieve.
2. We are WAY too hard on ourselves. Be kind and take care of yourself—really!
3. The animals would NEVER ask us to suffer on their behalf. They just wouldn't.
4. The biggest antidote to compassion fatigue is gratitude.
5. Express your feelings in your own way—memorialize, a ceremony or even a letter to your pet.

A NOTE FROM THE EDITOR

I discovered The Wildcat Sanctuary sometime in the year 2017. I started with a small donation and then graduated to a big cat sponsor. I knew I wanted to sponsor one of the tigers, but I didn't know which one to choose. So, I went to their website and read about each and finally decided on Griffen, one of three brothers who arrived at TWS in 2016. The reason I chose him is because it was noted that he "chuffed" a lot and I love the sound of a tiger chuffing.

I guess sponsoring cats at TWS is kind of like eating potato chips—you can't eat just one. And I couldn't stop being a sponsor with just Griffen. I also sponsor a tigress named Daisy. Daisy didn't have a great beginning in life but now she gets to live a great life. In addition to the two tigers, I sponsor Bell, a Serval who arrived at TWS with her mother Ava and brothers Jalapeno and Chili; Bengal sisters Ashes and Cinders; and last, but certainly not least, Bobcat Essey.

One of the many hats I wear is that of co-owner and publisher of a small publishing company. While we specialize in crime and mystery fiction, we always knew we'd like to do more. Especially if it involved something one of us was passionate about. About a year ago, I discussed with my partners the idea of publishing a compilation of the memorials written for each of the cats who found their forever home at The Wildcat Sanctuary. I told them how beautifully written and moving the memorials were and that I thought it would make a great book. They both liked the idea, but then I had to convince Tammy Thies, the Executive Director at TWS that it was a good idea. Obviously, I was able to do so, and this book is the result. As part of our contract with TWS, we agreed that the majority of the proceeds from the sale of FINALLY, FOREVER FREE will go directly to the Sanctuary.

If you have this book in hand and are reading this, you must be a lover of animals, most especially the wild ones. I urge you to help in any way you can, even if it's something as simple as signing a petition to end the breeding of wild animals for exhibition. Read the articles at the end of this book; they are very enlightening. And, if you haven't already, you *should* watch the documentary entitled *TIGER KING*. It accurately depicts the plight of wild animals in captivity.

Verena Rose, May 2020

The Memorial Garden

Aerial View of The Wildcat Sanctuary

Memorial Stones Created by a Local Artist

TIGERS

2006
TIGER - MEME

There's no doubt that Meme, a 25-year old Bengal tiger, is a favorite at the sanctuary. If her beauty and charm don't win your heart, hearing her story surely will.

Just a short time ago, Meme was an indentured servant at a breeding farm right here in Minnesota. Her world consisted of a 10′ x 10′ dark and cold corn crib, with barely enough room to turn around. There was no grass to lie in, no room to run or walk, no insulation from the harsh winter cold.

She was fed primarily roadkill, evident by the carcasses and bones that stood knee-high on the floor of her cage. For twenty years, her only purpose in life was to produce, for profit, litter after litter of cubs for the animal trade.

When Meme's owner decided to get out of the business, he felt his only option may be to shoot his three tigers. This was to be Meme's final reward for years of service to her owner.

Luckily, those words fell on the right ears. Our sanctuary was notified of the owner's intentions and we were determined to rescue these tigers. Two were placed with a sanctuary in the south, but due to Meme's age, no one felt she would survive the trip.

Therefore, Meme became TWS' first and, at that time, only tiger. Meme arrived with open wounds on her face and hips from rubbing herself raw against her small cage. The initial examination was not optimistic. She had severe arthritis and a bladder infection.

But with care from our veterinarian and staff, Meme now has a new lease on life. Life at the sanctuary must be heaven compared to her past. She has a heated den filled with straw for the cold

Minnesota winters, a tiger perch, complete with ramp and railings, a tire swing, tons of toys, fresh food every day and ample space to romp around.

In the summer of 2003, we achieved our goal of increasing the size of Meme's habitat. Once released into her new space, Meme did the final inspection herself. A stretch up the new tree, which she anointed as her new scratching post; a roll in the freshly mowed grass; and a walk over the rocks— just because they were there!

Meme truly enjoys the winter. After the holidays, we picked up a truckload of donated Christmas trees. We gave Meme the largest of the lot, leaning it against one of her perches. She couldn't wait to exit her lock out area to get at it. She jumped right in (or should we say, on it?), tearing at the branches and licking at the sap. She provided many humorous moments; especially when she rolled over the tree and landed face first into the freshly fallen snow.

Meme continually amazes all of us at TWS. She has taught us that each day is special and that we should enjoy every moment. Meme has also taught us that to forgive is divine. We are very thankful that Meme has chosen to forgive mankind for her life of servitude. We can all learn a great deal from Meme.

In Memory

Her Memory Will Live On

With a very heavy heart I must tell you that we lost Meme last night.

As you all know, Meme the tiger was diagnosed with cancer about a year and a half ago. More recently, doctors at the University of Minnesota School of Veterinary Medicine determined that the tumors had spread, and that Meme's condition was terminal.

Despite the prognosis, Meme's quality of life remained good until the beginning of this week when Meme stopped eating. Yesterday, Meme began exhibiting signs of pain. Our veterinarians examined Meme and determined that treatment would not improve her condition.

The Wildcat Sanctuary staff made the painful decision that Meme should not be made to suffer and were present as she passed. Meme will be cremated, and her ashes spread across wildlife land where she will spend her first moment and the rest of forever living outside of fences.

I knew this day would come, but it was even more difficult than I could've imagined. Meme's resilience and forgiveness have taught me so much and should be a lesson for others. Meme was more than a blessing to TWS and our supporters, she was a miracle. Her spirit will be with us always. It is very hard for me to express my feelings right now. I am devastated by her loss but inspired and continually amazed at her life. She embodied all that TWS is about. She was a living story for so many other animals in need and proved happy endings can happen if we all work together.

2013
TIGER - KITA

In 2010, The Wildcat Sanctuary accepted nine cats as part of a big cat rescue from the Wild Animal Orphanage in Texas. This facility had to shut its doors due to a lack of funding.

Kita was born in 2004 and was originally rescued from a garage in Michigan, along with her lion companion, Tsavo. Unfortunately, Tsavo passed from surgical complications not long after arriving at our sanctuary.

Kita still tries to be one of the lions and roars along with Aslan's pride. Tsavo's memory lives on in Kita and her strength and courage to overcome such a loss is inspiring to us all.

Kita also suffers from ataxia in her back legs from an old injury, which makes walking very difficult. She's not in any pain, but it does create an annoyance when she wants to go anywhere in a hurry.

Even with this handicap and her loss, Kita remains a free spirit and doesn't let it stop her from enjoying life. She will happily show anyone how great it is to be a tiger by stopping and rolling around on the ground, giving you a chuff or a happy moan.

In Memory

Losing a resident is the most difficult thing we have to deal with working at a Sanctuary. It becomes even more difficult when changes are occurring in the organization and we're always focusing on the future for sustainability.

But sometimes, we just need to stop and take the time to grieve. The loss of Kita was sudden and unexpected. Even though she had a disability, she had no self-pity and enjoyed life.

She didn't have full control over her backend, due to an earlier injury in her life. But that didn't stop her from gong in her pool, playing with enrichment or lounging on her perch.

She became close friends with Layla, our matriarch of TWS, over the past few years. They would often play along the fence.

In October, the keepers noticed Kita was having less and less control over her back legs. Her mobility decreased rapidly. The decision was made to help her pass with dignity.

She was the same kind spirit that she'd always been. She was even chuffing in her indoor area. Her spirit was strong, but her body wasn't. It was time to let her spirit be free.

You will forever be missed Kita and never forgotten. May you be reunited with your friend Tsavo.

2014
TIGER - SIERRA

Wildcat Sanctuary accepted nine cats as part of a big cat rescue from The Wild Animal Orphanage in Texas after it shut down due to lack of funding.

Sierra was born in 2000 and originated from an exploitative breeder in Ohio, along with another tiger, Ekaterina. Sierra is a white tiger.

This breeder charged the public to pet and have photos taken with adult lions and tigers that were declawed and chained down to a platform. The breeder was eventually closed down after multiple allegations of animal attacks on visitors. Sierra and Ekaterina were featured in an investigative report by *20/20*.

The Wildcat Sanctuary originally offered a home to Ekaterina and Sierra, however instead they were placed at Wild Animal Orphanage. So, after WAO's closing, here they are today, finally able to call The Wildcat Sanctuary their forever home.

Sierra is a very relaxed cat. She enjoys curling up in her hammock and taking a long nap in the sun. She can get a little frisky though for a new toy, especially for her tug toy.

She also likes stalking Ekaterina from inside her pool. She'll put her ears down and wait until Ekaterina is just close enough, then charge out of the pool and run around chasing her.

In Memory

I sit here typing because I don't know what else to do. I am beside myself. In a few short hours, we will say goodbye to a dear resident of ours. Every loss is difficult, but this one seems so unfair. To know that letting her go is the best gift we can give her is not a lot of solace right now.

Am I wrong to just wish for a miracle? I know each of us has our own time. Sometimes it doesn't feel like it is their time, but fate intercedes, and we have no choice but to say goodbye.

Sierra the tigress has a calm and welcoming presence. She has a joy of life and is loved by all. But now, she is so tired. Struggling with respiratory disease, we knew recovery would be long. But Sierra was so strong and had minor symptoms just a short time ago, so even the veterinary team was hopeful.

So many loving people have rallied by her side to help. Her caretakers have been with her every step of the way making her comfortable and doing all they could to pave the road to recovery.

Veterinarians, radiologists, and respiratory specialists have gone above and beyond their duties to treat her, consulting, prescribing and continually monitoring her progress.

They performed radiographs, a trachea wash, and so much more, all in an effort to diagnose and help her recover. After she left the hospital, they've been in constant contact, making adjustments to her treatment as necessary. We were all optimistic and hoped for the best. No one was ready to say goodbye.

But today, Sierra showed us she is tired, more tired than before. Though she seems comfortable, this has taken a toll on her and she just wants to sleep. Today is the first day her roommate, Ekaterina, seemed worried.

She chuffs at Sierra from across the hallway and it's the first day Sierra doesn't chuff back, even though she is awake and lying down.

Just a short time ago, Sierra and Ekaterina were playing with Christmas trees in the snow and Sierra was enjoying her outdoor hammock. I know Sierra will be back enjoying days like that in her new life. It feels selfish to wish those days could still be here at TWS, but it's what I'm feeling right now.

I know she has so many wonderful friends to meet her on the other side—those who've already left the physical world but remain a part of TWS always. She has so many staff, sponsor parents, volunteers, and former caretakers who love her and will deeply miss her.

Ekaterina, her habitat mate will also mourn her loss. Every one of us wants her to stay, but as always, we listen to the cats. Sierra clearly shared her intentions today and we must respect that.

Sierra—know you are loved and cherished. Please visit us often. No time is too soon. For now, just sleep peacefully.

2015
TIGER - LILLY

Lilly, the tigress, was born in 1996 and came to The Wildcat Sanctuary in 2006 after her owner was tragically killed by another tiger, Tango. She now lives wild at heart in a free-roaming natural area thanks to our supporters.

Authorities called The Wildcat Sanctuary to help with the emergency. However, it was too late for both the owner and Tango as they were both dead. Lilly, along with the other tiger there named Titan, were seized and placed with our Sanctuary.

Lilly was severely underweight and suffered frostbite on her ears and tail. The Wildcat Sanctuary was informed by authorities that Lilly had originated from YOR Exotics, where she was found as the last surviving tiger a few years earlier.

In order to survive there, Lilly had consumed her cage mates after they had passed away from starvation. We can only imagine the terror she has managed to survive.

At TWS Lilly was a happy and healthy cat. She shared a large, free-roaming habitat with Titan, her love. When they first arrived, they didn't live together. However, after years of living next to each other, often chuffing, and rubbing on their shared wall, it was obvious they wanted more.

After a few weeks of play dates, Titan and Lilly were merged together and they couldn't have been happier. Lilly was very boisterous and liked to show Titan off as her own. Titan liked to stalk Lilly when she wasn't paying attention, sneak up on her while she was at the pool and try to push her in. Then, the two would go running around and usually end up in a big tiger pile. After everything Lilly had endured, it was so great to see her playing and enjoying life.

In Memory

Why is it that, no matter how long you prepare for a loss, it still seems so sudden when it finally happens? It must be because, no matter how long we prepare, the time we have with our loved ones is never long enough.

This was certainly true with Lilly, our tigress. At 19, Lilly had a known heart condition. We'd hoped and prayed that, when it was her time, she would go quickly and painlessly. Our wish was that it would happen peacefully, as she lay next to the love of her life, Titan.

And that's exactly what did happen. Though she went as we wished for her to go, our hearts still ached, and the tears still flowed knowing that she will not be with us another day.

After enduring long years of neglect and surviving starvation not once, but twice, Lilly deserved nothing less than going peacefully and swiftly. She never had a bad day living at The Wildcat Sanctuary and she lived life to the fullest up until her very last breath.

Lilly was always a tom boy of a tiger, protective over Titan, and always knew that the humans were here to be her servants—and she reminded us often of that. She kept her wild side, and who could blame her after all she had been through?

But when it came to Titan, her heart softened, and she was sweet and docile. She was in pure bliss, as long as he was by her side. Even while being treated for a heart condition and having a few spells over the last several months, we did not know she would be leaving us so soon.

To all outsiders, she seemed healthy. She was muscular, had a beautiful coat, was very active and no one could ever believe she was 19. But her caregivers knew that inside, there was a ticking time bomb and there was not much we could do to prevent her future fate.

Lilly was lying next to Titan during evening rounds. She left us that night and we could see she went peacefully. Titan had already said his goodbyes to her and greeted his caregivers with a chuff the next day on morning rounds. It was a very somber morning. A solemn quietness overcame the Sanctuary as we mourned the loss of a tiger with a true wild spirit.

Lilly, your past may have been marred by a cycle of abuse, but your years of presence at the Sanctuary were a lesson of resilience. And your future in your new wild, life will be exactly what you dreamed of…free…until you are once again united with your true love, Titan.

2015
TIGER - LAYLA

In 2010, The Wildcat Sanctuary accepted nine cats from the Wild Animal Orphanage in Texas. Unfortunately, the facility had to close down due to funding issues.

Layla was born in 1991 and originated in Mississippi as a privately owned exotic pet. Layla has a very calm demeanor but occasionally gets the sudden urge to run around her habitat, usually with a piece of food hanging from her mouth.

Given her age and her shy temperament, this usually makes for a good laugh for anyone watching. She is also very curious but slow to accept anything new. She really enjoys lounging in her pool on hot summer days and soaking up some rays on her perch.

Layla is a favorite among the staff. She has a funny way of talking, it's sort of like she is trying to whisper a moan, very adorable.

In Memory

Layla, our 25-year-old tigress, now reigns over the sanctuary from her new forever wild life.

Layla came to us through the largest big cat rescue in history. Almost 60 big cats needed placement in 2010, after a facility in Texas closed down. I was placement coordinator for all the big cats, and it took countless hours and a little over a year before all the big cats had been relocated to their new homes.

The first day I walked through the facility, there were tigers as far as the eye could see. How was I going to choose who we could take, and who would be placed first? It was a heart wrenching decision.

Many of the tigers were chuffing and rubbing, playing with plastic kegs or living with companion tigers. Then there was Layla. She was a geriatric tiger.

Her enclosure was on the edge of the property, she had little in her enclosure because she was a known climber and they were worried about safety in her open top enclosure. She was laying on a concrete den, just staring through me, not even acknowledging my presence.

I knew we only had so much space back at The Wildcat Sanctuary, but after the first trip, her face continued to haunt me. She looked void in spirit, but physically in good shape for an older cat. She was beautiful and had such an elegance about her. I just had to find a way to bring her to TWS, even if she only had a short time left.

Happily, she lived five more blissful years here at the Sanctuary. It took her a little while to warm up, but the glaze in her eyes faded and her heart softened. She quickly became a favorite of everyone.

At 25, she enjoyed life. She would trot after cubs Jeremy and Simon along the shared fence and even roar at Tonka, intimidating the biggest boy at the Sanctuary. She had stunning beauty but would also show her playful side—a refined spunkiness of sorts.

We could see her health declining in waves this summer. She had small masses developing on her face and a few nose bleeds. There were days she was more tired than usual.

But after treatment, she rebounded and would be back to stalking and being spunky. We'd also find her lounging in her new pool or napping between her hammock and the trees. She had a good life.

Recently, she slowed down again, but it was different this time. It was the first time the glazed look in her eyes returned. The look that had haunted me the day I met her.

Saying goodbye was very difficult for each of us, but it was time for her to reign over a new world. We let her enjoy her last days in the beautiful summer sun, lying in the tall grass before it was time to let her go.

Layla, your beauty inside and out will never be forgotten. You truly were a queen to us and the Sanctuary.

2016
TIGER - TITAN

Titan, born in 1996, came to TWS in 2006 after his owner was tragically killed by another tiger, Tango. Authorities called TWS to help with the emergency, however it was too late for both the owner and Tango. Titan, along with another tiger named Lilly, were seized and placed with us.

Titan was severely malnourished upon arrival. We believe his owner fell on hard financial times and just could not afford the proper diet for the tigers. Those close to the owner said she truly did care about the animals but sometimes that just isn't enough, especially when it comes to housing potentially dangerous exotic animals.

Today, Titan is thriving and living a very plush life here at the Sanctuary. Although he came with Lilly, they were not living together before they arrived. After a few years of living next to each other, it was obvious they wanted more. So, we decided to merge them together.

There were a few scuffles at first, but once they figured out their places, they have become inseparable. Lilly passed away in the summer of 2015. Titan has adjusted well to living alone again and can often be found playing along the fence with tigress Sabrina.

Titan is a very relaxed cat, taking everything in stride. The pool is definitely his favorite thing in the summertime, and he loved to chase Lilly in and out of it splashing around. Another of his favorites has to be the fire-hose hammock; big enough for two and very cozy.

January 7, 2016

As you know, Titan will be 20 years old this year. He has been through so much in his life and done so well here at the Sanctuary.

Lately, he has been picky about his food, which is not like Titan at all. A few medications have helped his appetite, but we felt he needed a full exam and diagnostic tests performed by specialists at the University of Minnesota. We wanted to have a clearer picture of what medical issues he may be facing.

Though he has been eating well this last week and back to his social self, initial test results are most consistent with early signs of cancer.

We will have full results shortly. He is being given medication to assure he's comfortable. Of course, we will continue to provide him loving care hoping he has many more days to enjoy here with all of us.

January 8, 2016

After his big day being transported to the University of Minnesota for diagnostics, Titan came right up on morning rounds to chuff at his caretakers.

From the outside, he still looks like our boy Titan. A magnificent tiger who has beaten all the odds. Unfortunately, his test results came back today with the diagnosis of advanced leukemia and anemia.

We are treating Titan with oral medication to keep him comfortable. As long as he continues to eat, be active and show no signs of pain, he will be with us.

He has been strong through this, just as he has been with all of the battles he has faced in his life. He deserves to leave with dignity when it is that time, and we will give him that gift. But for now, we celebrate his life and enjoy our time with him.

In Memory

Titan, Lilly, and Tango—Together at Last

I cannot believe we had to say goodbye so soon. Even though Titan was recently diagnosed with leukemia, we thought he had several happy months ahead of him.

His blood results came back that the disease was further along than first diagnosed. Autoimmune suppressants were recommended to slow the cancer, but unfortunately, it slowed Titan down completely. It was time to reunite him with his brother Tango, and love, Lilly.

There is no other cat, besides founding tigress Meme, that embodies The Wildcat Sanctuary's reason for being more than 20-year-old Titan the tiger. So much so that, over the years, he became the face of the Sanctuary through videos, brochures, posters, and our *No More Wild Pets* campaign.

He was a tiger that had beaten all the odds. He was a former exhibit cat that had seen starvation not once, but twice. He tragically lost his brother Tango, after Tango killed their owner.

He arrived in 2006 with Lilly, full of anger and fear. It took months before he would greet his caregivers without a roar. It took a year before any man with facial hair or a hat could approach his habitat without him charging at the fence.

But his tragic history is not what defined him, it was his capacity for forgiveness. Love and patience prevailed. He learned to trust again and became one of the most charismatic cats at The Wildcat Sanctuary. When he let go of his anger, he found peace and became a gentle leader for our cause. His gentleness remained even through his last days.

Titan had two major loves during his life. His brother Tango, who he lived with from birth until Tango's death in 2006. And then Lilly. Lilly knew they were meant to be together from the moment she laid eyes on him.

It took two years of living along a shared wall before they were personally introduced. After a few play dates, they would spend the rest of their lives together until Lilly passed away last year due to a heart condition.

Titan was a strong and kind leader. He chuffed hello, enjoyed patrolling his habitat and saying hello to Sabrina along the shared wall. His habitat was located in the heart of the Sanctuary near the Memorial Pavilion, appropriate for such a leader.

On warm summer days, you could find him swimming across Tiger Splash and then lounging on the ledge with his head on the grass. He also enjoyed enrichment. Lilly always allowed him to play first, out of respect.

And this majestic leader would rip into the paper and run like a kitten across their habitat. He loved to show this silly side to our donors and volunteers as well. He enjoyed doing this even during this last month with his holiday enrichment.

Titan was also humble. And I know he looks to the new generation of rescued big cats to continue to guide our work and rescue more cats in need. We can honor him by saving others. And with your continued help, we will.

Titan, you have led us this far on our journey to create a world of compassion for animals. We will honor your legacy by carrying on such an important mission. Love to you our gentle leader and enjoy your new-found freedom.

2017
TIGER - ZEUS

Zeus, a Bengal tiger, has called TWS home since 2010. He was born in 1998 and arrived here with five other big cats and three bobcats. They were all living at Wild Animal Orphanage in Texas, when they were forced to close their doors. In all, over 400 animals were rescued with this shutdown.

Zeus is a very special guy with a goofy personality that can make anyone smile. He was born in captivity, hand raised, and has only ever known people. While he has lived next to other tigers, he really isn't too sure about them. He is very chatty with people though and often moans and chuffs to anyone in hearing range.

He is very laid back and enjoys playing when he is in the mood. Plastic kiddie pools are his favorite-when the keepers put one in his habitat he immediately runs and dives into it and begins licking it and rolling around. He is irresistible and everyone who meets him instantly falls in love.

In Memory

This Christmas, a tiger got his wings

Family comes in all shapes and forms. This Christmas Day, as many were with family and friends, our sanctuary family sadly had to come together to help tiger Zeus get his wings.

There isn't a day of the year, hour of the night, or a holiday that our staff isn't there for our cats. This Christmas was no different. When Zeus needed us, we were all there to help him go on to his new wild life.

At almost 19, Zeus had a good life. But the most special thing about Zeus was all the good memories he gave us. Even though he was a very calm tiger, he had a big personality and presence. He enjoyed giving joy to others.

From the moment we met him in 2006, he became part of our family. He never missed a moment to say hello, trot along the fence and made sure to put a smile on our faces. He did the same for volunteers, interns and donors. Zeus had a special friendship with every person he met.

Zeus was full of life and happiness. He chuffed continuously, honked hello, and showed us his belly. He made the most out of every day for himself and for us. He loved enrichment, paw painting, swimming. But most of all, he loved his transport crate and seeing other areas of the sanctuary.

Zeus had lived in many habitats over the years and had fun in every one of them. He liked all the neighbors he met, except for Ekaterina—she was naughty to him along the fence, and that was the end of that. He never went near her again.

Even in his last days, Zeus made us happy. We saw him slowing down, he had arthritis and some GI issues. But just a few days before he left us, he had a burst of energy and was playing in his habitat, trotting down the fence and chuffing away.

At that moment, we hoped he was getting better. But, in reality, it was his last hurrah. He quickly declined after that day, and pain medication could no longer make him comfortable. Even when we knew it was time to say goodbye, he still had it in him to chuff to us, because that was Zeus.

With the help of our vet team, he left us as peacefully and calmly as he led his days. He told us when it was time, another gift he gave us. And we'll always have our special memories, but there will never be another Zeus. His contagious joy will be missed every day!

So how did Zeus find his way to TWS to bless us with so many wonderful years?

It was in 2006, when I heard a facility in Texas was financially failing and they had over 60 big cats. Back in 2000, we took in our first tiger, Meme. Other cats, including Meme's son and an intact female, had been placed at this facility in Texas.

When I heard of their problems, I flew down to see how I could help. Sadly, the only help I could provide was finding sanctuaries for over 60 big cats. There was no saving the facility.

I asked about Meme's son and companion and was informed they had passed away. I was introduced to Zeus by very compassionate caregivers. They informed me he was born at the facility, which was unexpected since the animals weren't supposed to be allowed to breed. I will never know if Zeus is related to Meme, but something brought me to him and to the other big cats in need.

It was one of the largest placement efforts in our industry and was the first time in history we were able to get coordination of dozens of sanctuaries working together.

I was able to coordinate placement of all the animals through collaboration and support of so many sanctuaries. TWS became home to nine of the cats including Zeus, Sierra, Ekaterina, Layla, Lakota, Harley and Salem.

Our family always changes with each passing. Luckily, our hearts are limitless. There is always the capacity to show another animal our human compassion.

Thank you for being a very special part of Zeus' family. We know how much Zeus meant to you, too.

2019
TIGER - EKATERINA

Ekaterina's a female Bengal tiger who came to The Wildcat Sanctuary in 2010. She was ten years old at the time and had been part of a national news expose, featured by ABC's *20/20* investigative series.

A notorious Ohio breeder would charge the public for the opportunity to go inside cages with big cats to interact and take photos with them, including Ekaterina. When the breeder/exhibitor was finally closed down, we offered a home to Ekaterina then. But, unfortunately, she went to the Wild Animal Orphanage (WAO) in Texas instead.

Later, that facility shut down due to lack of funding. We were able to rescue nine cats from WAO to live out their days here at the sanctuary. We were happy Ekaterina was finally at her forever home and would never have to worry about moving again.

Ekaterina always liked being the center of attention. You can hear her voice from far across the sanctuary. She just can't resist 'chatting' with any caretaker who happens to be close by. She's also the cutest sleeper with all four paws up in the air, just as content as she can be.

And she's always loved enrichment, whether it's man-made or nature-made. She'll scrunch up her nose and stick out her tongue when she gets a new scent. This is called the flehmen response. Cats and many other mammals do this to examine scents more closely and it makes for a very funny photo, that's for sure!

In Memory

We are saddened that 19 year-old-Ekaterina lost her battle with osteo arthritis and renal disease. For the last several years, we could see Ekaterina's health declining and put her on our Comfort Care program. This included pain management, laser therapy, her own soft bed and even moving her to an enclosure with less rocky areas and later to quarantine, which had lots of indoor space.

Her last few days were special for her and us. She was doted over by all staff receiving special attention which she loved. We did our best to make her final days as special as possible including clean bedding daily, elevated areas for drinking and eating so she didn't have to bend down, and even bringing in a television and running movies, so she never felt a minute alone.

She thanked us in her own way with tons of chuffs and her famous vocalizations. Her happy noises. When her day arrived, she was surrounded by those she loved, and we were able to help her pass on very peacefully. Both a gift for her and us. Her last days were special, but so was her life.

She was rescued from a roadside zoo with her habitat mate Sierra and sent to a facility in the south. Once that facility failed, we and other sanctuaries stepped in to provide homes for over 50 big cats. Ekaterina and Sierra were just a few of those who called the sanctuary home.

For years before her rescue, Ekaterina was used as a photo prop. The public could pay a fee to follow a caretaker into her habitat, sit on her back and even pull her tail. A short search on the internet shows just how many interactions she was forced to have. After Ekaterina grabbed a photographer during an undercover story on *20/20*, authorities finally intervened.

At our sanctuary, Ekaterina was never forced to do anything. She loved life to the fullest and was quite the showoff in her younger days. She loved her weeble wobble zoo toys, playing in the snow, and most of all saying hello to all the humans at the Sanctuary. She always came up to see if we had a treat or new toy.

Sadly, being declawed for display, her arthritis set in at an early age. It became more difficult for her to walk up each visit. She would often call from her platform or take naps along the fence line so she would already be close when her human friends passed by. The sanctuary is noticeably quieter without you Ekaterina, but your chuffs will be heard in our hearts forever.

2020
TIGER - NIKITA

Nikita's a female Bengal white tiger who came to The Wildcat Sanctuary in 2012. She was seven years old at the time and had already survived a horrible life of abuse.

Nikita was owned by the notorious Ohio breeder, exhibitor and ex-convict Sam Mazzola. As a typical pay-to-play cub, he used her from a very young age as a photo prop to make money. Nikita grew up in a small, cement slab cage with other tigers. She had to fight for her food, becoming dominant and dangerous.

Mazzola would travel around with his exotics, bringing in over $20,000 per event. He'd force his bears to wrestle anyone who paid $1000 for the chance, and thousands did. Employees were seen using a bat on one of the tigers, too. We can only imagine the abuse Nikita endured.

When Mazzola died of asphyxiation in 2012, authorities divided up his animals and placed them at various facilities. Nikita went to a backyard facility where she lived alone in a 20' x 30' cage. But finally, she was safe and loved. Until Ohio laws became much stricter regarding private ownership of exotics. Her current owners couldn't meet the new regulations, so looked to place their cats at a sanctuary.

We were happy to welcome Nikita to her forever home. No more being on exhibit, no more moving from place to place, no more abuse…just love and a serene environment for her to blossom. And she has! She's a much more docile tiger today, calmly sitting for operant conditioning and not as fearful of cameras as she used to be. Today, she trusts her caretakers and knows what true compassion feels like.

How Nikita's changed

From Outreach for Animals Tim Harrison:

"I was contacted by Tammy Thies of The Wildcat Sanctuary in Minnesota to do some prep work on a white tiger being kept in a backyard near Ashland, Ohio. Upon my first visit to Denise and Jose Flores' property, I was amazed to see a well-run rescue facility that they called Tiger Paws.

*"The big cats they cared for were cats that had been abused by other so-called "rescue groups" but were really used for photo ops, traveling road shows, etc. The white tiger Tammy was coming to relocate to her facility was Nikita, as I found out, to be **the most aggressive and violent big cat that I have ever met (wild or caged).***

"Denise told me her sad story of abuse (struck with aluminum ball bats to "train" her, etc.) Denise stepped in and rescued her from the notorious Sam Mazzola (World Animal Studios near Cleveland, Ohio). If you want to know Sam's story, checkout the Animal Planet TV Show, Fatal Attraction's - "Terror at Bear Farm" (I also appeared in that sad episode).

Thanks, and stay safe, Tim"

In Memory

Nikita. Just her name speaks of strength, intelligence, and a powerful grace.

She was all those things and more, but to list them would not do her justice. Having to say goodbye to her so soon at the age of 15 is heartbreaking, made even more so by seeing how far she's come.

Nikita was always one to hide her discomfort or pain. When she started to show us, we knew it was time to act immediately for her. Sadly, even with our rushing her to the emergency clinic, the diagnosis was not a good one. She was in the end stages of renal failure.

Though we wished it wasn't so, all we could do for her was give her the dignity to pass in peace and suffer no more. A promise we try hard to keep for our residents at TWS. We'll always choose what's right for the animals, always, even if it's so painful for us.

Anyone who follows TWS knows Nikita and her painful history of abuse and neglect. She was born at a facility well known for breeding and selling animals for profit. A notorious animal abuser named Sam Mazzola bought and raised her, using her as a photo prop for anyone willing to pay him.

His abusive ways were not just to animals, but people as well. A Google search brings up dozens of articles documenting his exploitations and convictions.

One can only imagine what Nikita saw at this facility. The abuse suffered from living in a small cage on a cement slab, having to fight for her food. Being forced to pose for photos, struck with objects like aluminum bats to keep her submissive and under control. Seeing her fellow cage mates in similar or worse conditions took a toll on her.

Tim Harrison, a fellow rescuer from Outreach for Animals, described Nikita as "the most aggressive and violent big cat that I have ever met (wild or caged)." If you'd met Nikita then, there was no questioning his statement. She had no trust for humans.

She'd never been given a reason to trust. It'd been broken in her at Mazzola's facility. She picked the only way she could survive. To be stronger and fiercer than what hurt her.

After Mazzola's death, she was rescued by an Ohio couple who took her in. They showed her not all humans were like Mazzola. Not all wished her harm or would demand things from her.

There she started to learn what compassion was, though her trust was going to be a hard thing to win back. When more restrictive ownership regulations were passed in Ohio, TWS was contacted by the couple. They were looking for a reputable and safe home for their big cats.

And that's when, in 2012, Nikita came to her final forever home at TWS. She was just as fierce and dangerous. When we heard the story of her past, knowing the horrible abuse she'd suffered, it was understandable.

We don't blame any of the cats who come to us for how they behave. It's how they've learned to survive. They don't speak our language, and we can only show them our intentions through our actions.

I share her history, an understanding of Nikita, because I wanted to share the real Nikita who was hiding under all that fear and aggression. The quirky and kind of dorky side to her that she finally became comfortable enough to show us.

Her love of paint was immense! She so enjoyed getting nose deep in the vegetable paint and would spend the afternoon with it. It was so nice to see her enjoy something in earnest rather than fear.

The first time I met Nikita when I started at TWS, she was one of the cats who had a long list of dos and don'ts. All ways to help keep her stress down as well as safety for the staff. She'd roar, jump at the fence, and become defensive when others approached, especially if she didn't know them. It was clear that showing Nikita we could be trusted was going to be an immense task.

Meeting Nikita, I really wanted to show her we knew she deserved respect. She deserved to be allowed freedoms and joys. I saw her change. She seemed to enjoy the company of other cats around her, chuffing at them or engaging them through the fence, especially Shazam.

It was the first time I saw Nikita wasn't truly broken. She still had compassion herself toward other cats.

When I started working with her daily, it took a great deal of time to gain her patience, to work around her without her being upset. Feeding time was typically when she'd be calmest. She'd lay down and eat, but she'd never take her eyes off us, even then.

This past summer, there was a moment that brought a lightness to my heart, even as it brings tears to my eyes now. I went down to Nikita's habitat to see if she wanted to participate in operant conditioning. It was up to her, of course.

When I called for her and showed her the snacks I brought, she was laying on her back, belly up in the sun. Another great thing to see, that she was comfortable, that she felt safe enough to show her belly and laze about.

I'd knelt down in the grass by her fence and called her again. But all I got was a one-eye stare from her comfortable position. So I figured her answer was "no" and I just sat there to spend some time with her.

It surprised me when, after a minute, she slowly rolled onto her side, sat up giving a bit of sneeze, then getting up with a rather exaggerated stretch. I thought she was going to walk off into her shrubs, away from where I was. Her typical "not interested," which was fine. If she wanted alone time, she deserved to have it.

But she walked over and stood there staring at me for a moment. Then, she laid down right there by me. We shared a bit of time in silence, enjoying the sun. It was one of those moments when all the work we do, all the hours and the hurt of goodbyes we feel, all the pain and sorrows that our residents come with, show us how worth it is to do this.

Seeing her calm and willing to sit there with me for the time she did, just to say "Okay, I suppose you're an okay human, I'll trust you enough to share a moment" are reasons to keep going….even when the sorrow feels so heavy it's almost crushing.

She also allowed me one photo of her that day. She didn't growl, she didn't get upset that I asked to take one. She let me. I even got one chuff, just one meaningful chuff. Then, she stood up and walked off calmly to have her time alone in her shaded trees. I cherish that moment greatly with her, and I'll never forget it.

When we said goodbye to Nikita after having rushed to try and help her, that was what I saw, that time with her. Not how she looked just then at the hospital. But instead, her calmly walking forward into the brush, moving to her next life, free of the pain she saw here.

She didn't have to run away, she could walk calmly and safely into that light, into her next life without fear or anger.

Thank you, Nikita for giving us the time to show you that not all of us are like those in your past. Thank you for that gift, and showing us that no one is ever truly broken, you just need the right compassion and understanding to grow.

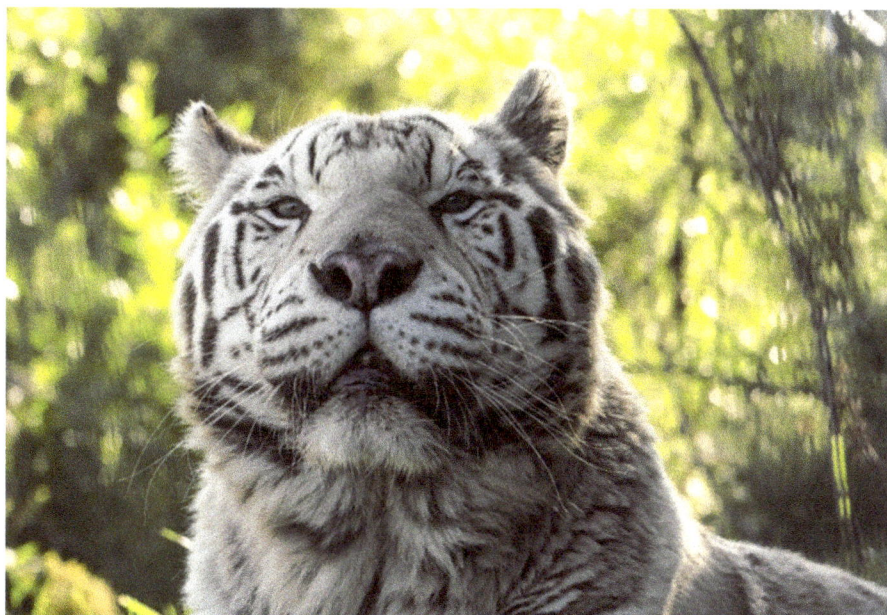

2020
TIGER - MOHAN

Mohan's a male Bengal tiger who came to The Wildcat Sanctuary in 2017. He was 15 years old at the time and had many physical issues he'd been dealing with.

When authorities contacted us about helping two tigers at an out-of-state facility, they told us we'd probably have to euthanize one and the other was also in very bad shape. Thankfully, we were able to give them both a good life after intervening with the veterinary care they so desperately needed.

At the time, Mohan could barely put weight on his front paws. His claws were overgrown and embedded into his soft paw pads.

Plus, he suffered from degenerative joint disease of the knees, due to untreated cruciate ligament injuries. His rear legs were permanently bowed, and he had rear muscle atrophy.

Surgery wouldn't be an option, but we knew we could make him comfortable and more mobile with joint support and pain management.

Life at the Sanctuary

Today, Mohan is one the sweetest tigers and beloved by everyone. He's definitely a gentle giant. He loves soaking up the sunshine and can even get up on a low platform built especially for him. His favorite thing to do is lounge in the shade, just enjoying the summer breezes.

Mohan has such a positive attitude and never gives up. There's never a day he doesn't look forward to! He's an inspiration to us all. We're so thankful we were able to intervene to help him live out his days in comfort.

In Memory

On the way into work, I saw the perfect message. Love courageously.

I knew this would be my last morning with Mohan. The last morning with all of us. All goodbyes are so hard, but this one especially.

We knew for a few weeks that this day was coming, so we made every moment count.

Mohan enjoyed the wonderful summer weather we've been having. He took many tiger naps in the sun and in the shade, as the breezes blew through his whiskers.

He shared quiet moments with his caretakers, and even a last dip in the specialized pool we ordered for him.

We tried so hard each day to hold back the tears and celebrate his life and all the joy he brought to us…and to you. But his legs, knees, and hips were all failing. Walking was becoming more difficult. Yet he was determined to do it to come say hello, chuff, and show us he knew he was loved.

And he was right. He was loved so very much. If love and support could have healed him, he would be running through the grass and still with us today.

Mohan is a miracle tiger not because of what he overcame, but because of what he endured.

Since we rescued him three years ago, he struggled with walking. He'd been in terrible pain and had received no medication to help. His untreated injuries had led to calcified ligaments, bowed legs, debilitating arthritis.

We did everything we could to help relieve his pain. From laser therapy, to oral medication, to daily mobility walks, we felt blessed to be able to make him comfortable.

But diagnostic imaging showed the damage could not be repaired. The only thing we could do was keep him comfortable until he could no longer bear weight on his back legs.

Of all the hundreds of cats I've rescued over the years, Mohan is the first cat I was never able to see run, due to his injuries.

It breaks my heart that that simple pleasure was taken from him. Even Bengal cat Spartacus, with his spinal deformity, found his own special way of running And so did our tigress Daisy.

But Mohan didn't think life was unfair. He found true joy in the smallest moments. How I loved seeing him play with such enthusiasm! Despite all the physical discomfort caused by captivity, Mohan was very happy.

And what made him special to so many was that he also made everyone feel just as special as he was.

Mohan, today we lead you to the pride on the other side, where you can run and finally live forever free. You deserve your new wild life. Enjoy, but visit us often. We look forward to hearing your chuffs in the breeze, and the wind moving the grass as your spirit runs free.

Mohan, you've made an impact on each of us. And we'll continue to fight for tigers like you…in your memory!

I can't think of a better way to honor Mohan than by making him a patron of our new Animal Care & Education Center. He epitomizes why we need this new hospital. It's vital for cats we rescue since so many – just like Mohan – need on-site urgent care.

LIONS

2010
LION - TSAVO

The Wildcat Sanctuary has accepted nine cats as part of a big cat rescue from the Wild Animal Orphanage (WAO) in Texas after they closed down.

Kita, a tiger, and Tsavo, a lioness, were originally rescued from a garage in Michigan. They both have had issues with ataxic hind quarters due to nutritional deficiencies but are otherwise very happy cats.

Thank you to Karen Berg who donated frequent flyer miles for Director Tammy Thies to fly to WAO and The Mahley Family Foundation and The Binky Foundation who each contributed $2,000 towards the placement of the nine WAO cats.

We still have work to do to find homes for all the WAO animals, but I'm extremely grateful for everyone who has set aside their differences to ensure so many of these animals have another chance at life.

The WAO keepers and interim board have been amazing, providing day-to-day care to all the animals with such little resources. They selflessly voted to close and place the animals when they knew it was in their best interest. Even the USDA, IFAW, ASA and GFAS are all working together to help as many animals as possible.

In Memory

Tsavo, such a beautiful lioness, had one of the greatest feline personalities TWS has ever seen. It is because of her love for life that made her passing, so traumatic for the staff, vets and all of those who had the good fortune of meeting her.

At The Wildcat Sanctuary, we spay and neuter our residents to prevent breeding, furthering our goal in ending the captive wildlife crisis. In addition, we spay and neuter to reduce the chances the cats will develop reproductive system cancers. We hope by doing this it will lengthen the life of the animal.

Tsavo was spayed eight days prior to her passing. She was recovering well, until staff found that she had opened a small section of her sutures and damaged a portion of her intestine. The staff and vets immediately tended to Tsavo, performing emergency surgery and providing intensive care.

While trying to stay optimistic, watching Tsavo's worsening condition was heart wrenching. We tried absolutely everything we could do for this poor girl. Unfortunately, it was not enough.

This tragedy has been one of the hardest things the staff and vets have had to cope with. It is hard to comprehend that this time our efforts to lengthen an animals' life has actually contributed to her leaving us too soon. She may have only been with us for a couple of weeks but seeing her silly expressions and goofy antics made us feel as though she'd been a part of our family for years.

We'll always remember her running across her habitat to greet us as fast as she could, playing with her roommate Kita and making her funny noises. Remembering her joyful personality will help our tears slow and our hearts grow stronger.

Everyone that met this amazing girl fell in love immediately. Tsavo was a one-of-a-kind cat and will be missed dearly. She was a great reminder that the best things in life are often the simplest. It is for this we will be forever thankful for meeting Tsavo, even if we only knew her for such a short time.

"There is no pain so great as the memory of joy in present grief."—Aeschylus

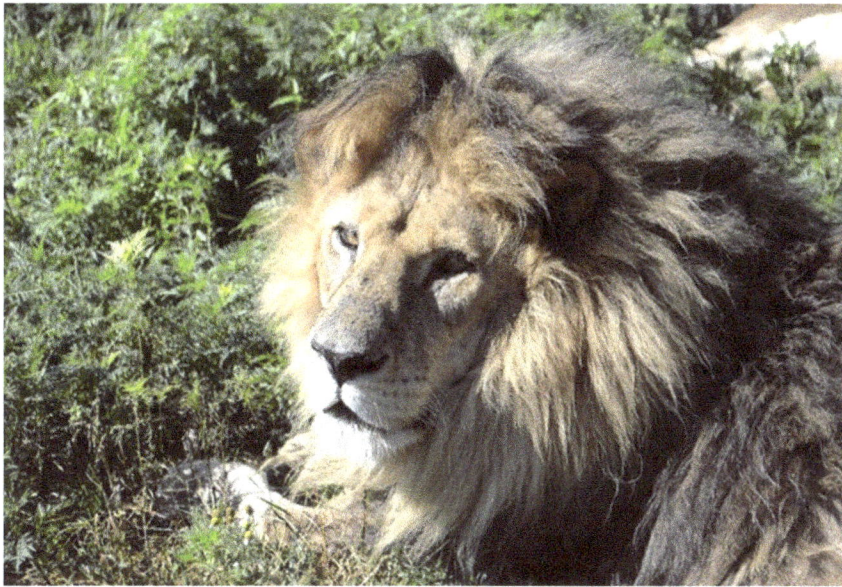

2014
LION - ASLAN

Aslan and two lionesses were part of a big cat rescue from the Catskill Game Farm in New York. With the closure of their animal park, the Game Farm auctioned off 950 animals and made east coast and national headlines.

Many worried that some of the animals would wind up in the hands of unscrupulous dealers, or that animals, such as deer or goats, would go to people who run 'canned shoot' operations where hunters pay to shoot fenced-in animals. It is described as one of the largest animal rescues of its type.

Wildlife Watch intervened on behalf of the three lions to ensure a safer fate through placement at TWS.

Aslan was born in 1996. Along with his pride Asha and Shanti Deva, he arrived at the Sanctuary in 2006. Everything was very new to him and he had no trust for humans. Luckily, he had his pride by his side to reassure him that everything was going to be alright.

Over the years, Aslan's confidence has grown. Since moving into their free-roaming habitat in 2009, he has let us see his true personality. He has fun rolling down the hill with Asha at feeding time and can now sleep peacefully even when people are around. He enjoys his enrichment, especially the scent of Vick's vapor rub. He even joins in during the girls' painting sessions, showing off his unique artistic side.

In Memory

It was an unseasonably warm winter day. The snow was thawing, and patches of grass appeared all throughout the sanctuary. The sun was shining.

Aslan was spending the morning doing what he loved most—napping in between his girls Asha and Shanti Deva. They were curled up in a patch of exposed grass soaking in the sun's rays. Asha was snug on his left side and Shanti was a few feet away on his right. This is what he always lived for. This is what we spent the past six months ensuring he received.

The vet and I approached the enclosure during our morning rounds. Aslan was a special part of everyone's routine so we could monitor his health closely. Six months ago, he was diagnosed with serious and chronic hepatitis of the liver. We made the decision to provide treatment as long as he could remain with his pride and be pain free.

Aslan in his elder years

Today, I was looking at Aslan who now has a very blonde and thinning mane—a side effect from some of his medications. This was quite the contrast from the full and dark mane he had in his younger years. His body was now that of an aged cat. But he was enjoying this day to the fullest. He was still the king of our sanctuary. Some even referred to him as the "tree of life"—a symbol of magnificent beauty and existence.

We had seen a steady decline and knew his time was limited. But we did not think it would end today. The pride was together and seemed more connected than ever. As I observed the lions lying blissfully in the sun with their eyes closed, I asked that Aslan give us a sign when it was time to let go. But for now, he would get to spend a peaceful day with the pride.

Shortly after I left the sanctuary that afternoon, Aslan had a serious seizure. As the caretakers rushed to the enclosure, Shanti Deva and Asha were trying to coax him up and were nudging and pushing him. When the seizure subsided, all three of them were coaxed into their indoor building.

Aslan had given us the sign. It was time to let him go with dignity. The seizures would only get worse and his body would only deteriorate more. He deserved to leave the sanctuary as king, the same way he arrived.

Aslan's Tree of Life

Our compassionate vet and staff made his last moments as peaceful as possible. Aslan remained in his area overnight so Asha and Shanti Deva could mourn his loss.

When I was informed of his passing, I had just taken this photo on my cell phone. I was several hours away, but it seemed fitting to take a photo of such a spectacular tree, maybe the "tree of life" in honor of Aslan.

He is now able to be free and king of his wild life. The pride is still together in spirit and one day will be reunited. Until then, we will take wonderful care of his girls, Asha and Shanti Deva.

Thank you to all of you who helped us provide Aslan six additional months of a happy life with the pride he loved so much. He spent his last day beautifully and doing what meant the most to him. We have your support to thank for that.

Aslan will be deeply missed but will always be a part of The Wildcat Sanctuary.

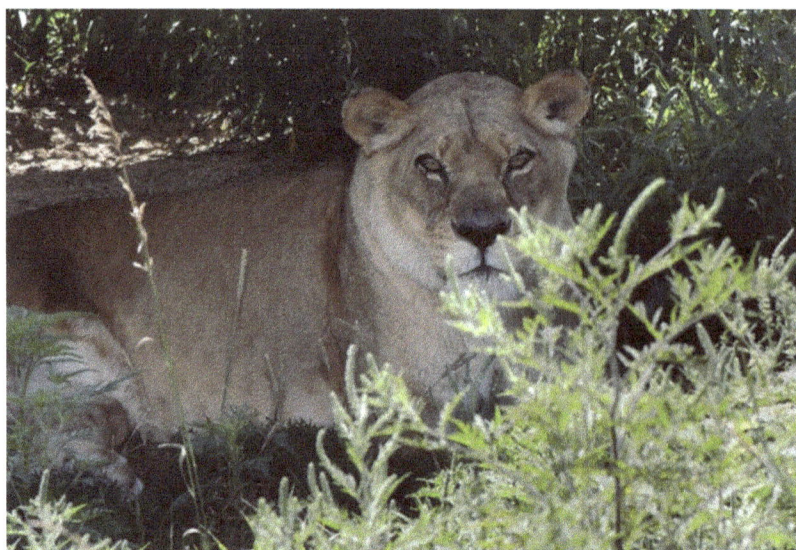

2015
LION - ASHA

Asha and two other lions were part of a big cat rescue from the Catskill Game Farm in New York just before Christmas 2006. With the closure of their animal park, the game farm auctioned off 950 animals, making both East Coast and national headlines.

Many worried that some of the animals would wind up in the hands of unscrupulous dealers, or that animals, such as deer or goats, would go to people who run 'canned shoot' operations where hunters pay to shoot fenced-in animals. It is described as one of the largest animal rescues of its type. Wildlife Watch intervened on behalf of the three lions to ensure a safer fate through placement at TWS.

Asha was born in 1996. After healing from her physical and emotional scars from her confinement at the game farm, Asha has blossomed into a very jolly cat. She loves all kinds of enrichment that keepers give her, including boxes to shred, pumpkins for Halloween, and anything heavily scented like having perfume sprayed on her toys.

Asha and Aslan shared a special bond before he passed away in 2014. They often groomed each other before mealtime or rolled down the hill together like old pals. Most of all, Asha loved relaxing. In her hammock, on her cave or just lounging in the grass, she thinks being a lazy lion is great!

In December of 2013, Asha became gravely ill. Nothing else matters when one of our beloved cats falls ill. For a moment, you feel helpless, but it also brings clarity. Clarity that this is what all the hard work is for—to help cats like Asha.

Our founder, Tammy Thies, shared "I can remember the first day Asha arrived at The Wildcat Sanctuary. It was a cold and snowy winter day, much like today. She was in a large metal crate being lifted from a truck with a skid steer. Both the crate and the skid steer were rocking from her shifting side to side. Even through the crate, you could sense the sheer power of her. She was such a strong girl. She has been a strong girl every day since joining our sanctuary in 2006. That is until recently."

Even at 17, Asha has been an active lioness. Mealtime is her favorite time. So, when she wasn't as interested in eating one day, we knew something was wrong. Seeing one of our strongest cats appear weak is very emotional for each of us, but we know we have an important job to do. And, with wild animals, it often must be done quickly.

Taking a 400-pound lioness to the vet isn't an easy task or an inexpensive one, but our donors' support ensures big cats like Asha always receive the best of care.

TWS vets sedated and examined Asha at the Sanctuary. She was given pain medications, fluids, and supportive care here at TWS so she would be stronger for her trip the next day to the University of Minnesota's large animal hospital for diagnostics.

The University's expert team performed ultrasounds and it was determined surgery was needed. Asha had a baseball size benign cyst on her liver and a blockage in her lower intestine due to slow motility. Results showed this had been an ongoing issue for Asha. Surgery took several hours and then she was on her way back to TWS for recovery.

Asha received around the clock monitoring and care by her keepers, including medication and a special diet. Two weeks after her surgery, she was introduced back into her pride with Shanti Deva and Aslan. The reunion and recovery was just as emotional for us as her illness. Seeing the pride accept her back and immediately begin grooming her was heartwarming.

Asha's keeper Kathryn said, '*Tears came to my eyes when I saw Asha walk-up and nuzzle Aslan. And hearing the pride roar together for the first time again was a great moment.*'

Happy endings and specialty care for our residents is made possible because of our donors' generosity. This was a very serious surgery for a cat of Asha's age and size. We feel blessed that Asha will have even more days here at the Sanctuary.

In Memory

Asha has always been known for having such a zest for life. She was feisty, with a brightness about her that always shined. You would think that, being so assertive with humans, she would be the dominant lion in her pride. Instead, she would take Shanti Deva's lead on how to approach their daily routine. Enamored with Aslan, she followed him constantly.

Asha was such a vocal lioness, communicating very clearly what pleased and displeased her. Since she never hid her emotions, we knew exactly what she loved. And how she loved mealtime! Belly rolls with Aslan and curling up for a nap with Shanti Deva also topped her list of favorite things in life.

Being so bold and assertive, it was very obvious when things weren't quite right with Asha. You could see her eyes dim slightly and a calm set over her. Almost a year and a half ago, we knew there was something dangerously wrong.

Asha underwent emergency surgery for a mass on her liver and slow motility that caused a blockage in her intestines. Amazingly, 14 inches had to be removed from her colon. We breathed such a sigh of relief when Asha recovered fully. She returned to her feisty self, thanks to the love of her pride. Life was good again for them. She would roll with Aslan and chase Shanti Deva as caretakers passed by.

Even though Asha said goodbye to her love Aslan earlier this year, she stayed strong in spirit. She found comfort in Shanti Deva who has always been the calming presence amongst the pride. We took comfort that Asha's bright zest for life continued, even with his loss.

But recently, we saw a little bit of that zest dim. It was different this time. We knew there could be no more emergency surgeries for this 19 year-old lioness. She had bravely conquered all she could. She was a little quiet, slept more than normal and was picky with food.

An exam confirmed another mass in her abdomen and depleted red blood cells that were not regenerating. It's never an easy decision, but we knew that this strong lioness deserved to go bravely, before her light faded entirely.

With heavy hearts and tears, we did the most humane and difficult thing, we chose not to wake her up from sedation and allowed her to join Aslan. We're sure Aslan met her with belly rolls and nose nudges. Saying goodbye to her was sudden, but it's what we had to do. We had to do it for her.

Shanti Deva, the alpha of the pride, still rules over their habitat. She seemed to know it was time for Asha to join Aslan, even before we did. She continues to be calm and social with her caretakers. She remains very active and still loves to roar at her caretakers as they drive by after feeding time.

It's hard to get used to her single roar, when we've been used to the roaring chorus of the entire pride. But her mighty roar is a symbol of how strong she is and that she continues their legacy here at The Wildcat Sanctuary. We will love and pamper her here until it is time for her to rejoin Asha and Aslan as alpha of their forever pride.

2020
LION - SALTENA

Salteña's a lioness who arrived at the sanctuary in 2018. Though records on her birth are not clear, it is estimated she was 26 years old when she came to us. She and six other lions made the long, 6,000-mile journey to Minnesota from Argentina.

We were told Salteña spent her life living in a circus transport cage with her mate. The circus had abandoned them in 2011, leaving them starving and dehydrated. Authorities then placed them at the Mendoza Zoo in Argentina.

An animal welfare group in Argentina later reached out to us, asking if we could take in the last two remaining lions from the Mendoza Zoo. Thirteen other lions had already died at this very old zoo. Animals were not spayed or neutered, so thousands were in cages there. Some had already escaped, roaming the zoo grounds.

Since there was only one outside area there for the lions, Salteña had been sharing it with the last male lion, Chupino. When he was outside, she was inside a small, dark cage in the mountainside. We knew, at her advanced age, transport would be very risky. But we just had to give her this last chance to have the life she dreamed of.

Life at the Sanctuary

We held our breath as the transport truck doors opened. We had two veterinarians on hand to deal with whatever Salteña needed. Well, were we ever surprised when she let out many roars letting us know she had finally arrived!

Today, she enjoys her comfy straw bed more than anything else. She has one inside and one outside, whichever she prefers. And, though Chupino is totally smitten with her, Salteña calls the shots with him. She is a very confident lioness! To see her so content now, after so many years of neglect, is the greatest feeling in the world!

In Memory

Yes, we knew this day would come, but it is even more difficult than I'd imagined.

At 27, we had to help our Lady Salteña pass on to her new wild life. One free of bars, free of concrete and free of confinement.

Salteña's life was far from a fairy tale. In fact, it was quite the opposite. She experienced a life no wild animal should ever have to endure. She had been used for years as entertainment by a traveling circus in Argentina. There she spent her life in a tiny, rusty crate on wheels, barely able to stretch her legs.

She suffered malnutrition, hunger, and metabolic bone disease. Her teeth were broken and rotten from a poor diet and chewing on the bars. Eventually, she was rescued by a zoo. Though better, she still did not have grass under her feet. This zoo had limited resources and was eventually closed.

I remember being asked if it was the right thing to try and move an old geriatric lioness literally across the world. In many cases, I would have said humane euthanasia was the better option. But that was not even an option for her.

The zoo had been closed for several years. Sadly, that might mean she would pass away in her cage, as others had already done. I refused to let that be her fate. We knew it would be risky, but we had to try. We had to show her what life could be like.

During transport, I was contacted in the middle of the night that Salteña was not doing well. They were sure she was in emergency distress. Luckily, they just did not know Salteña.

At her age, she had some vision and hearing issues, which meant she slept very soundly. It was difficult to startle her, and she was having vivid dreams—the one way she could live the life she wanted.

The moment she arrived, we heard her strong roar and protest of being in the crate. It was music to our ears. Salteña's spirit was as strong in person as we had felt across the continents. She was in charge spiritually, even if humans had physical control over her entire life. If you asked me again, I would say yes it was worth the risk.

At the sanctuary, Salteña finally was able to bask in the sun and loved her soft straw-filled beds. She enjoyed the most freedom she had ever experienced in her life…until today.

Her move was not the only risk we took with Salteña. As soon as she and Chupino arrived, we knew how smitten he was with her. Living together on shared walls in Pride Prairie, you could see their relationship grow. But you could also see Saltena was alpha.

We talked about the pros and cons of allowing them to be together. We knew if one bad move took place, that could end Salteña's life. Even if Chupino was just playing.

Late this past summer, we began noticing Salteña's decline. Before she was compromised any further, we made another risky decision. We allowed her to be with Chupino for the afternoon, together in their large habitat.

As much as we planned, we knew this could be dangerous for her. We kept this special day quiet, not to hide the moment, but to cherish it as much as possible. It is a day imprinted in my mind and one I will never forget.

They had some very peaceful moments. But true to Salteña, as well as lion behavior in general, she wanted to assert herself. Chupino tried his best to let her, but he also had to defend his honor. This is normal and typical behavior—we have seen it with all big cats during introduction.

But it took a lot out of Salteña—she was exhausted. They did get to share a very special afternoon in the same space—a truly magical day. After we separated them, they went back to being best friends, separated by fences.

They both seemed much more comfortable that way—they did not have to keep their guard up. And could just spend the rest of their days together the way they had for so many years.

Chupino knew her time was here before we did. We were still hopeful supportive care would help her. Saying goodbye was difficult, but not as difficult as her previous life had been.

Salteña lived in a barbaric circus, then a closed-down zoo, and was not rescued until she was 26 years old. This should not have to happen to any other lion, tiger or wild cat ever.

We have treasured the last 16 months we've had with Salteña. And we were honored to provide her this last peaceful year of her life, alongside Chupino.

JAGUAR

2015
JAGUAR—DIABLO GUAPO

Diablo Guapo, a black Jaguar, lived at a big cat rescue facility in Colorado. Unfortunately, the facility was not receiving enough funding to continue caring for the animals. The Director made the very difficult decision to start placing animals at other facilities, undoubtedly a humbling and difficult decision, but the right one considering the alternative.

Diablo Guapo's a very beautiful and rare cat. Breeders were offering up to $17,000 to purchase him. The sanctuary in Colorado wasn't concerned about money. They were concerned about Diablo's well-being and placed him with us.

The translation of Diablo means devil. Not at all fitting for such an amazing creature. We changed his name to Diablo Guapo which means handsome devil. But we soon started calling him Guapo.

Guapo was born in 1996 and arrived at the Sanctuary in 2006. He now lives in a 6,000 square foot free-roaming habitat next to Shazam. Guapo and Shazam made fast friends and can often be found lounging along their shared wall. They have a special bond and share an equally special kinship with one another.

Guapo is a favorite among staff, volunteers and donors. He's probably our most recognized resident next to our tiger Titan. His laid-back attitude and goofy personality draw everyone in. One of his favorite things to do is paint; he's quite the artist. Using non-toxic washable paint, the keepers spread it on a canvas and watch the artist go to work.

In Memory

Gone in body, but not in spirit

How do I even begin to share this news?

Some cats have a presence that can't be explained. That was Diablo Guapo. His spirit and beauty resonated through you. And you didn't have to know him personally to love him.

For those who never met Guapo in person, you still knew him and could feel him. He never knew how his specialness transcended across the globe to all of you. Or maybe he did, and just never let on. He was very humble that way. He was such a calm cat who also exuded joyful bliss, especially while playing with enrichment or trotting down the shared wall with his friend Shazam, the leopard.

When he first arrived in 2006 from a facility in Colorado that was closing, we knew there was something very special about him. What a patient cat he was—through the transport, through several construction projects to give him better and bigger habitats, and even in his geriatric years, when his body couldn't get him down the shared wall as fast as he liked.

Each cat at The Wildcat Sanctuary has their own personality. Guapo was definitely the most distinguished. He was wise and appeared to be a guide for so many other cats to come, and to us caretakers as well. He felt bigger than himself, and the love each of you have for him confirmed just how special he was, and will forever be.

As he grew older, he was very at peace and comfortable. But he let us know his time was near. He was slowing down each day but remained the calm and distinguished cat we all knew. He was very vocal and continued to talk to us, even as his time shortened.

We all knew when we had to say goodbye, and that moment was as heartbreaking as I thought it would be. But what I didn't expect is, that in that moment, I could still feel his presence. It was a very different and peaceful feeling. I wondered if I was the only one that sensed it.

His body was gone, but he was still with us. Then, as we do with all of our bonded cats, we presented Diablo Guapo to Shazam so he could grieve. In the past, all the cats seemed to know even before we did that their friend had moved on. This time was different.

Shazam approached the fence and tried to play with Guapo. Even rolling over and purring as he had done for several years. I couldn't believe it, but it seemed Shazam also still felt Guapo's presence and that he was still with us, just no longer in physical form. It's hard to explain why these things happen when we have to say goodbye. But here at the Sanctuary, so many have.

When one cat passed in the early hours of the day, the wind picked up and Aslan's pride began the most lovely, roaring session. When another passed, a rehabber came onsite to release a snowy owl and it flew directly to that habitat and perched on a tree before flying back to freedom. Rain and snow have begun to fall during days when it was clear. And double rainbows have appeared.

Does something like this happen with each passing? No, some pass quietly. But each passing does cause us to stop and reflect and remember the love we have for each cat and the lessons they've taught us.

I believe Guapo and so many others still reign over the Sanctuary grounds. Their spirit and strength will live on through the air we breathe, the energy we feel and the love in our hearts.

Sometimes, it's impossible to put into words the love we have for each cat. We're so thankful to have been given the opportunity to know and love Diablo Guapo. And that love will transcend all physical space and time, just as Guapo has.

Dear wiseman, know how much you meant to each and every one of us and you will always be with us in spirit. Continue on with your important work, touching so many.

COUGARS

2007
COUGAR - LEVI

Levi is a very shy cougar who came from a wildlife park. Park staff loved him, but Levi did not like to be on display because of past abuse from a private owner. He stayed in his den most of the time when the public came to visit.

The park decided it was time to provide Levi with a different environment and placed him at our sanctuary. Levi now has a large outdoor habitat with access to the barn. He loves women but is very shy with men. He's a very special guy and near and dear to all of our hearts.

In Memory

For the Love of Levi. Levi's friends and caretakers helped him pass over in the fall of 2007. His legs really gave out and it came to the point he could barely walk. His kidneys and liver were also compromised. He was ready, we were not—but we respected his wishes. He was a majestic and wise man and will forever be with us. He shared so much of his strength with us.

Levi, who was one of the oldest residents at the Wildcat Sanctuary, has passed over the rainbow bridge. He is now in a place where he can run without pain, his spirit guides beside him, a place where he can truly be wild at heart.

Levi was the first cougar to find a home at TWS, and the story of his beginnings is unfortunately yet another tragic one. He was rescued from one terrible abuse situation and placed into another.

Luckily, The Wildcat Sanctuary rescued him and gave him his final safe haven. Somehow Levi knew he'd landed in the right place. Over many years of care, he was able to open his heart again. He was very patient with every move, from Georgia to Minnesota, Isanti to Sandstone, from one spot to the next.

In Isanti, he became more curious, meeting up with Max in the next enclosure. He'd peek around the corner to sneak a glimpse of Meme the tiger. He would listen quietly when someone read to him.

In Sandstone, he loved to sit under his favorite tree and watch the goings-on. He was especially on alert when the food bucket came around, even if he'd already had his share!

Unfortunately, the original abuse had taken a toll on his body. He had always had trouble with his back and legs, but he started to have extreme difficulty walking. We do not always have the chance to let them choose when it is their time, but Levi let us know and allowed us to give him the dignity he deserved in his passage.

2008
COUGAR - YUMA

Yuma is a 10-year-old cougar who resided at a safe haven sanctuary in Colorado. The sad part is that the sanctuary was not receiving enough funding to continue caring for the animals. The Director made the very difficult decision to begin placing animals at other facilities in order to ensure they received the proper care. It must have been so humbling to have been faced with such a decision.

Upon arriving at TWS, Yuma was sedated for a full physical. Sadly, we soon realized that Yuma had been declawed on all four feet and she had regrowth where the nails were growing back into her pads with even some bones exposed.

Usually, we could make the decision to correct this, but Yuma's declaw was not done by a vet. Most of her digits on her feet are crushed beyond repair. Amazingly, Yuma seems to have little pain. She can be seen chasing an empty milk carton or large Easter egg, both forms of enrichment, across her enclosure.

She is also one of the most vocal cats on our property and calls out like a goose whenever she sees a keeper or visitor.

In Memory

Yuma, a 12-year-old cougar, has passed. Two months ago, keepers noticed Yuma becoming increasingly lethargic. It was during this time that she stopped eating.

Initial x-rays showed a blockage. With the removal of about 1-2 pounds of hay from her stomach, we hoped she would be on her way to a full recovery. It was unlike Yuma to eat anything other than her staple diet. Staff believed it may have been something more serious.

She was kept in quarantine after her first surgery where she was the best patient a vet and keeper could ask for. Unfortunately, she still wouldn't eat. We kept thinking it was her time, but she kept fighting and clearly communicating that it wasn't.

She had two more x-rays and after the second, our veterinarian decided to perform surgery again. She had two spleens, or a split spleen (she should only have one) and a stretched pancreas. The spleens were removed since she wouldn't need them to live a healthy life.

Staff and vets believed this to be the reason why she was uninterested in food. Just a day after her surgery, she began eating every last morsel of food she was given. We felt optimistic that she would have a successful recovery.

Up until the past couple days, she didn't skip a beat. She was her loud, cheerful self and could often be found reminding her habitat-mate, Raja, that she was boss.

We are sad to say that the tough little girl had relapsed in the past couple of days. TWS staff immediately responded to her lethargic behavior and sought medical treatment.

Beautiful Yuma unfortunately lost her fight, and staff helped her pass comfortably. She is now in a place with her friend Cooter, where she can continue to be her vocal self, playing with her basketball.

2009
COUGAR - HOPE

We were called to help rescue up to seven cougars living on an Iowa farm. Within minutes of stepping on the property, our staff knew it would take all we had to hold back the tears.

The stench was incredible, the site horrific. A small cage was filled with two feet of fecal matter and other debris.

The remains of one cougar that had passed away was there in a barrel. A few feet away, a pen held the remains of three other cougars. Two additional cougars had been shot earlier after escaping from their small kennels.

And then we saw her, a small cougar who was still alive. She was the sole survivor in a cage no more than four feet high. She had no den and no tarp, nothing to shelter her from the elements.

Hope, as we immediately named her, was extremely malnourished and dehydrated, but still able to move on her own. We were there to take her to a better life at The Wildcat Sanctuary.

Today, Hope is a happy and socialized cougar. She loves life to the fullest and never misses a meal, but can you blame her?

She lives with another cougar, Josie, and they get along just like sisters. One day they irritate each other, the next day they can be found curled together in a heated den.

In Memory

Some of the rescued residents come to TWS scared at first, while most seem to desire a life of change from their past, a life of great care, a chance to be wild at heart. They all "hope" their lives will be changed for the better.

Of the many cats that we've rescued, cougar Hope has been a true ambassador for this theory. She came from one of the hardest rescue cases we'd seen. And she flourished into a confident, trusting cougar.

We're saddened that Hope has passed. At the old age of 20, she was starting to experience some difficult days due to hypertension. We made the decision to help Hope pass before she became too uncomfortable.

She made the most of every moment here at the sanctuary. Whether it was running around with her cage-mate, Josie, playing with her toys, or enjoying her daily meal. We are very proud to say Hope has truly lived out her life to the fullest after such a horrible start in life.

Twenty years is amazing, especially considering 14 years of Hope's life were spent in a tiny, filthy pen with no shelter. Hope was the lone survivor when we arrived, and she was starving. It is the first time our vet told me a rescue wouldn't make it through the night—that she was too far gone.

Hope proved us all wrong. Even though her ears and tail are partially missing due to frostbite, she's still a beautiful girl. She has a resilience and happiness which is an amazing gift she shares with us all. For the last six years, she's been a gentle, happy cougar who let go of her horrible past.

Although she is no longer with us, we want her story to live on. All captive wild cats in need of help deserve the same chance at "hope," a chance to live wild at heart.

Hope's story was featured in a *National Geographic Kids* article in November 2005.

2009
COUGAR - NOKOMIS

Nokomis, a cougar, was surrendered at six months of age when his owner in Oak Grove found authorities knocking on their door. Oak Grove had an exotic animal ordinance, so it was illegal for her to keep him.

Nokomis was being fed Whiskas canned cat food and all his baby teeth were gray and cracked. Our vet had to pull his baby teeth, but thankfully his adult teeth came in just fine.

Nokomis has grown into a beautiful adult cougar. He is one of our largest males but cries like a baby when he wants a caregiver to provide attention to him. Nokomis' favorite toy is anything he can destroy, like basketballs or stuffed animals. He also prefers to live alone and has made it quite clear that sharing his space with another cougar is not an option.

In Memory

It breaks my heart to share with you that we lost Nokomis. He wasn't responding to the treatment that would help his lung condition. As much as I wasn't ready to let him go, I knew it was the right thing for him. His passing has devastated me to the core; I really thought he would be okay.

He was a strong cougar who never had an illness since his arrival at TWS. It's amazing how things can drastically change in 30 days. Due to our office move, my office was temporarily set up in the hospital which allowed me to be with him every day until the end.

He was perfectly Nokomis in a body that wouldn't cooperate. His personality never wavered, and he believed we would do the right thing for him. I would have done anything to make the right thing something other than what it was. But I had to help him pass on. He fought as hard as we did, but he just couldn't get well.

It was one of my saddest days ever at the sanctuary. And something I am still struggling with. I know it's selfish to want him here when I know his life, though good, was still confined behind a fence.

Nokomis gave me strength each day and we had a very special connection that won't be duplicated. He purred to me whenever I was near. He would chirp whenever he could see me through the office window. He loved taking naps on top of his den.

He was an animal that accepted his life in captivity and came to terms with it. What an amazing amount of forgiveness and acceptance this takes for a cougar who should have been wild. Nokomis will forever be loved and missed.

2010
COUGAR - CHEYENNE

Cheyenne, a cougar, is one of the lucky ones who came from a Nebraska farm and found sanctuary. She suffered from severe dehydration, abscessed teeth, frostbitten ears and tail, and mats around her neck. Her only shelter had been a steel barrel with no bedding.

Cheyenne is still timid with humans, but caretakers work with her daily by giving her toys, enrichment and treats.

Cheyenne's health is complicated due to her teeth and being FIV positive. But she's shown us that she's a fighter. Because of her illness, she cannot share a habitat with another cat. Though she seems to enjoy stalking the bobcats from her new area.

In Memory

One of the greatest rewards as a caretaker is to help a fearful new rescue grow into a confident, trusting resident. It's our duty and mission to become their "friend."

Working on the cats' timetable is often a long process of consistent dedication and compassion to help renew their faith in humans. While many are only resistant for a few months, some take years. It is these residents and their accomplishments of which we are most proud.

With that being said, the hardest thing to do as a caretaker is letting our "friends" go and process that the special moments we share with them are only a memory. With great sorrow we must share that Cheyenne, the once apprehensive cougar, has passed in the early hours of Wednesday morning. To honor her and her amazing growth we want to share the journey of this beautiful girl with you.

About two and a half years ago, Cheyenne was rescued from deplorable conditions in rural Nebraska. Her life consisted of a small, feces-filled enclosure and a couple of rusty old oil drums to den in. She suffered from frostbite on her tail and both ears because of this inadequate shelter.

Without a source of water in her enclosure, she was severely dehydrated. Her inconsistent diet resulted in broken and abscessed teeth. This poor cougar was in trouble and desperately needed our help.

She was spayed, given a full veterinary exam and care, and was moved to quarantine once she arrived. Cheyenne was so afraid of humans that she hid in her den for three weeks!

She'd wait for nighttime to emerge from her den to eat and explore her new home. Caretakers would do rounds the next day, only to find her tracks in the snow and her food gone. We waited anxiously to just get a glimpse of her to ensure she was okay.

Staff and volunteers began reading to her softly from a distance. Our work was beginning to pay off and she started coming out on evening rounds. This was her first big step and an uplifting moment for all of us.

Over the next few months, she was getting more courageous by the day and reached her second milestone by coming into her lockout when it was time to eat. Caretakers began walking around her habitat feeding her small pieces as a reward if she followed. This was a big step in getting her used to us moving around her without fear that she was going to be hurt.

Cheyenne then moved to a larger habitat near other residents at the sanctuary. She continued to show emotional growth when we were present. She was sunbathing and regaining her wild instinct to stalk the bobcats in a distant cage. She was even spotted for the first time playing with a toy in her habitat, her mobile.

At last, it was Cheyenne's time to move to her permanent, free-roaming habitat in Cougar Cove. With 5,000 square feet all to herself, she had plenty of room to relax in her thick, tall grass and still be vigilant of her surroundings.

Soon after, her glow in the dark ball was in a different area each morning and she was seen napping in her hammock during the day. These small signs showed caretakers that her faith in humans was almost back.

It wasn't long before she began coming right up to us as we did rounds, and even lounging in the open grass sunning her belly in front of small groups. Caretakers were in disbelief when one afternoon she played with her enrichment while they were right by her.

She was so happy flipping the box around, smashing it and tearing it apart. She knew we were watching, and she didn't care. She was in her moment and we felt honored that she would share that precious experience with us.

It is as though Cheyenne was testing us as humans, to see if we could be trusted. Once she realized we could, it seemed she let us know it was her time to go. She quit eating two days before her passing. Staff looked into her eyes, saw her calming presence and knew it was her time.

Considering Cheyenne was confined for most of her life and her past mistrust in humans, the staff faced a tough decision. We all felt it would be best to leave her in serenity, sleeping in her tall grass on a warm April day with a gentle breeze in the air and the lions roaring in the distance.

She showed no signs of pain and seemed rather content that we were allowing her to go the way she wanted to. Although some may take more time than others to come around, it goes to show that with some help from the sanctuary, anything is possible.

We'd like to leave you with a quote we feel closely represents Cheyenne and her special growth with her caretakers:

"The glory of friendship is not the outstretched hand, nor the kindly smile, nor the joy of companionship; it is the spiritual inspiration that comes to one when you discover that someone else believes in you and is willing to trust you with a friendship." ~ Ralph Waldo Emerson

2012
COUGAR - CODY

TWS received a call from the United States Department of Agriculture regarding several cats that were in an emergency situation. They asked if we could accommodate any of the cats or network with other groups to help. We immediately contacted the closest rescue group to the animals, Exotic Feline Rescue Center in Indiana. EFRC agreed to go on site and upon their return from removing a leopard, they emailed us this message:

"Got the leopard, will go back for the rest Wednesday if you can take the cougar. We cannot express the outrage and contempt for authorities in allowing this to happen. The smell, the filth, the starving cats, the rotting carcasses are all inexcusable."

We agreed to take in Cody from this deplorable situation. Initial reports from EFRC said he was in terrible pain due to broken and rotted canines and needed immediate medical attention. He also needed to put on weight, get hydrated and be on antibiotics for several weeks before surgery could be performed to correct the issues in his mouth. EFRC generously agreed to keep Cody and do the work before Cody would be well enough to transport to Minnesota.

Cody arrived at TWS in late fall of 2008 in much better condition with his surgeries complete. He is so relaxed and takes everything in stride. He has had a long journey and seems to let it all roll off his shoulders and live for the moment. He lives in a free-roaming habitat in Cougar Cove. He adores his caregivers and playfully stalks any new volunteers or interns.

In Memory

The Wildcat Sanctuary's Sweet & Calm Soul

Cody may have spent the first twelve years of his life in horrific conditions, never knowing when his next meal was coming, his water bowl would be filled or if his cage would ever be cleaned. But more importantly, Cody resided at The Wildcat Sanctuary for the last four years of his life, the best years of his life.

From the moment we picked him up, we knew this boy was special. He was purring while being loaded into our vehicle, and continued purring for the majority of the 12-hour trip and well, he has never stopped. One would think coming from a past like his, Cody would not trust humans at all. But not Cody, he was the sweetest cougar, capable of melting your heart the moment you made eye contact.

He was such a gentle and calm soul, who always had a positive outlook on life. He was even purring as he went into his last moments with us January 17th. Sadly, Cody was also declawed early in life. The combination of this and years of malnourishment resulted in severe arthritis in his spine and knees.

He was a strong boy until about a month prior to his passing. He started to show difficulties in mobility and signs of pain. The vets prescribed pain meds to keep him comfortable. Unfortunately, signs of his pain came on so rapidly it was not long before his dose had to be raised to the highest level. Our veterinarian performed laser therapy. He was doing well at this level until the past couple days. And that is when we knew it was his time, but we were devastated that it all happened so soon.

I can only imagine how many times we have discussed how much we dreaded the day we would have to help Cody pass. Just the thought would cause tears to fill our eyes and our breaths to deepen. We would have to immediately toss the thought out of our head as the difficulty in letting him go felt unbearable.

Now here we are today, the day we feared from the moment we saw his freckled nose. Our hearts are broken, our eyes swollen, and our souls shaken. I will miss spending time with him during evening rounds; these moments were so precious and filled my heart.

In his four years here, not only did he win over the hearts of all of us humans, but he won the heart of Josie, a female cougar. The two became very close friends with each other over the years, often snuggling together in their hammock or in the grass. It is truly amazing how in touch the cats are with one another.

As Cody passed, the other cougars residing in Cougar Cove were quietly watching him from their rooms across the way. It was as if his calming energy had spread when we carried him out of the building. While there are typically cougars calling from every direction, everything was quiet. His energy had the ability to transcend to others, whether two-legged or four-legged.

When upset from helping another resident pass or just from having a hard day, I would go to Cody. He held such healing powers for my soul with his positive and loving outlook. I am so thankful to have met such a special animal.

Please visit us often Cody and may you walk along on evening rounds pain free. I will be sure to call on you for your gentle spirit to push me through difficult times. I'll meet you across from your old enclosure, the entrance of the memorial garden, the path to you being finally, forever free.

"There are souls in this world which have the gift of finding joy everywhere and of leaving it behind them when they go". ~ Frederick Faber

2013
COUGAR - MAX

Cougars Max, Mia, and Matty, along with four other cats, were part of a big cat rescue from the Catskill Game Farm in New York in 2006. With the closing of their animal park, the game farm auctioned off 950 animals and made east coast and national headlines.

Many worried that some of the animals would wind up in the hands of unscrupulous dealers, killed for their parts, or sold off in the illegal exotic animal trade.

Wildlife Watch intervened and negotiated placement of animals in sanctuaries, while others purchased animals to ensure their safety. It is described as one of the largest animal rescues of its type.

Matty, Max, and Mia live together in a free-roaming enclosure here at the sanctuary. Max spends his days relaxing with the ladies and enjoying some TLC from TWS staff.

In Memory

Over the past seven years, we have been fortunate to watch Max, the cougar, grow into a fatherly figure to the others residing in Cougar Cove. While his spirit was still as energetic as that of his youthful neighbors, his body was not.

Through additional care, we helped Max maintain his physical health as long as we could. Unfortunately, he was in renal failure and his physical symptoms were beginning to worsen. As a result, we sadly helped him pass.

Max arrived, back in December of 2006, with Mia, Matty, Aslan's pride, and Shazam. Their dispositions mirrored the physical wounds they arrived with.

Time progressed, and like the others, Max's abrasions began to heal. As his body healed, his personality began to come through. From his very first days at TWS, he has been a very observant cat. He was always looking around with his big round eyes, and wrinkly forehead, just taking everything in.

Shortly after being here, Max found himself living with the two beautiful cougars he arrived with, Mia and Matty. He absolutely adored them and was somewhat of a bridge between the two. When introduced, Matty and Mia were a little unsure of one another.

But with Max's affectionate, benevolent attitude, he was able to bring the girls closer together. He would frequently walk up to one, greet them with a head-butt and grooming, then go to the other to repeat the gesture. He would always let them play with the new enrichment first, happily sharing any goodies he had received.

His persistent efforts created a little love triangle, and the three were referred to as the "3M's." While they may be an "M" down, Max's accepting spirit lives on in the girls. Max was such an important part of their daily lives, we are sure they will miss him dearly.

It was not just the girls Max left an impression on. He held a fatherly presence for Cougar Cove. When resting in his indoor room, he frequently chatted with cougars across and down the hallway, especially Castle and Vista.

When outside, he would often be seen greeting his neighbors, particularly the five wild born cougars. He would vocalize with his unique call, "rahr-urr-ruh" signaling the others he was near.

Langley, Donoma, Carlo, Noah and Andre would come running up to return the greeting. They would sit along the fence waiting for their turn to be groomed by Max. They would then run off playing as usual.

Though he was an older cat, Max still loved to play with his enrichment. He was a great artist, completing several painted masterpieces with Mia and Matty. As soon as the indoor rooms were cleaned and shift doors were opened back up, he would come sprinting in to see what enrichment was put down for him and his ladies.

A couple weeks before his passing, he was in his usual spot along the shared wall watching over the young cougars, Noah, Carlo, and Andre. They were tearing at the remaining paper and boxes from the previous day's holiday enrichment. He watched as they shredded, rolled, and ran around with the paper.

It was as if he was a proud guardian in that moment, watching them have such a blast. But you could see he knew his body was going, though he still wanted to show the young guys he still had it.

He slowly got up and walked over to his flattened holiday wrapped boxes, smashed from the prior day's destruction. He began playing with it, though slower than in the past; while glancing up periodically to ensure the boys were watching.

May his mellow, guiding personality live on in the cougars that looked up to him like a role model. He provided his girls with the best thing he could, a connection to one another. One they can continue to build as he did for them.

And to us humans, he left great memories and yet another cat to deeply miss. Please come back often Max and observe those in Cougar Cove from your favorite resting spot, beneath the dogwood bush.

"Lacking a shared language, emotions are perhaps our most effective means of cross-species communication. We can share our emotions, we can understand the language of feelings, and that's why we form deep and enduring social bonds with many other beings. Emotions are the glue that binds."~ Marc Bekoff

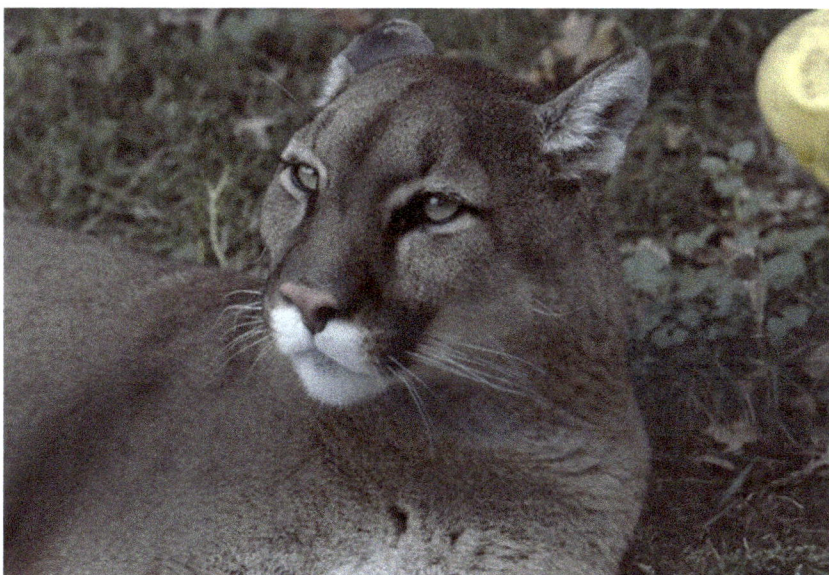

2013
COUGAR - JOSIE

Josie, a cougar, was a former wild pet. Her owners were educated about exotic animals, loved her dearly and had planned that Josie would be a part of their family for her entire lifetime.

Unfortunately for Josie, as they already had a 17-year-old son, they did not plan on the arrival of a new child. Josie's owners decided to put the safety of their child and Josie's needs first.

They could've sold Josie to a breeder or to a private citizen as a pet. Thankfully, the family wanted Josie to have the best life possible. That's why they chose The Wildcat Sanctuary as the place they wanted for her "forever home."

At the time, the Sanctuary was at full capacity. Josie's owners were persistent and contacted The Wildcat Sanctuary several times, insisting this was the right place for Josie to spend the rest of her life. We raised additional funds and built a new habitat in order to accommodate Josie and provide her a safe haven where she could remain wild at heart. She finally arrived here in 2001.

Today, Josie lives in a free-roaming habitat in Cougar Cove, with both wild- and captive-born neighbors. She is a sweet soul and receives special attention from her keepers in her advanced age.

When Tasha II was rescued from an Ohio facility, she and Josie became habitat mates. Tasha II had very limited vision and it was slow going, at first, since Josie didn't know what to make of her. But, with her kind disposition, Josie accepted Tasha II and they share their cougar kingdom amicably now.

In Memory

When walking around Cougar Cove, it was hard not to call out "where's Josie?" only to hear her respond with her duck-like quack. This Marco-Polo like conversation was a highlight in the staff and intern's workdays.

Sadly, now when passing by Cougar Cove, it's been difficult to resist calling out to her knowing she's no longer with us, but on her next journey where she was welcomed by her old pals Cody and Hope.

Earlier in April, keepers noticed a quick decline in Josie's appetite. Given this and her being 16 years old, we were nervous that her time was quickly approaching. Our vet team saw her immediately. Unfortunately, we discovered she had stomach cancer.

April 10th was a hard day for those at TWS, a day we lost one of our dearest friends.

For those who had the pleasure of knowing Josie, we found her to be a very nurturing cougar. Over the years with us, she's lived with several other cougars. Two of which she made very strong connections with.

She kept her relationships with them quiet at first. We'd often "bust them" resting with one another. After sharing our excitement of our findings with other staff, interns and volunteers, we'd begin finding their relationships becoming more public.

Her first pal was Hope. Shortly after Josie met Hope, we'd find the two girls snuggled up in the den with one another. They became like sisters, sharing every moment with each other.

Sadly, after Hope passed on, Josie would seek more human attention. It was as if she was attempting to fill the void of her dear lost friend.

So, we tried her with Cody, an older cougar with an equally endearing demeanor. It wasn't long before the two were spotted together throughout the day. She loved him very much and they took turns at grooming one another, while sharing a hammock in their indoor room.

Just as with Hope, her days with Cody were full of warmth, but limited. Her friends would pass, and she would be there to comfort a new rescue, making their time more enjoyable while with us.

Whether people knew her for 10 years or two months, she was like an old friend who you've known forever. She helped both animals and people through tough times or periods of adjustment. Her presence comforted us all at the Sanctuary, this nurturing little girl who just never stopped purring.

She is a reminder to us all that, even though we know at some point their time with us must come to an end, it just does not make it any easier. Days are longer, hearts are just as broken, and memories are clung onto desperately.

While with us for over a decade, she had seen many cats come and go. She had even helped Cody and Hope enjoy life through their last moments at the sanctuary.

Given their bond with sweet Josie, they will be sure to greet her on the other side, saving a spot in the tall grass for her to lie. She can peek her head out, with chin lifted and eyes squinted, just like her days at TWS. Where she can welcome those, who follow her paw prints, being the nurturing girl she is.

We will miss her waiting for us to call out "where's Josie?" so she could quack and come purring her way towards us, helping us through our days. We will miss you sweet Josie, you truly were one special friend.

"Each of us can look back upon someone who made a great difference in our lives, someone whose wisdom or simple acts of caring made an impression upon us. In all likelihood, it was someone who sought no recognition for their deed, other than the joy of knowing that, by their hand, another's life had been made better."~ Stephen M. Wolf

2014
COUGAR - MIA

Cougars Matty, Max and Mia, along with four other cats, were part of a big cat rescue from the Catskill Game Farm in New York in 2006. With the closing of their animal park, the game farm auctioned off 950 animals and made east coast and national headlines.

Many worried that some of the animals would wind up in the hands of unscrupulous dealers or be sold to people who run 'canned shoot' operations, where hunters pay to shoot fenced-in animals.

Wildlife Watch intervened and negotiated placement of animals in sanctuaries while others purchased animals to ensure their safety. It is described as one of the largest animal rescues of its type.

Matty, Max, and Mia live together in a free-roaming habitat here at the sanctuary. Mia is a stately old lady with lovely graying fur. But don't mistake her for feeble, though—Mia is never afraid to show her roommates who's boss!

In Memory

As caregivers, the most we can ever ask for is that our animal friends live long and happy lives, and when it is their time to leave, that they pass on as peacefully as possible. This is what we had with Mia the cougar.

Mia lived a long 17 years and arrived at TWS in 2006, with several other cats from the Catskill Game Farm in NY. At TWS, she lived with her confident beau Max and energetic friend Matty. Max was very special to Mia and when he passed away from renal failure last year, Mia found a new friendship with Matty in his absence.

Just a short time ago, Mia was rubbing on her ball, strolling through her habitat, and sharpening her claws while stretching on a log. She and Matty enjoyed the new enrichment balls that donors had provided. She was the happy Mia we had come to know and love.

Within just a short time, she began to lose weight and coordination in her hind end. It was symptoms we've seen before in our geriatric cats that have compromised kidneys.

A vet exam confirmed our fears—Mia was in advanced renal failure. Knowing we had done all we could for her we made the difficult but important decision to let her go peacefully and with dignity. It is never an easy decision, but one we knew we had to make for her.

Her last few weeks were joyous, and she spent a lot of time outside in the nice weather. Life was on her terms and she entered and exited the animal building at her leisure, ate whatever she wanted and spent some special moments with her caregivers through the habitat fence.

Mia was different from all the other cougars. She had a quiet side to her, compared to Matty and the "5 Wild" who also live in Cougar Cove. But, when it came to painting enrichment, the kitten in her came out.

None of us wanted to say goodbye. But the end of her journey with us was very special and peaceful. She led us every step of the way and we were able to make the end of her life as meaningful as her beginning here.

Mia, we will miss your expressive eyes and calming presence. Your name meant "dear" and "mine" which you will always be to us. Enjoy your new wild life over the Rainbow Bridge. Max is there waiting with purrs!

2016
COUGAR - SPRING

Spring, a male cougar, spent 9 years in a wire cage. As he was closely bonded to the only humans he knew, Spring did not know he was a cougar.

He had a difficult adjustment after his owners chose to surrender him in 2007. TWS provided all the love and care we could, but we were unfamiliar faces to Spring. He refused to eat his first week at the sanctuary.

Spring was very fearful and confused when we introduced him to the other cougars. He just wanted to run and hide. Fortunately, with time, Spring has come out of his shell and is now very social to his keepers. As a result of his solitary start to life, Spring still has trouble with other cougars. So, he lives alone, but he does not seem to mind at all.

Spring has a very calm spirit, a unique chirp, and a sweet face. He loves to playfully stalk his keepers and unsuspecting interns, as well as chat with them in his own native cougar tongue.

In Memory

Just a week before his 18th birthday, the Sanctuary said goodbye to Spring the cougar. He had been receiving special care for a number of years, but his last days still came too quickly.

You've heard the phrase "Gentle Giant" and that truly describes Spring the cougar. He was the largest cougar at the Sanctuary and had the sweetest demeanor. Spring even preferred to live alongside bobcats, because he was intimidated by other cougars and big cats.

He loved people, painting and he loved playing with his toy balls. For a big and senior boy, he had a young soul and enjoyed every moment to the fullest. And his joy was contagious to those that cared for and loved him. We know you felt it, too.

Spring's distinctive call, which sounded like "wow," could be heard throughout the Sanctuary. He never missed an opportunity to say hello, followed by his rumbling purr. And his distinctive expression, including crossed eyes, made it easy for everyone to know it was Spring the moment they saw him.

Spring was diagnosed with severe spondylosis and arthritis in 2011 and early renal disease. He received pain management and kidney support orally several times a day. Because of his arthritis, he could not groom very well but enjoyed being brushed/scratched through the fence and would position himself along the fence each time a caretaker approached with the back scratcher.

He was the only cat who had a special summer and a different winter home at the Sanctuary. He loved to nap in the shade of the pine trees in the summer, but the cold was hard on his arthritis. So come fall, he'd move into the quarantine area of the Sanctuary where he received an indoor room with his very own hammock.

He and his neighbor Salem, one of the smallest bobcats on the property who is 21, would compete with who could mark the shared wall the most. It became a big clean up job for the caretakers, but they were happy to support their antics.

It's the small things we notice that alerts us of a big change. Even though Spring still talked to us and purred nonstop, he started letting Salem win the marking contest. His last week, there was less cleanup for the caretakers and he spent more time on his hammock and we knew his health and heart were declining.

The day we said goodbye, the staff held a bedside vigil. He was peacefully sedated while lying on his hammock before being brought into the Scarlet Veterinary Center. Each staff member had the opportunity to personally say goodbye. We all circled around him as tears flowed down our faces.

Our veterinarian asked if we were ready, if Spring was ready. We said yes, even though our hearts wish we didn't have to make that decision. But, before she could administer the last drug, Spring took his last breath on his own, something we did not expect. It was a moving moment, and reaffirmed we had picked the right time.

As with all goodbyes, we do not take the decision lightly. Often, we question—are we deciding too soon? Spring assured us we had not. And, it's important to remember, if we choose a day too soon to ensure they do not suffer, they will forgive us. But, if we choose too late, we will never forgive ourselves.

Spring, thank you for all the joy you brought everyone. You are truly one-of-a kind. May there be many bobcat friends and toy balls where you roam free now.

2016
COUGAR - TASHA

A pet tiger was shot by authorities in Iowa after it had escaped and attacked the owner's dog. The owners also had Tasha and another cougar Raja in their possession and contacted TWS for help. Tasha and Raja came to TWS in 2007.

Tasha is a female cougar with a sweet disposition who "talks" constantly. She is very easygoing and loves all sorts of enrichment, like balls and whole prey. In fact, Tasha is so playful that she will often provide her *own* enrichment, tossing her food dish around or stalking nearby interns.

Unfortunately, as she approaches advanced age, Tasha has begun to experience kidney problems and other age-related issues. Tasha receives special supplements which are added to her daily diet, in order to keep her as happy and healthy as possible.

Tasha prefers to live alone and tends to hold herself in higher regard to other cougars. She has established herself as the princess of TWS.

In Memory

Sadly, we had to say goodbye to one of the strongest voices here at TWS, 17-year-old cougar Tasha. Tasha had been treated successfully for years for advanced renal disease and hip dysplasia. A few years ago, she began having seizures, but those also subsided. This week, the seizures returned, and her prognosis was poor. We had to make the difficult decision to let this joyous girl move on to spread her specialness elsewhere.

Every single day, Tasha brought a smile to our faces and was full of fun antics. She was a cat everyone at the Sanctuary looked forward to seeing. And she felt the same way in return. Her distinctive voice was much deeper than a normal cougar and her personality stood out.

She would run along the fence with her caretakers, stalk behind the smallest blade of grass, and be the first and last to greet everyone near the entrance to the Cougar Cove section of the Sanctuary. Her head bobble was precious, and her purr was contagious.

When she was younger and had more energy, she played for hours with her tug toy. She loved to entertain herself, as well as all of us. And if you gave too much attention to her neighbors, her distinct call could be heard to lure you back her way. No one could resist her. And why would you want to? She could bring a smile to anyone's face.

As social as she was to people, she was not that way with other cats and chose to live alone. She would not tolerate a cougar even on a shared wall, so bobcat Baby Jenga moved in to be her next-door neighbor.

Tasha liked being the queen of her castle, and all of Cougar Cove. She was the first to be heard in the morning and last at night. Oh, how we'll miss her being such an important part of our daily routine.

We love you Tasha and know your joyous spirit is no longer hindered by your body. May the rescued residents that follow in your footsteps enjoy their days at the Sanctuary as much as you did. And make sure as they arrive, they hear your special call welcoming them to their forever home.

You will always be a special part of TWS and a voice for those still in need of rescue.

2018
COUGAR—MAX II

As a sanctuary, we are a home for life to all our rescued residents. But at TWS, we take that even one step further. We follow and commit to providing a forever home for all the cats we refer to other reputable facilities and sanctuaries, too. If, for any reason, a sanctuary or facility cannot care for the cats we've referred or placed with them, we'll do everything we can to provide them a home for life. And that is the story with Max.

Celebrating a new home, a new birthday, and a new life!

Max turns 16-years-old this month as he arrives at The Wildcat Sanctuary! He is a kind-hearted cougar who suffers with arthritis. He has been receiving the best medical care to keep him pain-free. Because of your support, he will now be able to live his golden years at The Wildcat Sanctuary.

In 2011, we received a call from a private owner needing to surrender a cougar due to a divorce. At that time, we had just taken in cougar kittens Carlo, Noah and Langley, and we didn't have habitat space for him.

The Lake Superior Zoo had lost their other cougars due to old age and they agreed to accommodate Max. We support zoos that help rescue privately-owned cats, especially when there are not enough sanctuaries to take in every cat in need. We are thankful they used Max's story to educate people about why wild animals should not be kept as pets.

Max has spent the last six years at the Lake Superior Zoo. Due to flooding and a new facility plan, the zoo decided to renovate habitats, including where Max was living. When we heard of this, we reached out to the zoo offering a final and forever home for him.

Max moved very easily. And from the moment he arrived at the sanctuary, he acted as though he had lived here his entire life. We have never had a cat adapt so quickly to their new life. He explored both his indoor and outdoor areas and met his new neighbors, without missing a beat.

Max reminds us a lot of our cougar Spring who we recently said goodbye to. If Spring melted your heart, Max sure will, too.

He also has a gentle and social demeanor, was 4-paw declawed and has arthritis. We will make sure to provide Max with everything he needs to enjoy life to the fullest during his golden years.

In Memory

Cougar Max—his spirit was bigger than he was

With tears, we said goodbye to one of our sweetest residents, Max the cougar. After being treated for constipation, he had a few good days before he declined quickly due to a mass on his liver. Our hearts are broken, but also filled with love for this gentle giant.

His story is a little long, but every aspect of Max's story is so important to share. Have you ever known an animal is meant to be with you, but you do not know when and how it will happen? Life has a funny way of bringing things full circle and those are the moments you really want to pay attention to. Because something truly special will come into your life, just like Max the cougar.

I know we say every cat is special and they truly are. And we rescue so many gentle giants that have no reason to forgive us but do. Max was privately-owned in Iowa before needing a home due to a divorce.

When I received the call and heard his story, he really touched me, and I wanted TWS to be his forever home. But I also had to make the best decision for him, and we had just taken in the '5 Wild' cougars who were still in three separate groups.

A small, temporary pen would need to be constructed for Max, and that would not have been fair to him. We reached out to other sanctuaries, but it was at a time the industry was bursting at the seams and no one had space.

An accredited local city zoo in Duluth had been looking to help a rescued cougar. They had a habitat, trained staff, wonderful vet care and little foot traffic. They also wanted to help educate the public that wild animals should not be kept as pets. Max's story would do just that.

Several years passed, but we continued to follow his story. Max became the most popular resident at the zoo. He educated many about the plight of wild animals kept as pets and enjoyed his ambassador role. He chirped to guests, purred at caregivers, and was receiving first class care for his broken teeth and arthritis.

Then a flood hit the zoo and damaged enclosures. We learned from the USDA that they were looking for a home for Max. Of course, we jumped at the offer to take in this special boy, once and for all.

Max arrived at TWS a few years ago at the age of 16. His sweet disposition made his transition easy and he fit right in next to the other cats. Every day he was relaxed in his hammock, chirped hello and the roar of his purr was constant. He did not mind living next to big tigers like Zeus or rambunctious ones like Daisy. Max kept his own pace, a calm, confident one.

We knew with his degenerative arthritis that Max would not be with us forever, so we cherished every day—and so did he. He enjoyed enrichment, he crated on his own for habitat moves and was kind to each neighbor he met.

We were cautiously optimistic when on his first day ever of leaving food, the vet staff saw him immediately and treated him for constipation. We were hoping it was just that, but we know that can often be a symptom of something larger. The next few days, he was outside and acting like his old self.

Our hearts were hoping. But then he curled up in his hammock and became lethargic again. We knew it was something more. And as difficult as that realization was, again we had to make the best decision for Max. His liver was failing, and it was time to say goodbye.

Saying goodbye to any resident is so very hard. But saying goodbye to one who thanked us each day for our work with chirps and purrs leaves a little bigger hole. We all need that reassurance that we're making a difference in their lives, especially when there are so many we cannot save.

Thank you, Max, for playing a bigger role in your life by sharing your story. We will make sure it lives on—always.

2018
COUGAR - MATTY

Matty, the cougar, along with six other cats were part of a big cat rescue from the Catskill Game Farm in New York in 2006. With the closing of their animal park, the game farm auctioned off 950 animals and made east coast and national headlines.

Many worried that some of the animals would wind up in the hands of unscrupulous dealers, killed for their parts, or sold off in the illegal exotic animal trade.

Wildlife Watch intervened and negotiated placement of animals in sanctuaries while others purchased animals to ensure their fate. It is described as one of the largest animal rescues of its type.

For many years, Matty lived with her parents Max and Mia together in a large, free-roaming habitat here at the sanctuary until her parents both passed away. Matty is very active and interested in what's going on around her—especially in what all her cougar neighbors are up to.

She loves to crouch low and stalk anyone passing by her habitat. She will also let loose a fearsome cry every mealtime, reminding us daily that these cougars will always be wild at heart.

In Memory

Every loss at the Sanctuary is difficult, but when it's a sudden and unexpected loss, the pain cuts a little deeper. We never thought we'd be saying goodbye to active 14-year-old Matty the cougar so soon. Fourteen might be considered geriatric but is very young for our residents who often live as long as 20 years or beyond. Matty left us due to acute renal failure, just like her parent's Mia and Max did a few years ago.

Within just three days, she went from being a happy, healthy girl…and then she was gone. There's a big hole in all our hearts right now and still some disbelief.

If you met Matty, you know why. She was one of our most active cats at the sanctuary. She never missed a moment to play with the '5 Wild' cougar family along the fence line, play hide and stalk from the tall grass with her caregivers and then pop up purring as loud as could be.

It was rare to see her sitting still or just basking in the sun—she liked to be on the move and in the middle of all the sanctuary happenings.

As calm and cool as tiger Zeus and cougar Max were, Matty was just the opposite. She was a party animal. Full of energy and life. Taking on every piece of enrichment she was given—and she always won. Jumping to the tallest perch before launching off and on to her next adventure.

She came to us in 2006 with several other cats when the Catskill Game Farm in New York closed. But boy, does it seem like just yesterday. Twelve years later and she hadn't aged a bit, at least on the outside. She remained in good spirits even after the passing of her parents. Nothing seemed to get Matty down.

I'm happy she didn't have more than a few bad days on this earth, but her loss does take our breath away. In rescue, we're always providing comfort care to our elder residents and those that just can't beat the odds of the health problems they have from their past. So, sometimes we feel cats like Matty were cheated a little. And so were we. We just didn't know her time was coming so soon.

Matty, you left us too fast! But then again, you were never a cat who moved slowly. We enjoyed every day and every moment with you. Thank you for always being such a happy and energetic presence here at the Sanctuary. The other side is very lucky to have you!

2018
COUGAR - MISHA

Misha, a cougar, was two months old when she was placed with us in 1999 by Georgia U.S. Fish and Wildlife. A private citizen purchased her illegally as a pet and was given ten days to place her with a licensed facility. TWS was recommended as a facility that would be able to provide Misha with a lifetime of care.

Just a few days after Misha was placed with TWS, she became lethargic and vomited frequently. Shortly after, she went through emergency surgery due to an intestinal blockage. While living in her previous owner's home Misha had eaten many household items that became lodged in her intestine. Since the initial surgery, Misha has undergone two additional surgeries to help correct the damage.

Due to Misha's condition, extra care is taken to make sure she is not given any object which she may ingest that would cause further damage. Therefore, Misha's enrichment program includes items such as phone books, vegetables, and meat hidden inside cardboard boxes, all safe items for her to do as she pleases with.

Misha thoroughly enjoys ripping apart boxes and tearing each page out of phone books creating quite a mess throughout her habitat. Misha has overcome a great deal and grown into a beautiful adult cougar living with a roommate Max, a Eurasian Lynx.

In Memory

Where do I begin? I could never imagine a day that you weren't here with us. It's only been a day, but it already feels like a lifetime. You've been part of my family and the TWS family for 19 years.

I know 19 is a long, good life—but your leaving came suddenly. A blessing for you, but difficult for those of us that loved you so much.

I remember getting the call from the US Fish and Wildlife Service that an individual was ordered to surrender you after purchasing you illegally as a pet in Texas. I never knew how much I already loved you until he tossed your 8-week-old self into my arms and took off in his truck.

Your beginning had some rough days when you first were surrendered. You had an intestinal blockage from cat toys, a bandana tied in knots, and several rubber nipples from a baby bottle you ingested while living with your former owner.

After surgery, we couldn't risk feeding you with a bottle anymore. So, you were perched on the wood dining room table as we tried to feed you with formula and ground turkey from a bowl.

We had to wean you fast and boy was it messy. You, I and the table were covered in the mess. I remember you looking up with that adorable face and all I saw were two blue eyes and a head full of formula. Those days were so special and set the stage for 19 wonderful years with you.

It wouldn't be your last abdominal surgery though. If you could get it in your mouth, you did. No matter how careful we were, as a toddler and teen, you'd always find something you shouldn't.

As you matured into a beautiful adult cougar, you became so regal and sophisticated. But even in your princess pose, your play side would show through. You'd lift and motion with your right paw— your trademark move—to signal you'd trip your prey or people if they were on your side of the fence.

Though it was playful, it always reminded us that you were an amazing predator. Then, you'd frolic up to the fence and rumble the large purr you were known for.

Though you loved your human friends, you also made a special friendship with Max the Eurasian Lynx. He fell in love with you through a shared wall and your resentful acceptance gave him the best years of his life.

Once he moved in, you were such sweet friends and always near each other whether on the hill or perch overlooking the sanctuary. When he aged and couldn't get to the top of the perch, you curled up next to him underneath. That's how loyal you were.

After he passed, you ventured back to the top of your tall platform and took in the sun lying on your hammock. Close to the sky was perfect for you—because you were a sweet angel. I know everyone who knew you loved you as much as I did. I just knew you a little longer—which made me even luckier.

I can't express how much I loved you and how full you made my and Max's lives. Yes, each cat at TWS is special. But the cats who've been here since the beginning knew the start-up struggles and were so patient and such good teachers. I, and all the animals of TWS, have you and many other founding cats to thank.

I love you and miss you my dear friend. I am sure Max has been anticipating your arrival. Be sweet to him.

2018
COUGAR—TASHA 2

We received a tearful call from an Ohio woman asking us to help her and her cats. She is a USDA licensed owner who was committed to providing a home for her cats but realized what the future would mean for her and the animals she had in small cages in her backyard.

Though she wanted to provide more for these animals, she'd struggled financially to keep up and was fearful she wouldn't be able to meet the regulations the new legislation would require.

She researched different sanctuaries and contacted The Wildcat Sanctuary because she felt we could offer what her animals deserved—a home for life, where they wouldn't be uprooted again and where they would have the open space she couldn't provide for them.

Sadly, the story of her animals and what they've been through is as heart wrenching as many of those who died that day in Zanesville, Ohio. And, like most others, hers is not their first home.

Tasha, the cougar's, first home was sad. At a young age, she was used for breeding. She lived in a garage for 9 years, but one day escaped through a hole in the roof. Her owner didn't report her escape, fearful Tasha would be killed. But Tasha did finally return, scared and hungry.

Then, Tasha went to her second home, living in a 10' × 20' cage. Declawed by her first owner, it has left her tender footed and she also has vision problems. Her current owner says she trembles, shakes, and drools at the sound of machinery near her cage. But with all she has gone through in her 11 years in captivity, she still craves attention from her human caregivers.

The International Fund for Animal Welfare (IFAW) heard of our efforts and called offering an emergency grant to help with initial costs for Nikita and Tasha's transfer to The Wildcat Sanctuary.

Nikita and Tasha's story touched hearts across the country and was covered by several media outlets. Tasha felt right at home from the minute she arrived at TWS. She's such a gentle soul.

In Memory

We had to let go of our bright, shining star Tasha II today. Her health had begun to decline over the past year. Her vision and mobility were affected by a degenerative nerve condition. But she was still Tasha, shining bright and making everyone smile.

Within just a few short days last week, that slow decline sped up. And her bright personality began to dim. Her organs were slowly shutting down. It was when Tasha's mental state dramatically declined, and she stopped engaging in the daily activities that made her so happy, that she clearly told us it was her time.

Tasha's shining spirit brought so many people together. After escaping the garage of her first home, where she'd lived for nine years, she was rescued by a wonderful couple. But when laws became stricter in Ohio where they were, they contacted us to help Tasha and other cats. They knew we'd provide them a safe and wonderful life.

The First Time I Met Tasha

I remember seeing Tasha for the first time. If her cross-eyes, and head tilt didn't make her endearing enough, her pure bliss for life did. She was in a 10' x 20' area filled with more toys than you could count. And she played and showed off with every one of them before hopping on a platform, tilting her head, and inviting you to play through the fence.

Tasha brought so many special people together. Three wonderful sanctuaries came together to help Tasha and all the animals. It also brought the support of IFAW, Tim Harrison of Outreach for Animals and all of you together! And her former rescuers remained involved in all their lives.

She was so lucky to be loved by so many. And we were so lucky to have known her.

Tasha treated everything as a new playground. When she first arrived, her toys never stopped moving. She was dribbling them and in motion all the time.

As she aged, she loved her firehose hammock and loved to greet everyone with her signature Tasha chirp. But that wasn't enough. She always had to come up in person to say "Hi!" and to share her joy.

Now, instead of walking past Tasha, our bright shining star each day, we just look up to the sky and see her shining down on us. We feel blessed to have had you in our lives Tasha and thankful for all the new friends you introduced us to.

May you continue to shine bright with our pride on the other side.

2019
COUGAR - LIBERTY

We've rescued many cougars through the years, but Liberty's journey stands out as an example of what too many captive exotic animals have to endure. We arrived on a rural farm to pick up a cougar who was being surrendered by her owner. What we found astonished us: Liberty was no larger than a lynx. She was emaciated and dehydrated. We could not get over how small in stature this cougar was.

The owner explained that she had fed only milk to Liberty her first year of life and that Liberty had fractured both of her back legs, which had gone untreated. Liberty cannot extend her back legs fully, and she has a severe curvature of the spine and pelvis. The tops of her ears were dangling by a small amount of flesh and were about to fall off. She had urine burns on both sides of her tail.

The owner said Liberty wasn't eating or drinking very well, but Liberty ate four times the first night she arrived at TWS and eight additional meals the next day. She continues to love her food—in fact, she is the first to cry out in excitement when she hears the keepers at mealtime!—and has put on weight each day.

Liberty weighed 45 lbs. upon arrival at TWS in 2008. This is the size of a six- month-old cougar—Liberty is six years old. The initial fecal exam showed Liberty also had roundworms and *coccidia,* a type of bacterial infection. Though Liberty's journey has been rough, she finally has a life that will ring true to her name. She has become such a social cougar and her chirp can be heard constantly. For a small girl, she sure shows her roommate who is boss!

In Memory

Can you die from a broken heart? That's the question we're dealing with right now after losing cougar Liberty just days after Raja's sudden passing. After Raja passed away, Liberty was lost. We knew she'd need time to adjust to her new life, so caretakers have been giving her special attention.

She didn't want to drink or eat that much, so they provided her with bloodcicles and spent special time at the fence with her during mealtime. She didn't want to go to sleep in her room, so they placed warm straw in her cave and under her trees.

From the outside, it could appear Liberty was weak and depressed. But I ask myself another question? Did Liberty choose this deliberately? Even with her disabilities, including being blind, she'd always been a strong girl. Her voice carried across the sanctuary when she heard the caretakers coming with food. She was Raja's confidant right up until his passing.

And now she was a shell of herself. She had complications for so long since arriving with metabolic bone disease. And she had to be examined and given supportive care on several occasions to keep her going. Did she just hold on for Raja and now she could let go?

As caregivers, we turn over every stone to assure there isn't a scientific reason for their losses so close together. Could something be in the environment or the food? We're looking at all options, but I don't think we'll find anything. Sometimes the universe is bigger than us and the power is amazing.

What I do know is Liberty beat the odds so many times. From the day we picked this tiny adult cougar up from a farm. She was emaciated, her ears frostbitten off, and she couldn't extend her back legs. I'd never seen an animal in such frail condition.

But her spirit was strong. So strong.

She rebounded, and became very confident, and eventually was merged with cougar Raja. She adored her life with him. They were always together, or at least close by. She was the outgoing one and always calling out to their caretakers. She enjoyed enrichment, just like Raja, and both were very generous sharing with each other.

As the years progressed, she went blind but still used every inch of her habitat. She followed Raja and he followed her. They were extremely bonded and truly respected each other.

She continued to need supportive care including eye drops, medications, and subcutaneous fluids. She was truly a miracle. And now she's performed one more. She joined the one she loved so much. As heartbroken as we are, we know it's what she wanted. Trying to make sense of it is difficult, but I know it makes perfect sense to Liberty.

Raja and Liberty, we're at peace knowing you are together again—forever.

2019
COUGAR - RAJA

Tragically, a tiger in Iowa was shot by authorities after it escaped and killed the owner's dog. Once on the property, they discovered the owner also had two cougars named Raja and Tasha. They quickly contacted TWS for help. Raja and Tasha came to TWS in 2007, a true sanctuary where they would get the care and space they needed.

Despite Raja's rough start in life, he's a very happy cougar who's only social with the people he knows. He tends to retreat when other people are on site. But, once they pass, he's back to playing with his toys and cuddling with his roommate Liberty.

Liberty helped Raja come more out of his shell. She loves to yell at her caretakers for food, which has rubbed off on Raja. The only difference is, Raja's a little quieter than his vocal partner.

He loves hanging out on top of his platforms, watching his neighbors around him. He's always up for any kind of food enrichment and is always the first to come up during mealtimes. Though out of all the enrichment caretakers have tried with him, nothing is better than tearing apart a piñata!

In Memory

I am crying hard for cougar Liberty's loss even more so than mine. Cougar Raja's sudden loss due to renal failure has left more than us grieving. His mate and confidant Liberty is also grieving.

At 14, Raja was considered young in terms of TWS cats. Most of our cats live well into their late teens and early 20's. So, we were devastated by his quick decline and are left with our loving memories of this beautiful boy.

Raja came to TWS with another cougar Tasha I. They were privately-owned and surrendered after a horrible incident happened. Even though both cougars came from the same farm, Raja only had eyes for cougar Liberty.

Raja was the most stunningly handsome cougar I've ever seen. And his sweet, soft, and even somewhat insecure demeanor only added to his charm. He only trusted people he really knew and often retreated when volunteers were onsite. But as soon as it was quiet, he would come back out to greet us all with his sweet face and purr.

Raja loved cardboard boxes and became quite famous as a social media meme. But that wasn't Raja's style at all—he never gleamed for the limelight. Even when he'd perch up on his cave in the sun, creating the most beautiful backdrop I've ever seen, it wasn't for the photo opportunity. It was to take in the warmth of the sun and the energy of the world around him.

But what Raja loved most of all was his friend Liberty. They were introduced years ago at the Sanctuary after attempts to introduce Raja to other cougars failed. Upon their first meeting, it didn't take long before Liberty was curled up in Raja's lap on a hammock. They were best friends from then on.

Raja never noticed Liberty's disabilities. Coming to TWS with metabolic bone disease, she's much smaller than other cougars and about 1/3 of Raja's size. As years passed, Liberty became blind. But that never stopped her from leading Raja. She was the confident one and he followed.

Only when Raja began to get sick, did Liberty let him take the lead. She followed him everywhere and never left his side. As he grew weaker, he could no longer perch up on the cave in the sun but found a great spot on the ground.

Liberty would drape herself over him—even if she was napping on her back, her front and back legs would be lying on his head and backside. He more than tolerated this, he loved her companionship and support.

When it was time to let Raja go, all of our hearts were broken. Not just for our loss, but for Liberty's as well. We knew she needed time to grieve, too. The night of his passing, Liberty curled up in their favorite spot under the pine tree. She stayed there for quite some time.

Caretakers also saved some of Raja's fur and put that in some of their favorite spots. He is gone physically, but I know he hasn't left Liberty's side spiritually. I think she can feel that, too.

We'll give her extra attention for the days and weeks to come. We'll honor Raja by making sure we take the best care of what he loved so much. And when she's ready, we'll ensure she has cougars on her shared wall and can make new friends. Until then, she's doing well, eating and enjoying the sun.

Raja, you may never have asked for all the attention, but your sweetness was just too genuine not to be noticed. We'll miss you more than you know, and you and Liberty are connected by a power larger than this world. She is never far away. Friendship is truly forever.

CANADA LYNX

2006
CANADA LYNX - KODIAK

Kodiak, a Canada lynx and retired exhibit cat, came to us declawed on all four feet. As he gets older, it gets harder and harder for him to walk around.

Kodiak is very shy and exerts very little energy. He prefers to lie around and relax versus being active like the younger cats. His habitat accommodates his needs by providing multiple dens and easily accessible perches for him to lay on.

How many hours of the day can one spend watching a tiger? Kodiak would know. When he's not snuggled amongst warm, soft blankets in his newly insulated and heated cat room, he's keeping a watchful eye on his neighbor Meme.

We're not sure if he's locating her, making sure she's not in his habitat, or if she's just that exciting; whatever the case, Kodiak is addicted to spying on his neighbor.

Kodiak receives several different forms of enrichment (objects or activities to keep him occupied). We need to be a little more creative when it comes to ideas for Kodiak—due to his many allergies and sensitivities to different things.

From time-to-time, he is given his favorite toy: a leather glove. He loves leather gloves! A new addition to his enrichment protocol is a snack tucked into a paper-towel roll. Kodiak can smell the treat and he has to use his natural instincts to get to it. Enrichment works.

In Memory

It has been such a difficult few months with the loss of Meme, the tiger, and Kaya, my domestic animal companion. On May 2nd, 2006, we also lost Kodiak, our beloved Canada Lynx.

On the morning of May 2, 2006, a staff member asked me to check on Kodiak, our wonderful and wise lynx. He had labored breathing and in minutes we had him in transit to the vet. Kodiak stopped breathing in the car, we assisted him in his breathing, but it was not enough. Kodiak passed away in my arms.

Our vet performed a necropsy and Kodiak had two issues. He found that 80% of his intestine was compromised due to very advanced cancer. He also found a foreign body blockage that had ruptured the intestine and caused Kodiak's quick death. We don't know if Kodiak's intestine had been less compromised, if he could have passed the object or not.

It is times like this, that I replay the 'what ifs' over in my head. We try to be careful every day, but it seemed Kodiak had a toy that came from an adjacent cage where the small Bengal domestics were. Kodiak was not known for eating or digesting toys or objects.

It's difficult to know if the discomfort from the cancer contributed to him chewing on and digesting the object. We now know Kodiak would have still passed in the near future due to the cancer, but it is very difficult when I think any discomfort or pain could have been avoided.

2010
CANADA LYNX - KAJEEKA

George and Kajeeka, a pair of Canada lynxes, resided at a sanctuary in Colorado. The sad part is the sanctuary was not receiving enough funding to continue to care for their animals. So, the Director made the very difficult decision to start placing animals at other facilities in order to ensure they received the proper care they needed. It must be so humbling when one is faced with such a difficult decision.

George is very apprehensive of people and is very protective over his habitat mate, Kajeeka. The bond they share is amazing and very special. Kajeeka is deaf and blind, but you'd never know it by her spirit. She's so courageous and truly enjoys life. She gets up on her perches and can often be seen playing with her toys. She is absolutely in love with George and he takes his self-appointed job of protecting her very seriously.

In Memory

An unexpected tragedy hit us today. Kajeeka, our sweet lynx, has passed. She wasn't feeling very well the past couple of days, so we decided to have our vets look at her. Blood work and x-rays showed kidney failure, anemia and a possible mass on her kidney. We made the decision to help her pass so she would not have to endure any more pain or illness.

Our hearts go out to George, who was her guardian and loved her very much. The two were inseparable and this loss is going to be hard for him, so please keep him in your thoughts. After we helped Kajeeka pass, we brought her back to George for him to say goodbye.

Kajeeka had a pretty rough start in life, first being completely declawed and then losing her hearing and eyesight. She also lost one of her eyes completely. But none of those things slowed her down. She loved anything to do with scents; perfumes, Lawry's Seasoned Salt, catnip, you name it and she rubbed on it.

She loved George most of all, often claiming him as her own by peeing on him when anyone walked by. No matter what she was doing, George was always near. We still can't believe this happened. Kajeeka was such a wonderful girl, so full of life it's hard to believe that hers is over. She will live on in our memories though, and we'll do our best to comfort George in his time of need.

We are so glad we were able to know you Kajeeka, we hope wherever you are now all the colors are bright and the scents are never ending.

2012
CANADA LYNX - SHAY

When bobcat Sydney and Canada Lynx Shay arrived at TWS, the signs of past abuse were very apparent. Both had crooked mouths due to their jaws being broken as a result of blunt force trauma. Shay was extremely timid of humans and would shake and defecate if we got too close. They counted on each other for support.

They both have healed emotionally and physically, though Shay still prefers animal companionship over human. She is also losing her sight, but still does wonderfully getting around her enclosure. She now lives with George in a large habitat with indoor access.

In Memory

Sometimes, it's hard to say goodbye. But, when you know in your heart that it's the right time, it can make letting go a little easier. It was time to let our lynx Shay go.

Shay was a very reclusive cat but, given her experience with people, it wasn't surprising. She was severely traumatized and abused by her first owner.

Thankfully, Shay had Sydney, a Eurasian lynx she came with, to lean on. However, Sydney passed a few years ago and Shay never really found another she could be close with.

Shay was blind and mostly deaf. While we gave her every creature comfort we could, a warm building to sleep in, nutritious food to eat, and all the enrichment she could have, we could never give her the companionship she had with Sydney.

As the years went by, Shay became even more introverted than before, not enjoying enrichment as much. Given her eyesight was gone, she wasn't venturing too much into her habitat.

Life in captivity can be very hard for an animal. But with lots of space and fun enrichment, it can still be enjoyable. For Shay, life just wasn't enjoyable anymore and her health was slowly deteriorating.

We made the difficult decision to let her go so she could once again be with Sydney and be free of the terrible memories she held inside.

We believe we can make a difference here, giving animals who've experienced abuse, neglect and heartache a chance to be wild at heart. I believe we did that for Shay.

Goodbye dear Shay, I hope your new free life brings you nothing but joy and happiness.

2013
CANADA LYNX - GEORGE

George, a Canada lynx, lived at a safe haven sanctuary in Colorado. The sad part is the sanctuary was not receiving enough funding to continue to care for the animals. The director made the very difficult decision to start placing animals at other facilities in order to ensure they received the proper care. It must be so humbling when one is faced with such a decision.

George is very apprehensive of people and is very protective over his companion Kajeeka, who is deaf and blind. The bond they share is amazing and very special.

He originated from a fur farm where his life would have ended at two years old and his pelt used for a coat. Luckily, someone intervened.

George has a physical deformity, which is common in many fur farm animals. His knee on one leg is not attached and the bottom half of his leg faces sideways. An x-ray showed it could not be corrected with surgery and could only be amputated.

At first the leg didn't bother George, but within a year at The Wildcat Sanctuary, you could see it was beginning to cause him pain. We chose to remove the leg and George hasn't missed a beat.

In Memory

There are many different personalities when it comes to the residents here at TWS. We have the loud ones, the shy ones and of course the show-off all the time ones. And then there was George. George was calm, cool, and collected and never bothered with any of his neighbors' antics or dramas. He was the picture-perfect lynx, often lying on his perch with his face to the sun just enjoying the moment.

He needed nothing from us humans in the way of attention. But given his gentle nature, everyone who met him fell in love with him. Out of all the residents, he had the most sponsor parents and I believe it's because of his love story with Kajeeka.

George and Kajeeka arrived at the Sanctuary in 2006. Kajeeka was mostly deaf and blind and George was her caretaker. He would always let Kajeeka come and get her piece of food first and would never try to steal it away from her. They were always together, often lying under a tree or sleeping curled up in their hammock.

They also loved enrichment, anything strong smelling would get them rolling around and they loved to paint together.

Then a few years ago, Kajeeka became ill and passed away, leaving George alone. We worried he would not be far behind her, but he proved to be very strong. Even after losing a leg, due to genetic issues, he endured.

When we moved him to a different habitat, he surprised everyone by crawling up to his top perch, five feet above the ground, and this was his new favorite spot.

About midway through the fall this year, we noticed George was not moving around as much and his remaining back leg was starting to bow out when he walked. We decided to move him to our Quarantine area so he could have flatter ground and we could keep a closer eye on him.

More recently, he lost his appetite both for food and for enrichment. We brought him to the vet for x-rays. The x-rays showed a great amount of deterioration in the joints which meant there was pain involved.

He was put on a pain medication but, after a month, it was obvious it was not enough. After discussing with all the staff and vets, we made the difficult decision to help George pass.

We let him know that he was going home to be with Kajeeka again and would no longer have any pain. Separately, George and Kajeeka were halves but now together, forever free, they are whole. So, this is goodbye my dear George, may you ever rest peacefully with your love.

2017
CANADA LYNX - CLEO

In March of 2015, we received a very familiar call—a private owner whose life circumstances were quickly changing. It would be impossible for him to keep the exotic cat he so loved.

His Canada Lynx had spent all thirteen years of her life with him and his wife, living indoors as a household pet here in Minnesota. But, because of a divorce and a move to an apartment, it would be impossible for him to keep her. So, wanting to do the best for her, he contacted The Wildcat Sanctuary in hopes we could take her in.

Cleo had never experienced the outdoors or all the things a Canada Lynx loves; grass to catnap in, pines trees to smell, and snow under those big, gigantic paws. Though she's a wild cat by nature, she'd always been treated as a domestic cat by her owner.

Naturally, once she arrived, her first days at the Sanctuary proved to be a big adjustment for her. Everything was so new and scary. The caretakers gave her plenty of tender loving care, helping her acclimate to her new life.

Cleo had been fed a canned food for exotics her entire life. She never had the typical raw meat diet that Canada Lynx eat in the wild. It didn't take long for her to begin enjoying her new chicken diet while getting used to the sights, sounds and new neighbors she began meeting at the Sanctuary.

Cleo had been 4-paw declawed by her previous owner. Declawing involves amputating the toes of a cat up to the first joint. It is not just removal of the claws. To declaw a cat, the veterinarian cuts off the last knuckles of a cat's paw—cutting through bone, tendons, skin and nerves. In a person, it is equivalent to amputating each finger or toe at the last joint.

Sadly, almost 70% of the cats that come to The Wildcat Sanctuary have been 4-paw declawed before they arrive. Regrowth of bone and numerous bone fragments left under the skin can cause permanent lameness, excruciating pain, or arthritis. During Cleo's intake exam, we found she has regrowth on 50% of her toes which will need to be monitored and repaired.

In Memory

After a long battle with renal disease, we've let Canada Lynx Cleo finally be free.

There are so many reasons why wild animals shouldn't be pets. The many stories we hear break our hearts. And some are still sad, even though they find their way to the sanctuary. But we know we gave them all we could for the time they were here, and that's the most we can ever do.

For most of her life, Cleo was kept as a pet in a household. And even though she was loved by her family, she never got to experience what being a lynx truly was. She was in her teen years before she was surrendered to the sanctuary due to a divorce.

Experiencing grass under her feet for the first time should be exhilarating, but for her it was frightening. The interior of a house was all she knew. She'd imprinted on the humans that raised her and didn't imprint again. She was declawed and had spinal arthritis from a past injury. She had chronic GI issues which would not allow her to eat a raw diet like the other wild cats at the sanctuary.

Most cats transition in a very short time to their new wild life here. But Cleo put up a wall and wouldn't let us in. So, we watched Cleo from a closed-circuit TV to make sure she was okay and adjusting to her life at the sanctuary. We loved her and hoped that she would realize just how special she was to us all.

She was given a comforter and stuffed animal. And we'd often find her curled up with both. After a few months, she'd run along the outdoor shared wall with geriatric bobcat, Salem. Sometimes for play, sometimes to assert her dominance.

But even with the best medical care for her ailments, enrichment, indoor and outdoor areas, Cleo the lynx always appeared a little unsettled. A wild cat caught between two worlds was always an internal struggle for her. Now, she can finally be free.

Cleo, we loved you more than you'll ever know. We tried harder than you'll ever understand. We've given you the last gift we possibly can, to finally live your forever wild life. We hope you enjoy your newly found peace. We will miss you!

2019
CANADA LYNX - SHALICO

Shalico is a male Canada Lynx who arrived at The Wildcat Sanctuary in 2006. He was about six months old at the time he was surrendered. Shalico and his brother proved just how easy it is to buy exotic animals over the internet. Both were purchased through the internet by two college students from a breeder in Montana.

Once the college student who purchased Shalico realized it was illegal to own him, he surrendered him. Unfortunately, Shalico's brother had not been surrendered, too. Instead, his brother was seized by authorities from the other college student.

We tried to reunite the two brothers, but sadly never heard back from authorities. When we called to get a copy of health records, the veterinarian told us the other lynx was very sick and having seizures. Luckily for Shalico, he's never had any of these health problems.

Shalico's been a ball of energy since the day he arrived. He found companionship with a bobcat named Morgan. She's been his little shadow since the day they met and continues to be his little cuddle buddy. Their special friendship has been covered by media outlets.

We'd hoped Shalico could've lived out his days with his brother, but he's found happiness living 'wild at heart' with Morgan. His favorite treats are freeze-dried shrimp treats and he loves rolling around in perfume enrichment!

In Memory

I just feel broken. There is no other way to say it. I've spent the last 13 hours standing next to Shalico counting his breaths and waiting for the slightest response. Before that, I spent 11 hours alongside him in diagnostics and emergency surgery for an intestinal mass.

And I wasn't alone. So many talented veterinarians and technicians were right beside me. No one wanted to give up. Everyone was trying to give him the chance he needed to return to us. But he didn't.

I replay the days and hours back in my head. My rational side knows clots and aspiration is a risk of any surgery. It could happen to anyone or any animal, but I keep asking myself why it had to happen to him. At 13 years old, my heart feels like he was cheated of time…or maybe more so that I was. It hurts. It hurts like hell.

His loss cuts deeper than others and my tears keep flowing. Then I have the guilt that my deep hurt for his loss is disrespectful to others that I was able to deal with in a more rational way. When I tell myself to act like an adult and just "buck up," then it feels disrespectful to him.

I keep hearing my inner voice and it is just as devastated. Any moment of silence just brings back the sadness and loneliness of him leaving. This is grief. And I know you have all felt it too. So how do I move past it?

When I look at the words I have written above, I realize it is all about me. How I feel, how I will miss him. But in reality, it should be about him.

How silly he was and that he acted like a teenager who never grew up. How bobcat Morgan idolized him from the first moment she saw him—running up to him and cooing and remaining that way for a decade. How his mews rang across the sanctuary whenever he wanted anything…which was all the time. They were like adolescent tantrums followed by him pawing at the ground or towards what he wanted, and he always got his way.

Shalico has been with us since he was just a few months old. Purchased off the internet by a college student, the university gave the student a quick ultimatum and that's how Shalico found his way to us. He was the most gorgeous and sophisticated lynx in the winter with his thick fur coat. And once that shed in the spring, his lanky and disheveled carefree side came out.

Morgan and he had lived with other cats at the sanctuary, but they were a special duo. She followed him like his shadow, but also was no pushover. She loved Shalico deeply but is also independent, so I think she will be okay on her own. And I know I will be too, but for now I just need to feel the sorrow, love the memories, and experience the loss.

In Shalico's last days he brought so many people together. In such a time of sadness, I have also never felt so much love and compassion. Seeing the vet teams in action, the outcry of support from all of you online, to the staff ensuring every cat at TWS still received their personal attention, it made me realize how lucky both Shalico and I are.

His time may have been too short but surrounded by love for every moment is so much more than other animals and humans ever get to experience. And for that I am forever grateful.

Shalico, may you get everything you want where you are now. Morgan will hold down the fort here until it is time for you to be together again. Love you, my friend.

2019
CANADA LYNX - KITTY

Kitty is a female Canada Lynx who came to us in 2005 when she was 10 years old. She'd been rescued by a woman who saw Kitty being mistreated. She brought Kitty into her family and took great care of her. But when the family had to move for work, they were stuck with a difficult decision.

Though Kitty was legal to own in their current town, it was illegal to own a Canada Lynx in the town they were moving to. This happens so many times to people who own exotic animals. Though it might be legal when they get them, laws change, families are relocated or split up, and the animal is left homeless.

Luckily, this family did quite a bit of research. They made an emotional decision to place Kitty in a sanctuary. After even more research into healthy and happy sanctuaries, they chose to contact us at The Wildcat Sanctuary.

They accompanied Kitty on her arrival to help her make a smooth transition and they continued to sponsor her for several years to make sure she continued to get the best care. This is very unusual since most owners rarely continue to help with the expenses of their cats once we take them in.

Kitty loves her new home here, surrounded by the sights and sounds of so many other wild cats. She's a wonderful little girl who loves to sit in her hammock, sunbathe on her platforms, and roll in the new spring grass.

She also loves watching her bobcat and lynx neighbors run around and play, though she'd never want to join in on the action. She's much happier sitting in the grass or sunning herself on her highest perch.

She's one of our oldest residents now, in her mid-20's. She's far exceeded the life expectancy of a captive Canada Lynx. We cherish each day with this very special girl.

In Memory

We lost our snow angel this holiday season

Kitty, the Canada Lynx, received a peaceful exit to her peaceful life, surrounded by so many who loved her. At almost 25, Kitty had been declining. From losing most of her eyesight, to arthritis in her back hips, we could see her time was getting closer. But she still loved her daily routine.

The last few days, her routine changed though. She got up less and last night, though comfortable, didn't want to get up at all. That's when our staff knew it was time to say goodbye. Kitty's passing was very calm, and she's now free.

Sometimes when I write these memorials, I just feel broken inside. But as I sit here and write these words about Kitty, I'm sad for her loss, but my heart is full of love. She leaves that warm, comforting feeling she always brought throughout the years she lived at the Sanctuary.

Kitty came to us in 2005, from a very nice woman who took her in from another owner to give her a better life.

Over the years, Kitty always had a calm and even presence, even the first day I met her. She arrived by airplane. When we went to pick her up at air cargo, they couldn't find her. They mistakenly unloaded her with the luggage, and we were told she was at baggage claim.

We had to rush to the airport, park the vehicle and make a mad dash down to baggage claim. There, we found beautiful Kitty in a crate, rotating on the carousel with suitcases, calm as can be. So calm, that no one in the airport seemed to notice a large Canada Lynx in their presence!

Next to her calm demeanor, her white toes were her other signature mark. You can't look at those beautiful toes of hers and not melt to the core.

Even though she appeared to be a sophisticated lady, over the years she had some tricks up her sleeves. And she'd implement them just as calmly as everything else.

She lived next to Jasper, a Lynx cross, who she didn't like very much. I could never figure out why—he was a total doll. Kitty refused to fight with him because that would mean she'd have to show him some attention.

Instead, she'd back up her rear end to his wall and defecate through the fence into his habitat. Now, in the wild and captivity, cats mark their perimeter. But this was more than that. This was definitely a snub to him.

Kitty had a sophisticated, yet quiet way of getting what she wanted. And she had a routine. From her power walks to her meals being brought directly to her—she could get us to cater to her every whim.

Over the years, she lived with other cats from lynx Kodiak, Shalico and Ramsey to bobcat Buddy, who were all males and often pining for her affection. She never engaged with them. Instead, she quietly claimed her habitat and napping space and eventually took over a lot of the area.

She'd even stay in her den or room to ensure the staff would bring the food and any medication directly to her. Then after receiving it, you'd see her outdoors doing her power walks throughout her habitat.

When she began losing her vision in her elder years, those power walks became extremely important. She knew every inch of her habitat and never tripped or ran into anything. Even when lions Salteña and Chupino moved next door, this little lady was never intimated. She was out walking, came up to the fence line and took in their sounds and smells.

Behind all the confident calmness, Kitty had an overwhelming sweetness. She touched everyone's hearts and, even though she lived to a ripe old age, our hearts hurt that she's gone…for now.

Kitty, thank you for being so easy to care for and even more easy to love. You deserve your wild life to be everything you dreamed of.

CANADA-EURASIAN LYNX

2010
CANADA-EURASIAN LYNX - JASPER

Jasper, a Canada-Eurasian lynx-cross, came from a fur farm that was closed due to neglect and poor conditions. At eight weeks old, he was left to starve to death in an empty bathtub, covered with a piece of plywood.

Being one of the lucky ones, Jasper doesn't seem to carry any lingering effects of his previously nightmarish life. Jasper's arrival at the sanctuary gave him a new lease on life.

Jasper has grown healthy and strong. He truly enjoyed being roommates with Otis, until Otis passed away due to pancreatic cancer. Now Jasper lives alone and seems to be doing okay with his newfound independence.

Jasper's favorite time of year is winter. We learned that Jasper's favorite winter pastime is playing on large piles of snow created from our winter chores. Clearing paths through the snow in Jasper's habitat can create quite a huge mound. Jasper can't contain himself, he's so happy. He runs to the very top where he performs his famous "snow dance." He literally jumps up and down and dances on top of the pile!

In Memory

Jasper has passed but he leaves behind an important message. He had a difficult start to his life, but he never held a grudge. He had a personality of peacefulness that I've never seen in another wild animal.

He enjoyed and accepted every person and animal that came into his life. But his best friend of all was Otis, who passed a few years ago. Jasper was so calm and easy going. He even participated calmly in his medical treatment to curb his recent onset of seizures.

Jasper taught me so many life lessons while he was alive. But his death may have taught me the most important…all living things are connected in this world…and never underestimate this.

Jasper was the third permanent resident of The Wildcat Sanctuary and was one of my closest animal friends. His seizures had subsided, and he was stable when I left for my recent trip to Africa.

This trip was extremely special and enlightening. I learned so much from the beautiful animals living out their lives in the wild. As well as the extreme poverty, but also joyful resilience, of the people in Africa.

For years, I've heard and used the term Rainbow Bridge when animals pass. But in recent years, we've often seen a full rainbow within a few days prior to or after an animal passes at the sanctuary. We've always looked at it as nothing more than an interesting coincidence…until my trip to Africa.

On the day of my arrival in Lewa Conservancy, the brightest and most vibrant full rainbow appeared. I had never seen anything so strong and beautiful.

But with that came a heavy aching. My mind went right to thinking about the Rainbow Bridge. A frantic email home revealed everything was good and the animals were fine. My new friends in Africa comforted and told me that maybe the rainbow in Africa means something different than at home. "No worries—it's all good" I heard repeatedly on my trip.

The week continued full of animal tracking and visiting local schools. Each day, I felt blessed to be having such an experience. The sense of peace, appreciation and healing were overwhelming.

Late into the trip, our group proceeded to Pombe Point. A high point that overlooked all of Lewa. It was breathtaking. Within a few minutes of arriving, an amazing full rainbow appeared, not only one, but then another above it. A complete double rainbow.

I had seen a full rainbow the first day, but never a double rainbow. Tears filled my eyes—of happiness and sadness. I couldn't explain really why, but the Rainbow Bridge again came back into my thoughts.

It would be several days before I could be in communication with TWS again. But when I finally did contact home, I emailed TWS saying I've seen not only the full rainbow, but a double one too. I said I knew something had happened. They confirmed Jasper had passed at 4:30 pm on the day I saw the double rainbow.

My heart broke, not only from his leaving, but not being there with him. I know he was in the best and most caring hands as he left us, and I find peace in that.

But I'm in shock with his passing and also the great connection to him that I felt all the way from Africa. I no longer believe the Rainbow Bridge is just a phrase. I'm not sure I know exactly what it is or what happened, but I do know that I'm now so thankful and aware of the connection between the earth, animals and people. It is a magical thing.

Jasper, thank you for your message and rest in peace with Otis on the other side of the Rainbow Bridge.

EURASIAN LYNX

2007
EURASIAN LYNX - OTIS

Otis, a Eurasian Lynx, came to TWS at the age of four months from a Canadian fur farm, along with his sister Lindsey. Here at our sanctuary, Otis has been given a safe haven where he can remain wild at heart.

From the beginning, Otis bonded with fellow TWS resident, Jasper, a lynx-cross. The two roommates are virtually inseparable and can often be found lounging together in the grass. As much as Otis loves his buddy, a new stuffed animal really gets him going. Luckily, Otis has left his old life behind and enjoys the little things in life, like spending time with his best friend and playing the afternoon away.

In Memory

It's been a very difficult few weeks. We lost Otis, the Eurasian Lynx, to pancreatic cancer. It was so sudden, and I am glad that he didn't have to suffer long, but it has been devastating for both Jasper and me.

Otis had been sick over the last few weeks and his first visit with the vet showed a low-grade infection and some hints of pancreatitis. When he continued to deteriorate, we suspected a possible bowel obstruction. Last week, we decided to do surgery and found that Otis had pancreatic cancer. We chose to let him pass since it is terminal cancer and his was pretty advanced, given his signs of illness over the last few weeks.

My heart hurts and I will miss this special boy very much. I was so blessed to earn his trust over the last 8 years. His amazing bond to Jasper is also what I will always remember. Otis was able to live every moment of his life exactly how he wanted—beside Jasper. And I am so very thankful for that.

Jasper is a little confused and grieving in his own way. I am trying to spend more time with him and give him more things to do. He's been looking around for Otis, especially at mealtime. I know he will forever miss his special friend.

2017
EURASIAN LYNX - MAX

Max, a Eurasian lynx, was the typical exhibition cat. He was owned by an exhibitor who took him to schools and other events for show. One day, though, Max made it quite clear he no longer was interested in the leash or the profession. Luckily, the exhibitor found The Wildcat Sanctuary and chose to retire Max to us.

Max is a well-adjusted cat, but he will still growl today if he even sees a leash. Obviously, his memory of his former life stays with him.

At The Wildcat Sanctuary, Max now enjoys roaming a 7,000 square foot habitat with the love of his life, cougar Misha. It was quite a surprise to us all when we noticed Max was grooming Misha through the fence.

So, one day, we allowed for a play date and they have been together ever since. It makes us feel wonderful being able to provide companionship for life for our rescues, even if they are from another species. Sometimes those are the best, most lasting friendships.

In Memory

What can I say? Whether it's 10-month-old Esteban or now 22-year-old Max the Eurasian Lynx, writing these memorials and saying goodbye never gets easier. But what it does give me, gives us all, is a break from the grief to remember what made each of them so special. Sharing the story of their life and how you helped us make each day count is how we get through these hard times. So, thank you for letting me share just how wonderful Max, the Eurasian Lynx was.

In Max's early years, he was an exhibit cat. He traveled around the country to schools, Renaissance Festivals and auto shows. When Max was no longer compliant for his owner, he was fortunately retired to our sanctuary in 1999.

Max was a happy boy who had affection for his caregivers, but even more affection toward other animals. He was friendly to his neighbors, and a love connection formed between he and Misha the cougar in 2001. They lived together ever since. Their friendship was featured in National Geographic Kids magazine, as well as other articles.

Max was a cat who was very at peace with himself. He would purr at his caregivers, call to his friends across the sanctuary, and always followed Misha around with his signature Max grunt, followed by presenting his rear end. Even though it was a compliment, Misha never perceived it that way and would give a playful swat to his back side.

His favorite spot in his habitat was up on the hill where he could watch other cats and keep an eye out for the food cart. Mealtime was an exciting time for Max and something he always looked forward to.

As he aged, he had chronic kidney disease and some muscle atrophy. Caretakers and your support provided Max with the stairs he needed to still enjoy climbing his perches and platforms.

In the last days, Max was very weak, but still had glimmers of that signature personality. He was calm and comfortable, but his body could not keep up with his internal beaming personality. He deserved to be free where he could shine as bright as he needed.

I know Misha still feels his warmth with every ray of sun, his head butt as she cuddles in her hammock, and hears his famous grunt as the wind blows.

Misha has been doing well on her own since his passing. She's spending a lot of time in her tallest hammock on her tallest platform. She purrs when we talk to her and seems peaceful knowing she had a long, lovely life with her dear friend.

Max, it is not an understatement when we say you were happy with yourself. That is truly a special gift. Shine bright forever and always.

2018
EURASIAN LYNX - LINDSEY

Lindsey, a Eurasian lynx, was one of 30+ kittens born on a fur farm in Saskatchewan, Canada. Sadly, fur farms still prosper in both the United States and Canada. Had Lindsey's path not led her to The Wildcat Sanctuary, her life would have ended prematurely on the fur farm at the age of two.

Unfortunately, there are many others like Lindsey who are not as lucky and suffer unimaginable fates in fur farms each year. Luckily, both Lindsey and her brother Otis were given a second chance to live out their lives at The Wildcat Sanctuary.

Understandably, Lindsey arrived at the Sanctuary filled with mistrust. She was very aggressive and quickly developed a reputation of being a bully among the other residents. But our keepers have worked very patiently with her to bring her around.

She now enjoys living in the Wildcat Pines section of the Sanctuary and her habitat is filled with lots of pine trees, a hammock, and perches for her to play on. Like a lynx in the wild, Lindsey enjoys hanging out in the pine trees where she has a hidden vantage point on everything going on around her.

In Memory

I can't believe I'm writing another memorial so soon. This time for Lindsey. My heart is torn open. But at the same time, I'm beaming with pride for who she was and how she helped me grow.

At nearly 20 years old, Lindsey the Eurasian Lynx wasn't geriatric to us. At least she never showed it. She was a very independent and strong lady, like every female Eurasian lynx I've met in my rescue work. So, it shouldn't surprise me that she hid her cancer so well. But it still hurts nonetheless.

As one of the first 10 founding cats of the sanctuary, Lindsey was very special to me. She'd seen it all alongside me—from the crazy days of starting the sanctuary near Atlanta, Georgia to our move to Minnesota. She arrived at a young age, back when we took in cats from fur farms.

She was unsocialized, but not from fear, rather from determined independence. Lindsey called the shots. Even at just five pounds, that didn't stop her. I think that's why I loved her so much. That bold spirit taught me the most important lesson about rescuing wildcats and running a sanctuary.

I was young, naïve and my heart was wide open. I thought if I loved each rescue enough, it could fix anything. It could reverse all they'd been through. But you can never love the wild out of a wild animal, and you shouldn't want to.

I used to think if you loved them all enough, they'd love you back—it's what I hear from private owners now. Love does fix all, just not the way I envisioned. All the love in the world didn't make Lindsey stop swatting or growling as a kitten. All my love didn't make her sweet and docile. But she taught me to love her for what she was—a lynx. A lynx caught between two worlds.

When I backed off, gave her space to be out in tall grass with trees, she grew up becoming an independent and strong wild cat. She powered through everything—sanctuary moves, habitat moves and in turn did only what she wanted. She didn't like to be locked out for cleaning, so she made it our job to find creative ways to make it worth her while.

She intimidated even our savviest caretakers. And then the most amazing thing happened. Lindsey would purr, rub and present her beautiful backend when I approached her habitat. After finally giving her the respect, and independence a wildcat deserved, she respected me back and gave me what I'd longed for—to know she knew I only meant to be a friend, not foe.

She always remained strong and lived every day on her own terms. She loved being in the center of her habitat, taking naps under her pine tree. She never complained and had a routine to her day.

As the years progressed, her outward affection for me grew and she would always greet me at the fence. After her lessons early on, I no longer expected it, but I very much appreciated it. It was her way of saying thank you for letting her be who she was—a lynx.

At 20, she had arthritis and her huffs to the staff were less threatening. But she still demanded and received the respect she had gained in her prime years. She never showed any outward signs of being uncomfortable or having trouble breathing. The first morning she didn't come up for her morning medications to demand her treat, we knew we had to intervene.

During sedation, her heart rate became erratic and she stopped breathing. She passed just moments before we were going to help her move on. But that rang true to Lindsey's spirit—it had to be on her own terms. Our vet team found that she had an advanced case of lung cancer—something that surprised us all. She masked the symptoms as wild animals do.

Lindsey—Heaven is as big as you make it. You can have as much space and freedom as you want. And your friends are there for the moments you want to say hello. Thank you for teaching me the most important lesson of all—wild is wild.

2020
EURASIAN LYNX - LEISHA

Leisha, a female Eurasian lynx, came to live at The Wildcat Sanctuary in 2005 when she was six years old. Her owner surrendered her when city ordinances became more stringent. Insurance issues also came up that prevented ownership of an exotic pet.

There are so many reasons why private ownership of wild cats is NOT something we support. These are just two of so many reasons owners have no idea about when they purchase a wild cat as a "pet."

Leisha arrived at The Wildcat Sanctuary a very socialized cat with a very healthy appetite. She'd been well cared for at her previous home and adjusted quickly to sanctuary life here.

She loves empty milk jugs and scents of all kinds. But the one thing she is not too fond of is another lynx. We tailor all of our cats' habitats to fit their personalities. Since Leisha has made it very clear that she does not want to live near another lynx, she doesn't.

She thoroughly enjoys the special habitat where she roams near the bigger cats, the cougars, lions, and tigers. She may look like a smaller cat, but she obviously has a big cat personality!

In Memory

At 21, it was time for Leisha to move on to her new wild, life in the sky. She'd been diagnosed two years ago with slow growing cancer in her jaw. She really beat the odds by being so strong. But now, her body just couldn't fight any longer.

Leisha came to us 15 years ago after being privately-owned. Her very first day at the sanctuary, we knew Leisha had a personality all her own. She greeted us with her traditional 'huff,' her way of reminding us things would be on her terms. And things really were, each and every day, until the day we said goodbye.

Some might say she was a little rough around the edges, especially since she'd intimidate new staff and interns at feeding time. But, in reality, Leisha was very predictable. She loved mealtime yet was a bit impatient about the service.

She loved to nap in her hammocks—up high in her younger years, and lower more recently. She was easygoing about which habitat she lived in. She enjoyed living in different areas throughout the sanctuary, but only if she lived alone. That was her one dealbreaker. She didn't like to share her space.

She was extremely confident and only needed to assert herself on rare occasions. She lived next to tigers, lions, and cougars. The roars and yowls never bothered or intimidated her. And during feeding time, she could hold her own in a building full of rowdy big cats—though of course she was always separated in her own room.

You couldn't let her 'huffing' fool you. If you stayed by her habitat long enough and she realized you weren't scared off, she'd actually begin to purr, and head butt the fence. It was her way of weeding out the weak.

She also liked enrichment. Scents were her favorite and her face would be full of drool, and her tongue sticking out. These were the times she didn't mind showing her silly side.

As she got older, she lost her hearing. It didn't cause her any problems, but caretakers would spend more time waking her from a deep sleep to come take her medication. Her naps got longer and more frequent, and we could see her slowing down.

The last week of her life, Tammy was so happy to capture her out on her platform in the sun—her favorite thing to do. What a good long life Leisha had. The only other wish we had for her is that she'd been able to live it wild. She would've been great at living wild with that strong, independent personality. We're so blessed we could give her the next best thing.

Enjoy your new wild, life Leisha. The lions, tigers, cougars, and your humans will miss you each and every day!

BOBCATS

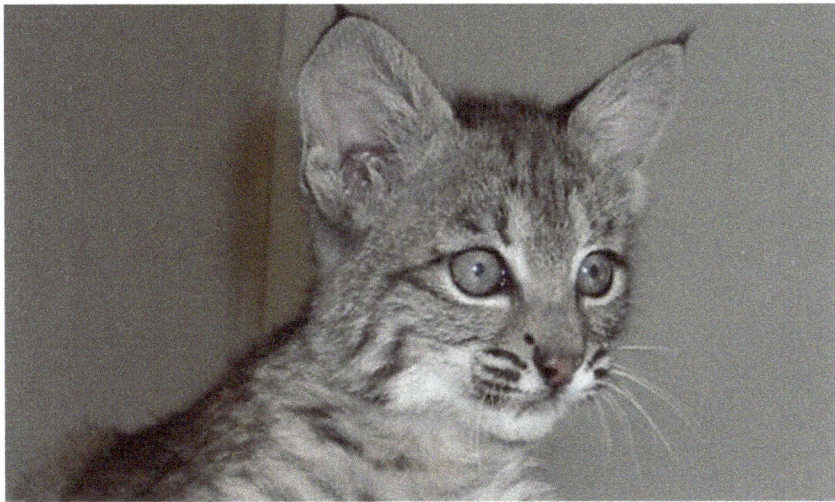

2007
BOBCAT - MAYA

Maya's first owner bought her off the internet from a breeder in Montana. But it took a lot of research to find the truth. The owner refused to admit that he had purchased her because he eventually discovered it was illegal in Minnesota and didn't want to be prosecuted.

At first glance, this little bobcat kitten seemed quite healthy. But soon things changed. It was horribly sad, but not a surprise given where she originated. Many bobcats now in our care who came from this breeder have had significant neurological and health problems.

Maya's short little life was a blessing but devastating at the same time. It is our job to keep them safe and healthy when they come to TWS and it is heartbreaking when we can't. Sadly, Maya passed very soon after her arrival.

2008
BOBCAT—COOTER

Cooter, a bobcat, arrived at TWS in 2006 with four other cats from a facility in Colorado. At that time, Cooter was an elderly bobcat and we were blessed to have two additional years with him.

Though his eyesight and hearing had mostly gone, he was still one of the happiest bobcats I had ever met. He would spend an entire day batting at his water bottle mobile that hung from his enclosure ceiling.

In Memory

In the last month of his life, it became more difficult for him to eat. So, we decided to schedule an exam and assumed he had a bad tooth. Instead, we found a large malignant tumor in the back of his mouth that had spread to the jawbone.

Thankfully, we were there and able to help him pass over the rainbow bridge. Even with tears of sadness, I am so happy to have met this boy who enjoyed every moment of his elder years. He taught me that life is fun and grand no matter what your age. I will miss his vocal greeting and his hours of batting the mobile. But now he is, finally, forever free and I am happy for that.

2009
BOBCAT—MURRAY

Murray is a 25-year-old bobcat who lived at the Fejervary Children's Zoo in Davenport, Iowa. The city council voted to close the zoo and to relocate all the animals. Given Murray's age and proximity to The Wildcat Sanctuary, we made an exception to take Murray in, even though we are already operating at capacity.

We don't know how long Murray will be with us since he's showing signs of old age with arthritis and kidney disease. But he will have a home at TWS for as long as he is comfortable.

His hearing and eyesight are poor, but we soon learned his nose works just fine! Murray loves the smell of catnip and Lawry's seasoned salt. A very special thank you to The Mahley Family Foundation for funding Murray's habitat.

In Memory

It is with a heavy heart that I share that Murray, our 25-year-old bobcat, has passed away. Murray, also known as Mur Man and Old Man Murs, was one of a kind. His journey in life led him to TWS last year after the zoo where he lived closed its doors. We don't know much about Murray's previous life, but we do know he led a happy albeit sleepy life here at TWS.

Although Murray was quite old and had difficulty seeing and hearing, we found that his nose still worked perfectly. The very first day he arrived we gave him some Lawry's seasoned salt in a box. With his stiff joints he crawled right in and immediately began rubbing and drooling. Scents were his number one, favorite thing.

He was also particularly fond of napping. Napping in his den, in the sun in his chute to his enclosure, or in his outdoor den, he basically napped all day. We are all so happy we could give him his time of rest after being on display for so many people for so many years.

He deserved his retirement and we believe he lived it to the fullest. Murray will be forever missed and loved.

2010
BOBCAT - AMOS

Amos, a male bobcat, came to us in 2010. We'd been contacted by a woman from Washington state regarding her pet bobcat. She was going through a divorce and could no longer care for Amos, a 15-year-old bobcat.

We decided Amos would be a good fit here so, once the weather was warm enough for airline travel, he was sent here. He was 15 years old, but you'd never have known it by the way he acted. He was as spunky as they come. He was such a vocal guy as soon as he stepped out of his crate on that very first day, he was vocalizing to staff.

Amos lived next to two other bobcats named Henry and Haley. Unfortunately, they did not get along with Amos very well and Amos let them know to stay out of his way.

Unfortunately, Amos was poorly declawed and had fairly severe arthritis in his paws. He was very shy at first and would not take any food from us. Finally, after a few days here, he decided to eat some tuna mixed with cooked chicken. Talk about a picky eater!

After that, he was eating great and even eating some raw chicken, which has more nutritional value than cooked chicken.

We'd also found that he loves enrichment. Any kind of new scent made him rub and drool. Even though Amos was a geriatric cat, he was still a little spitfire. He had the most unique voice and was very vocal. He was the newest addition to the bobcats that sing for their food.

Since Amos was so old, he had some problems with arthritis and spondylosis. When he began plucking his sides, we thought it had to do with his spinal pain. Our veterinarian came up and did blood work and took some x-rays. We were worried about possible kidney issues but found nothing wrong.

Then, when one of the caretakers went to check on Amos, she found him in a spunky mood but with problems standing and walking. He was crated and taken to the vet the next morning where x-rays showed a mass in his abdomen. Amos had intestinal cancer.

We did not want him to suffer anymore and helped him pass. It's hard when they are here for only a short time, but Amos adjusted so well and won our hearts right away. We will miss him very much especially his little tail flick during feeding and his cute black nose.

Thank you to his sponsor parents who helped provide him a wonderful life and vet care the short time he was here.

2010
BOBCAT - LAKOTA

Lakota is a 15-year-old bobcat who came with Harley and Salem, two other bobcats. We received a call that Wild Animal Orphanage (WAO) in Texas was closing down. With over 400 animals to place, we knew we had to help. These three bobcats, along with five tigers and a lion, now have a forever home at The Wildcat Sanctuary.

Unfortunately, Lakota is deaf and blind and has hematomas in both ears. He was also poorly declawed, and it shows in his feet and legs. He needs a little help to find his food, but he's still capable of jumping up onto a fire-hose hammock so he can take his long naps.

When they first arrived, they all needed immediate vet care for a flea infestation and multiple types of parasites. But as soon as their treatments are complete, they will be living next to Sebastian the serval. Given they are from Texas and the shock of our Minnesota winters would be too much, they will have access to a heated building all winter.

In Memory

Lakota recently arrived from a Texas facility that was closing down. He was a very calm cat in a body that had many problems. Lakota was blind and deaf, but still was a happy cat who loved his habitat mate Salem. When he arrived, he would circle on occasion—a sign of a neurological issue, but still enjoyed naps with Salem, the outdoors, and his fire hose hammock.

Recently, he began to circle more frequently and became very disoriented. We tried a few treatments and supplements, but nothing helped. It wasn't fair for Lakota to live in a body with a brain that no longer worked the way it should.

He was with us for such a short time and was already loved by so many, including Salem. We are sad his stay with us was so short, but so happy we were able to give him the gift of a free spirit when it was needed.

Whenever a new cat arrives at the Sanctuary, it feels like they have been a part of our family forever, no matter if they have been with us only a few months. Their passing is just as difficult. Lakota, you were loved by so many and you will never be forgotten.

2013
BOBCAT - HAMLIN

We received a call from a Minnesota owner of four bobcats looking to relinquish them. His 3-year old granddaughter had a very close call while near one of the cages and the owner was also scratched severely, requiring stitches. His family convinced him to reach out to The Wildcat Sanctuary in order to spare the bobcats' lives.

The four bobcats had been purchased online from a Montana breeder. The owner's intention was to breed them here in Minnesota and eventually kill them for their pelts.

Montana breeders have been selling kittens for decades, for as much as $1,750. They will ship the cats anywhere, apparently with no questions asked, as long as the buyer can pay.

Many of the cities and states where these wild cats end up have laws and ordinances that make it illegal to own them. But, for years, nothing has been done. It is outrageous and heartbreaking that we have been called on to rescue so many, just like these four.

Sadly, in order for the owner to remain detached, none of the bobcats had been named. We agreed to take them in, since we were concerned about the safety of this family and the lives of the bobcats. All of our permanent habitats were full, so we quickly built temporary enclosures for them.

These bobcats lived in 4×8 wire suspended cages in the owner's backyard. The pick-up went extremely well, and the owner was very helpful. Once we safely captured and transported the bobcats back to the Sanctuary, our veterinarian performed intake exams, as well as spay and neuters, on them.

Three of the four bobcats needed full dental treatments due to advanced dental disease. Two of the bobcats were spayed and neutered right away, with the remaining two scheduled soon after. All were treated for intestinal parasites, too.

Having never felt grass under their paws, this would be the bobcats' first opportunity. It was a joyous moment when they were released into their habitat here at the Sanctuary. They began acting like kittens, exploring their new areas, tossing their enrichment high into the air, batting it around and rolling in the grass and on the different scents.

We could hardly contain our tears as we watched them jumping from hammock to den, marking/hugging everything in sight. What a great day providing a home to these wild cats in need, giving them a second chance at life!

A family member of the owner has since shared this: *"Thank you for taking them! I am very glad he chose to let them live. I told him that you provide the most amazing life for the cats."*

We are so thankful they are with us, too!

Hamlin now has a name

When the four Minnesota bobcats were rescued from their owner's backyard cages, they had no names. One of our top supporters, Russell Cowles, had a wonderful idea for recognizing one of our volunteers.

Hamlin looked healthy during his intake exam and was scheduled for a special neuter for his cryptorchid. He had fleas and intestinal parasites but was in good condition otherwise.

It's been a few months since Stelter, Brianna, Felicity, and Hamlin were rescued and brought to our Sanctuary. And my, oh my, how life has changed for them!

They are so happy they literally kiss the ground they walk on!! No longer timid, they have spent so much of their time exploring around the tall grass and flowers of their summer habitat. The trees, hammocks, pools, perches, and indoor dens have also been such treats for them. Imagine how life has changed from what little they had before to all we have been able to give them now.

In Memory

We were shocked and devastated at the sudden and unexpected loss of sweet Hamlin the bobcat. Hamlin died suddenly from a bone fragment that was found lodged in the soft tissue at the bifurcation of the trachea. This is an extremely rare occurrence in captivity, but also could happen in the wild. The location of the bone fragment was not operable.

Bones, muscle, and organ meat are all a crucial part of a wild cat's diet. This is the first time something like this has happened at our sanctuary and we are so saddened by the loss.

Even though he was only with us a short time, his curiosity and loving nature made everyone instantly fall in love with him. He came with three other bobcats this past summer from a private owner here in Minnesota. Once here, he was the first to venture out of his crate and feel grass under his feet for the first time.

He discovered so many other new experiences, too. Like lounging on a fire hose hammock all snuggled up with Felicity and shredding his very first paper towel roll enrichment. One would think after enduring a life in a tiny cage above the ground, some anger and resentment of humans would exist, but not for Hamlin.

He was always happy to see the staff and would purr and rub on the fence to get our attention. One of the reasons we gave him the name Hamlin, other than after one of our volunteers, is that he was a ham and loved the limelight.

We are so glad he was able to experience freedom while he was here. I can honestly say watching him, Stelter, Brianna and Felicity run, play and be bobcats is one of my greatest memories and a victory for all exotic pets in the world.

So goodbye sweet Hamlin, you are now finally, forever free. We will never forget you and be forever grateful to have known you.

2013
BOBCAT - MAKISHA

Makisha was a privately owned bobcat in Washington state. When her owner began having health issues, she decided to try to find a stable home for her. Two amazing animal lovers took it upon themselves to help Makisha and her owner find a suitable sanctuary and contacted The Wildcat Sanctuary.

The original plan was to fly Makisha to our Sanctuary, but after two days of canceled flights, The Wildcat Sanctuary's staff ended up having to drive to meet them in Montana. It was a long round trip drive from Minnesota to Montana and back, but Makisha was an excellent traveler.

Makisha found her forever home here at the Sanctuary in 2010. As with all of our residents, Makisha received an intake exam from our veterinarian. We microchipped her, performed a physical exam and X-rays, as well as blood work.

Overall, her health is very good for a bobcat her age. She had ear mites and a severe ear infection which was treated upon her intake. The permanent damage to her left ear is a result of the ear infection she arrived with.

Makisha is a geriatric bobcat and she also has anemia. We provide her a stress-free life and hope she will be with us for years to come.

Despite her age, Makisha is as playful as a kitten. She will stalk and pounce at passing caretakers and loves to carry toys with her around her enclosure. She really blossomed once she arrived and began living life to the fullest here at the Sanctuary.

In Memory

We are so sorry to say goodbye to Makisha, a very strong and independent bobcat. Earlier this summer, we'd noticed Makisha limping. She was seen by the vet and had a large cyst or tumor on one of her front legs.

The fluid was drained, and she was put on some medication for the pain, but the fluid buildup and swelling were likely to return. She was doing well on her pain meds for a while, but the fluid had returned and her limp worsened, especially when we received a couple of inches of snow.

She was seen again by the vets and the tumor or cyst had tripled in size. With winter and snow fast approaching, we knew it was only fair for Makisha to let her go peacefully with no more pain.

Makisha was with us four years and was one of the most beloved bobcats. She was 16 when she arrived at TWS but had all the spunk of a 6-year-old. She loved enrichment to the max, rolling and drooling as soon as you placed it on the ground.

She wasn't very fond of people but, if she knew you had enrichment, would watch you like a hawk until you left it for her. She really enjoyed painting also, but you had to get it from her quickly because she also liked to pee on it once it was complete. Perhaps it was an artistic sealant!

Makisha was a very independent girl and really only tolerated anyone she might live with. She found a mutual, understanding relationship with two servals who were also independent and the three maintained happy but separate lives. Makisha usually was the one to get to the enrichment first while the others enjoyed getting the food first, a win-win for all.

It's so hard to make these decisions for the animals when they have no voice to tell us how they feel, but it was clear she was in pain and her time to go. Makisha is now free from pain and I hope wherever she is there is a never-ending flow of Lowry's seasoned salt, her favorite enrichment! Makisha we miss you already and will love you always.

2014
BOBCAT - CEDAR

Cedar the bobcat was rescued from an Idaho homeowner in May of 2009. He was living in deplorable conditions in a trash-laden pen under a woman's patio. His wire cage was filled with garbage, feces, and rotting chicken.

The woman was hospitalized for unknown health reasons and could no longer provide for the bobcat and two wolves she still maintained on the property.

In previous years, the woman had upwards of 30-plus wolves and was identified by local authorities as a "hoarder." The wolves were rescued by Wolf Haven International in Washington State.

His intake veterinary exam determined he was a neutered male who'd been declawed on all four feet. He had two rotting teeth that needed treatment and was overweight after being fed an improper diet of canned cat food and yogurt.

After some time to adjust, Cedar settled in quite well at TWS. He enjoys his fire hose hammock and grassy enclosure and the freedom to roam his natural habitat, as he chooses. The memory of living in a filthy pen under a patio has faded, thanks to the love and quality care he receives here at TWS.

In Memory

Cedar the bobcat peacefully passed away in his sleep. Though it was unexpected, we find comfort that he was able to pass on with dignity. For many years of his life, he lived in a small, wired enclosure filled with debris and garbage. We don't know Cedar's exact age, since he came from an animal seizure out of state. But much of his paperwork documents him to be 20 years old.

After arriving at TWS in 2009, he was shy and reserved. He'd spent time with several roommates, but generally kept to himself. So, he was moved to a large free-roaming habitat where he could live as he wanted.

He was often found on his hammock where he enjoyed taking long and quiet cat naps. He loved mealtime and would always be waiting right up front for his caregivers. Since he loved hammocks so much, we hung one high up in his feeding area for him, too. It was great seeing him up there, peeking out from his hammock, keeping a close eye on everything, including the food cart.

His routine was the same the day and evening prior to his passing. He ate well, soaked up the sun on his hammock and strolled through the tall grass. We were all saddened when he didn't come out for morning rounds.

Seeing him curled up in his normal sleeping position was bittersweet. He was gone, but he left in the most peaceful and dignified way possible. Initial results from the University of Minnesota show no distress and Cedar passed of natural causes.

Cedar, like every resident, is special to all of us. His sponsor parents also mourn his loss but are remembering him with a memorial plaque and commemorative brick. His story and legacy will remind us that each animal deserves peace and dignity. And because of our donors and sponsors, Cedar was able to experience just that.

Goodbye, Cedar. You will be missed by all.

2014
BOBCAT - SIDNEY

Sidney, a bobcat, was found living in a warehouse in downtown Minneapolis during an unrelated police raid. Prior to her release to TWS, Sidney spent ten noisy days confined to a kennel at animal control alongside several barking dogs.

At TWS, Sidney has a much more peaceful environment surrounded by trees, grass, several perches and dens, a much more appropriate atmosphere for a bobcat. Sidney has had a home here at the Sanctuary since 2001.

Sidney is a beautiful bobcat who has won the hearts of all the TWS staff and volunteers. For quite a while after coming to TWS, Sidney had enjoyed living in her own private space. Although Sidney was perfectly happy living on her own, we thought she could be even happier living with other bobcats.

In the spring of 2004, we created an opening in the shared wall between Sidney's habitat and her bobcat neighbors. Along with giving Sidney new friends to live with, it also increased the habitat size for all of the bobcats involved.

With this new bigger living arrangement, Sidney now has the best of both worlds; she can socialize with other bobcats or she can go to another area or den for some alone time when she's had enough of her roommates.

Sidney enjoys enrichment as much as the next girl does. A simple box filled with catnip can capture her attention for hours. Sidney also enjoys spending a hot summer day by the pool.

In Memory

I can remember the first time I met her. I was called to Animal Control to pick up a bobcat who had been a former pet. I walked down the concrete hallway, kennels on both sides. Barking dogs jumped at the fence as we continued down the tight path.

Dog after dog lunged at the fence and then we came upon a kennel with a sheet draped over it. I peered in and there she was. This gorgeous girl walked toward me, let out a small noise and began to purr. Amongst all the barking and strange surroundings, she calmly walked into her crate. Her first step to life at The Wildcat Sanctuary.

This beautiful, calm, and happy demeanor continued every day during her life here with us. Sidney lived to be 19 years old. Though we had so many years together, it still seems too short.

She was happy every day, no matter the circumstances. She enjoyed catnip, painting, attention from her caregivers and napping with her bobcat friend Scooter. She would always come to say hello and purr the second she saw you. Her happiness was contagious.

Since 2012, we have been monitoring Sidney's blood levels, which were suspected to indicate cancer and hyperparathyroidism. She had chronic arthritis, but still loved to jump and run. She continued to slow down over the past few months, like all geriatric animals. Every day was precious and every day we made sure it was peaceful.

The last few days, we moved her to an indoor kennel in the hospital. Just like the day I met her these surroundings did not bother her. She purred when I entered, slept soundly in her cat bed and was calm and happy, but that's the way she deserved to leave. Pain free and content. Her kidneys were shutting down, so we had to do what was right and say goodbye.

Even though her first and last days were in a kennel, because of the donors' and sponsors' generosity, every day in between consisted of tall grass, toys, sun, enrichment and companionship of her own kind.

Sidney was a joy to care for and will be forever missed. Her sweet personality and sure bliss to see us is in our hearts forever.

Thank you for giving us the gift to care for you for so long.

2014
BOBCAT - FELICITY

We received a call from a Minnesota owner of four bobcats looking to relinquish them. His 3-year old granddaughter had a very close call while near one of the cages and the owner was also scratched severely, requiring stitches. His family convinced him to reach out to The Wildcat Sanctuary in order to spare the bobcats' lives.

The four bobcats had been purchased online from a Montana breeder. The owner's intention was to breed them here in Minnesota and eventually kill them for their pelts. Montana breeders have been selling kittens for decades, for as much as $1,750. They will ship the cats anywhere, apparently with no questions asked, as long as the buyer can pay.

Many of the cities and states where these wild cats end up have laws and ordinances that make it illegal to own them. But, for years, nothing has been done. It's outrageous and heartbreaking that we have been called on to rescue so many, just like these four.

Sadly, in order for the owner to remain detached, none of the bobcats had been named. We agreed to take them in, since we were concerned about the safety of this family and the lives of these bobcats. All of our permanent enclosures were full, so we quickly built temporary habitats for them.

The bobcats lived in 4' × 8' wire suspended cages in the owner's backyard. The pick-up went extremely well, and the owner was very helpful. Once we safely captured and transported the bobcats back to the Sanctuary, our vet performed intake exams, as well as spay and neuters, on them.

Three of the four bobcats will need full dental treatments due to advanced dental disease. Two of the bobcats were spayed and neutered right away, with the remaining two scheduled soon after. All were treated for intestinal parasites, too.

Having never felt grass under their paws, this would be the bobcats' first opportunity. It was a joyous moment when they were released into their habitat here at the Sanctuary. They began acting like kittens, exploring their new areas, tossing their enrichment high into the air, batting it around and rolling in the grass and on the different scents.

We could hardly contain our tears as we watched them jumping from hammock to den, marking and hugging everything in sight. What a great day providing a home to these wild cats in need, giving them a second chance at life!

A family member of the owner has since shared this: *"Thank you for taking them! I am very glad he chose to let them live. I told him that you provide the most amazing life for the cats."*

We are so thankful they are with us, too!

When the four Minnesota bobcats were rescued from their owner's backyard cages, they had no names. Charlene Boden won the naming rights of the blue-eyed single female through our eBay auction. She chose the name Felicity for her, which means "Happiness." The name couldn't be more fitting since she's now enjoying true happiness in her new home at The Wildcat Sanctuary.

She's having so much fun with enrichment and everything we give her. She's the most acrobatic of the four of them when she plays. Blue-eyed bobcats are rare, so she is indeed a beauty!

It's been a few months since bobcats Stelter, Brianna, Felicity and Hamlin were rescued and brought to our Sanctuary. And my, oh my, how life has changed for them!

No longer timid, they've spent so much of their time exploring around the tall grass and flowers of their summer habitat. The trees, hammocks, pools, perches, and indoor dens have been such treats for them. Imagine how life has changed from what little they had before to all we've been able to give them now.

They've all been spayed or neutered and are free of parasites. Since they arrived with dental disease, three of the four will be having dental procedures this week. We're looking forward to finishing their new, large, free roaming habitats so they'll be able to move into those before snowfall. Life just keeps getting better and better for these four! We're so thankful to have supporters who help us provide the best of care for the cats we rescue.

In Memory

We have 106 residents, 47 are senior or geriatric with 27 of those being over 15 years old. The hardest part about rescuing so many cats is that they will one day leave us. It never gets easier and it tends to come in waves. It can feel too much to bear sometimes. But we know we have to continue, we have so many animals that count on us.

Even with all the heartache, we know we're giving them a life of dignity and our job is to say goodbye while keeping that dignity intact. I feel so blessed to have the caretakers, managers and veterinarians that we do. They're so empathetic towards each animal and there is always love and appreciation for every individual cat, even as we say goodbye.

Felicity was one of the most beautiful bobcats we'd ever seen. She had a silky silver coat accented with ice blue eyes. She didn't crave human contact but enjoyed her life. She was a bobcat who was truly wild at heart.

Felicity spent most of her life confined to a small suspended wire cage in a backyard before coming to The Wildcat Sanctuary. She was purchased to be bred and pelted for her fur.

She felt grass under her feet for the first time here at The Wildcat Sanctuary. Felicity spent her days rolling in the grass or snow, rubbing on enrichment and she especially enjoyed playing in her vegetable paints.

Saying goodbye to our older cats is hard enough but saying goodbye to a younger cat is even more difficult. Felicity was just seven years old and seemed quite healthy. She would play, come up to eat and spend her nap time on top of her den, which was her favorite spot.

Felicity passed away from a bacterial infection that was sadly resistant to the antibiotic treatment we provided. As the infection progressed, she had a high temperature and her liver was shutting down. The findings were confirmed by blood work and a necropsy.

It was a sudden loss that shocked us all. But we're so grateful she was able to do what she loved up until the day we said goodbye. She did not suffer and went peacefully while being monitored by caretakers who loved her so.

Felicity, your beauty was more than just your eyes and fur coat and you will be missed by us all.

2017
BOBCAT - BUDDY

Buddy, a bobcat, was seized from a person who had him illegally in California. TWS was contacted because the owner's paperwork showed he was purchased from a breeder in Minnesota and authorities wanted to track down the person who sold him.

We agreed to take Buddy into our program. He was incredibly thin when he arrived in 2006 and had terrible scarring on his neck from an ill-fitted collar.

After a few months, Buddy put on weight, put on a beautiful silver coat, and now can always be found purring and rubbing on his enclosure wall. He loves all sorts of enrichment and is the first to mark his new toys.

In Memory

Buddy was privately-owned before arriving at The Wildcat Sanctuary almost a decade ago. He always took life in stride. And he wasn't too hyper or grumpy. Instead, he was calm and personable.

That mellow demeanor was the same at feeding time. As other cats grumbled for their food and got excited, Buddy always took his sweet time. It was the running joke how long caretakers had to stand out in the cold waiting for Buddy to finish his meal. He would eat a piece, look up and around, get distracted by a blowing tree branch, before going back for his next bite.

In his elder years, he enjoyed an indoor temperature-controlled room. That way, he could take as long as he wanted, and everyone stayed warm—including Buddy.

About 7 years ago, Buddy started having a weepy eye. It was thought he had a bad tooth, but after several dental radiographs and vet visits, no bad tooth could be found. But the problem persisted and was treated with antibiotics.

A few years ago, he was diagnosed with a chronic condition that was inoperable in his sinus cavity. We were informed it would get worse but could be managed for quite some time with more antibiotics and pain medication.

He enjoyed several more years in his tall grassy outdoor habitat. He lived with Canada Lynx Ramsey, but they had more of an annoying brother relationship, rather than best friends. Buddy liked to meet the new neighbors as they moved in and always came over to say "hi" to his caretakers.

His favorite pastime was marking the outside of his water bowl and creating a mess for the caretakers in the hallway area. Even in his old age, he could spray quite a distance!

At 18 years old, he was slowing down. He slept a little longer, his walk was a little slower, but he was still our Buddy boy. But we could see old age was settling in.

Most recently, he began to have nose bleeds and the day we said goodbye, we could see he had some discomfort. We promised ourselves, his sponsors and most of all Buddy, that he could stay as long as he wanted, unless he became uncomfortable. Because then he would be staying for us, not him. And as always, our decisions, no matter how difficult, need to honor them.

So that is what we did. He left us true to form. As calmly as he lived every day and as peaceful as Buddy was.

Your beautiful face and calming presence will be deeply missed. We feel blessed to have had you as part of our lives as long as we did.

2018
BOBCAT - TRACTOR

Tractor, a bobcat, was living in a suburban home where he was making it difficult to have visitors and was marking territory by spraying. He was bonded to his owner and initially had a difficult time accepting his new caregivers.

But now that he's been with us for many years, he loves living wild at heart. He lives peacefully in a habitat with other bobcats and enjoys the freedom to do as he pleases here at the Sanctuary.

People always wonder about the names some of our cats have. When his owner told her father "I got a bobcat." The father's response was "Why do you need a tractor?" And the name stuck.

Tractor likes all sorts of toys including balls, hammocks, and catnip boxes. But his favorite things in the world are vegetables—he'll pass up a piece of chicken any day for a cucumber or pumpkin. It's a great form of enrichment for him and keeps him busy as the other bobcats watch, wondering what in the world he's doing!

In 2010, caretakers noticed a change in Tractor's walking due to arthritis. Specialists were able to perform an innovative surgery to help Tractor.

In Memory

At 20 years old, time and arthritis caught up with bobcat Tractor and it was time to help him move on to our pride on the other side.

I remember the call eighteen years ago that brought Tractor to our sanctuary. A couple had purchased a bobcat kitten to live alongside their domestic cat in a suburban house. When they told their friends that they'd bought a bobcat, their friends asked, "Why do you need a tractor?"

That was how he was named. For good reason, it never crossed their friends' minds that they would purchase a bobcat as a pet.

A few years into adolescence, Tractor began urinating in the house and outlets and started a small fire. He also wasn't friendly to visitors, so his owners reached out to us to provide him a forever home. We were informed that he loved dry kibble, pounce treats and vegetables. They were concerned that raw meat could turn him "wild."

Upon arrival, we had to encourage him to eat raw meat by wrapping green beans in deli meat. Luckily with a lot of patience, we were able to transition him to a proper diet for a predator so that he didn't have organ failure or a vitamin deficiency.

Tractor didn't understand why he had to start a new life at the Sanctuary. And he blamed us. He began showing his wild nature and never warmed up to his human caregivers. Instead, he lived his life befriending other cats and helping them adjust to sanctuary life.

Over the years, he befriended Scooter, Bella, Libby, and Athena. In his later years, he lived with Athena and Libby and could be found curled up in the hammock with them.

When he was in his early teens, he was diagnosed with hip dysplasia, a painful and debilitating disease. A hip replacement could not be performed, since the aftercare physical therapy would not be possible.

So, specialists performed hip denervation surgery, alleviating the pain from the disease. What a difference that made for Tractor. He could jump, run, and climb again!

Even though Tractor didn't show his affection towards us humans, we loved him with all our hearts. And to show that, we'd provide him his favorite treat—cucumbers!

At first his roommates thought he was crazy and couldn't figure out why a bobcat would be so excited over a vegan treat. But soon they joined in and all enjoyed their ongoing vegetable snacks and enrichment.

Thank you, Tractor, for being such a good friend to new residents who needed a little reassurance. Your work is done and now you get to move on to your forever wild life. Enjoy your new-found freedom.

You will never be forgotten. We love you.

2018
BOBCAT - SALEM

Salem, a bobcat, is in her late teens. She was rescued along with two other bobcats, Harley and Lakota. We received a call that Wild Animal Orphanage (WAO) in Texas was closing down and had over 400 animals to place. So, we knew we had to help.

These three bobcats, along with three tigers, found a forever home at The Wildcat Sanctuary in 2010. When the bobcats first arrived, they needed immediate vet care for a flea infestation and multiple types of parasites. Salem is also partially blind and deaf and has a hematoma in her left ear, but these minor health issues do not stop her from living her life to the fullest.

Although Salem is getting on in years, she is still very spry and light on her feet. She is usually the first one to eat and loves scents for enrichment. We are so happy we were able to step up and provide Salem with the life she deserved.

In Memory

Sadly, we had to help Salem pass over the Rainbow Bridge this week. They say cats have nine lives, but no one proved that more than our dear bobcat Salem. She left us at 24 years old, but not before living all nine lives to the fullest.

To say we're at peace with her passing may seem strange. Our hearts hurt that we'll no longer get to see this sweet girl every day. But our hearts are full that we were able to know and love her. Having our animal friends live to a ripe old age is the most we can ever ask for.

Salem was a very sweet and social bobcat. One could easily mistake her for being docile because of her social nature. But Salem was completely in control. She was confident around humans and even more so around new residents she met, no matter their size.

She loved to chase cats along the shared wall, or brooms when the staff were sweeping the hallways of her building. She found fun in everything! She loved to nap in boxes, roll in catnip and was always at the fence purring hello.

Salem was once owned as a pet on the east coast, then transferred to a facility in Texas that eventually closed down. TWS was her third and final home. Salem arrived in 2010 with hematoma of the ears which caused her left ear to curl and form scar tissue.

Over the last few years, her calls for attention could be heard from the intern bunkhouse. And caretakers catered to her sweet demands. Lowering her hammocks for easy access and as her sight and hearing waned, we made sure to slightly rattle her hammock to wake her up so as not to startle her. We provided catnip and essential oil scents to keep her stimulated and spent a lot of quality time with her.

Salem had survived 2 former homes, intestinal blockage surgery due to slow motility, amputation of her front leg due to an injury, loss of sight and hearing due to age. Despite all that, she was still a happy and active girl for many years.

We knew Salem was special and she made each of us feel the same way. She slowed down little by little and when her engagement with the things she loved declined, we knew she was telling us her ninth life was almost over.

We honored her by helping her pass on to a place where she has limitless lives. We love and miss you! Salem, thank you for the wonderful moments and memories!

2018
BOBCAT - LIBBY

The Wildcat Sanctuary never stops helping animals, even on holidays. Never was that more apparent than when Libby, a privately-owned bobcat in Minnesota, was transported to The Wildcat Sanctuary on Memorial Day of 2010.

Her owner contacted the Sanctuary when she was having trouble securing homeowner's insurance. It can often be next to impossible to acquire insurance when you own an exotic pet.

Libby had been purchased several years earlier from a Minnesota game farm who sold bobcats and lynx as pets. Breeders and dealers often don't share problems like this that you might encounter as an exotic cat owner.

Now that Libby is enjoying life at The Wildcat Sanctuary, she lives with other bobcats in a large free-roaming habitat filled with pine trees, perches and hammocks.

She is very tolerant of her human caretakers and gets along excellently with her bobcat roommates. She loves all sorts of enrichment, especially painting with non-toxic vegetable paints.

In Memory

Our Silent Soldier

Even at 19, it was unexpected to say goodbye to bobcat Libby. She had what appeared to be congestion for a few days. After not responding to antibiotics, she was sedated for a thorough exam. A large inoperable mass was found in her throat putting pressure on her trachea. The only choice we had was to let her go peacefully.

Libby arrived at TWS on Memorial Day years ago. She was a former pet and was surrendered to the sanctuary after her owner lost their homeowner's insurance for having an exotic animal.

She quickly made friends with bobcat Tractor, who passed away earlier this year. It took her longer to win bobcat Athena over, but she finally did.

Libby always looked so innocent with her large saucer like eyes, but you could never underestimate her. She was a very strong girl who marched at her own pace and didn't lend herself to too much drama.

But when she needed to, she asserted herself with her roommates and her caretakers at feeding time. Mealtime was when she spoke up. Yes, meat was her primary diet. But, of all things, she enjoyed avocados, too!

In photos, she was often in the background. She preferred it that way. The limelight wasn't for her. Instead, she had a steady routine to her days that she liked to follow. She did enjoy enrichment, especially catnip and that's when she'd let her silly side show.

Libby, our silent soldier, you were brave to the very end and your sweet and strong presence will be missed. May you and Tractor march together again in your new wild life.

2019
BOBCAT - HARLEY

Harley was one of our oldest bobcats here at The Wildcat Sanctuary. She came to us in 2010, along with Salem and Lakota, two other bobcats from Wild Animal Orphanage (WAO) in Texas.

WAO was closing and, with over 400 animals to place, we knew we had to help. These three bobcats, along with several tigers, found a forever home at The Wildcat Sanctuary. When the bobcats first arrived, they needed immediate veterinary care for a flea infestation and multiple types of parasites. Ever since, Harley has been a very healthy bobcat.

Harley, as her name might suggest, is a bit of a wild child. She is very vocal and loves to grumble while eating her meal. She has one of the most unique faces we have ever seen on a bobcat, which only makes her much more special!

She loves sunbathing in her hammock, rolling in catnip and perfumes, and showing off to her neighbors just how beautiful she really is. She is one sassy lady who just loves her TWS forever home!

In Memory

I'm so sad to share that we helped 20-year-old bobcat Harley on to her new wild life. We could no longer keep her comfortable with the spread of the carcinoma in her leg. So, we had to make the difficult decision to let her go.

We always use the phrase 'wild at heart' when talking about our residents, but these words truly embody who Harley was. Content at the sanctuary, she always had a wild side and kept her distance from her caretaker humans.

Formerly declawed and kept as a pet, Harley ended up at a facility in Texas with two other bobcats, Salem, and Lakota, before needing placement at The Wildcat Sanctuary in 2008.

For years, she enjoyed their companionship. But as she aged, she wanted her own space and we gave it to her. She much preferred her habitat in the brush, watching wildlife in the woods nearby. She had her very own "bird tv" as she lounged on the fire hose hammock she loved so much.

And though she enjoyed boxes, scents, and other enrichment, she enjoyed it even more when no one was watching. She was camera shy, so we respected her privacy.

Harley may have not rubbed and purred along the fence to us like other bobcats, but that did not mean we loved her any less. Love is not about reciprocation. It is about loving selflessly and giving Harley the best life she wanted—on her own terms. And that is exactly what everyone did.

Harley, sadly you could not live wild, but we were able to give you the next best thing—living wild at heart.

Now you truly get to live as your spirit was meant to be. No more fences confine you. And every choice is yours. We will miss you each, and every day, but smile knowing you are finally, forever free.

2019
BOBCAT - SCOOTER

The Minnesota Wildlife Rehabilitation Center received a call from a West St. Paul, MN resident. He was rescuing his neighbor's "pet" bobcat. Apparently, the neighbor said the bobcat was destroying his house and he was planning to let it go free outside. Not a wise decision for a captive born animal who wouldn't be able survive on his own!

Since the Wildlife Rehabilitation Center only works with wild born animals that can be released back into the wild, they referred the caller to The Wildcat Sanctuary. Scooter was surrendered to us in 2001, within hours of the call.

The staff immediately fell in love with him! They couldn't help but be taken in by this little bobcat who was only a few weeks old. His sweet face and his little pink nose still make him a standout.

Over the years, Scooter's demeanor has changed. He went from being a docile eater, to a noisy cruncher. Now, in his old age, he's reverted back to being a more relaxed eater. He loves sunning himself, purring at his caretakers, and eating on his own time schedule.

No matter whether it's dinner time or not, he wants his food when he wants it! And who could say no to a face like his? We were so happy to be able to intercede and bring Scooter here to live out his days at the Sanctuary. He truly lives wild at heart, along with all his bobcat and big cat friends!

In Memory

Through tears, I'm writing this trying to comprehend that I had to let Scooter the bobcat go after 18 years together. Even though it was the right choice since his kidneys were failing and he'd lost a substantial amount of weight, it's so difficult for many reasons.

"Scooter Booter," as I called him, was one of the sanctuary's founding residents. As we celebrate our 20th Anniversary of saving lives, I'm also grieving that the ones who started it all are passing on to their new finally, forever free life. It feels like more than a passing of a loved one, it also feels like a passage of an era. But mostly, it's difficult because I won't get to hear Scooter's rumbling purr again as he eagerly greets me to say "hello" or see that beautiful face and HUGE pink nose.

Surrendered as an adolescent, we've all been a part of Scooter growing up…and growing old. Scooter was the most tender-hearted boy to me and other staff. But when it came to food or protecting his territory, a switch flipped, and Scooter was 100% wild bobcat. This was true from the moment I met him.

Walking into a private home, it was dark, and all the blinds were drawn. I heard low grumbles from across the room as the owner explained the bobcat wasn't very fond of him and could get very possessive.

As I approached, I spoke softly to Scooter. He began approaching, then running, and to my surprise, jumped into my arms and rested his head on my shoulder. That was the first time I heard that loud motor-like purr. Eighteen years ago, I was pretty naïve about how to approach a rescued bobcat. I know better now, but I'm very thankful for Scooter's response.

As he aged, the tender-hearted side took over. He didn't have the energy for anything but to love and be thankful for his caregivers. We provided comfort and hospice care over the past few weeks. Staff and I spent time with him each day. He received a menu of food items for his declining appetite, new scents to rub on, blankets to curl up in.

In his elder years Scooter lived alone, but we made sure he wasn't lonely. When he was younger, I introduced him to bobcats Tractor and Sidney for companionship. It took two years before they could safely live together because Scooter was so territorial and possessive. But once the final merger took place, they were inseparable for many years.

When Tractor needed hip surgery, he had to be out of their habitat for quite some time during rehab. Scooter never accepted him back. But Tractor found a new family with the female bobcats at the sanctuary.

Scooter and Sidney lived happily together until Sidney passed away of old age several years ago. Since then, we tried other friends for Scooter. But he never accepted them. Instead, he chose his human caregivers to be his closest friends. And I was blessed to be one of his favorites. I felt the same way about him.

Scooter loved enrichment—especially anything he could rub on and of course mark. He claimed everything with his signature spray, then he would roll on it. Pizza boxes were one of his favorite items and we gave him those recently, too. Scooter kept life simple.

I do find peace that he had 18 wonderful years because of our donors' support. But right now, I just need to sit with my aching heart knowing time will help heal the loss. Scooter Booter, thank you for making me feel special. I sure hope we did the same for you. I love you very much and please give Sidney and Tractor a bobcat head butt from us all.

CLOUDED LEOPARD

2015
CLOUDED LEOPARD - SCARLET

When TWS posted the story of the planned rescue that fell through for Bhutan the snow leopard, a curator for a city zoo was inspired to contact our sanctuary about providing a home for a clouded leopard named Scarlet who needed placement.

In 2012, Scarlet was 12 years old and had arrived at the zoo about a year earlier with her male companion. Sadly, her companion died within a few months. Scarlet had been living in an indoor holding area since then and the zoo was having financial troubles, so they were unable to build an outdoor area for her. The curator wanted what was best for Scarlet, so she contacted TWS.

Director Tammy Thies said, *"What makes this rescue so special is how rare her breed is in the wild and in captive breeding programs. We are honored to provide Scarlet with the retirement home she deserves."*

Clouded leopards are considered endangered. As of 2011, there were only 69 clouded leopards living in 24 institutions that participate in the Clouded Leopard Species Survival Plan. Scarlet is no longer able to breed and is not a part of the Species Survival Plan.

She'll spend her years of retirement in a large, free-roaming habitat with indoor access at the Sanctuary. Being the best climber in the cat family, she will enjoy tree branches and high platforms in her habitat.

Clouded leopards live throughout the forests of Southeast Asia. The smallest of the big cats, they are secretive and rare in the wild, preferring to remain alone and hidden from view. They have the longest canines and tail, compared to body size. Even though they are small in stature, they are morw closely related to the big cats than to small cats.

Scarlet underwent an intake exam and remained in a quarantine area at the Sanctuary for 30 days before she was released into a free-roaming habitat. Trail cameras were set up to document her activity while she acclimated to her new home.

During her intake exam, we discovered some devastating news. A pre-implanted microchip helped us find out more about her past. Being a rare cat, Scarlet was part of the Clouded Leopard studbook where her genealogy was tracked. She was bounced around through several breeding facilities and non-accredited zoos and actually was lost in the system. We contacted the SSP to inform them of her whereabouts and status.

But the exam also uncovered health issues. Her rear-end was necrotic and swollen and she was incontinent. It was definitely painful, and she was self-mutilating due to the discomfort.

A tumor on her mammary gland was also discovered and a biopsy was performed. And the most devastating news was that her initial blood work came back positive for feline leukemia. The feline leukemia virus (FeLV) is a disease that impairs the cat's immune system and causes certain types of cancer and is contagious between cats.

In many organizations, this would be a death sentence for Scarlet. But we owed it to her to perform more tests, treat some of the health issues and see if, with the right support, she could begin to heal and continue to have quality of life.

Two weeks later, a follow-up exam was performed. Her back-end had dramatically improved with antibiotics and pain medication. The infection had subsided, and the inflammation decreased. The mammary tumor was malignant, but our vets felt they had clear tissue margins and the prognosis was good.

And the second IFA feline leukemia test came back negative. This meant she has exposure to the disease, but currently is not shedding the disease. Our team made the decision that she deserves the best chance at a good life at TWS. But it will take special care to provide for her.

Because feline leukemia is spread by close and persistent contact between infected and non-infected cats, Scarlet will now require a permanent habitat that is separated from the rest of the TWS population. This will ensure the disease cannot spread to the other cats. She'll also need to be officially quarantined in terms of care, utensils and feeding. She was temporarily moved indoors for ongoing observation.

Our vision for her permanent habitat will provide her an indoor shift area, a 2000 square foot enclosure that has ample landscaping for coverage for her shy nature, logs to climb and claw, and hammocks to lounge on. Given her future habitat site is in the quarantine area, only a small team can work on the construction.

Outsourcing the habitat vs. volunteers building it will ensure it is erected quickly with the least possible chance of cross contamination to our other residents. The fence company completed the new fencing of her habitat in January 2013 while a fundraising campaign began to finish paying for the rest of her planned new home.

May 2013

For those of you who don't know Scarlet's story, she came to us with a horrible infection on her rear end. This was likely due to incontinence which could be from a genetic malformation. We have been treating this with antibiotics for months and finally it was cleared up enough for her to undergo surgery for a more permanent health solution.

Thanks to Dr. Scott Hammel of Veterinary Surgical Specialists, Scarlet can now enjoy life pain free. Dr. Hammel performed an episioplasty which will allow Scarlet to urinate more freely thus preventing urine building up on her rear end causing the infection.

Scarlet has endured so much in her lifetime that finally giving her this basic freedom from pain is truly a blessing. Her surgery went very well, and she is now on the road to recovery. She will receive a check-up in two weeks to make sure everything is healing as it should be.

The future here for Scarlet looks bright. We are currently working on her new habitat and as soon as she is all healed, she will be free to enjoy the great outdoors once again. Two of our fantastic volunteers built her a special log jungle gym to stretch her wild side on, with high climbing logs and private coves to lounge under.

Scarlet remains a very private, shy cat but we're hoping that, with her new pain free life and new habitat to explore, she'll break out of her shell and be the wild cat she deserves to be.

May 2014

Emergency surgery was performed on Scarlet today after a medical exam confirmed pyometra. Pyometra is an infection of the uterus that occurs because of hormonal changes in a cat's reproductive tract.

Scarlet is not spayed. The majority of our residents are spayed/neutered upon arriving at the sanctuary. That decision was made by medical experts since Scarlet had so many other health issues that needed immediate attention when she arrived at the Sanctuary.

Scarlet is receiving the best of care and is being monitored closely by her caregivers. We're optimistic, but also realize this was a serious surgery.

Scarlet, who arrived shy and elusive, has come out of her shell. She naps up high on her hammock and loves to scratch her log. We hope she'll be back out in her habitat very soon.

January 2015

Recently, it was observed that Scarlet's eye appeared to be cloudy. She underwent surgery for a luxating lens that was removed. Her ophthalmologist felt Scarlet should regain the majority of her vision back in the eye. The surgery was successful and has a short recovery period. Scarlet was able to return to her habitat and get back to her daily routine within a few days.

In Memory

Farewell Special Scarlet

Sometimes, the best decision we can make for them is the hardest one for us. That was the case recently when we helped Scarlet, our clouded leopard, pass on.

In 2012, we received a request to take in a very special cat, a rare clouded leopard named Scarlet. Scarlet also arrived with special needs and behavioral issues clouded leopards are known for in captivity. But to us, Scarlet was just special because she was Scarlet.

When she first arrived, she was elusive and shy, highly stressed and sucked her tail so much her skin was exposed. On top of that, she also had chronic health issues and underwent several treatments and surgeries after arriving at the Sanctuary.

With the love of her caregivers, Scarlet blossomed at TWS. Her personality started to shine, and she greeted her caretakers for meds and meals. She loved sleeping up high in her fire hose hammock and sharpening her nails on the logs. She also liked to forage for her food in trees, teaser balls and even from her suspended toys.

Over the past few years, Scarlet became brave—and even sassy. It was a blessing to see her emotionally doing so well, even though we knew her health was declining. She became a ball of energy and very brave.

She even began operant conditioning to encourage her to keep her little paws (and big claws) on the floor vs. reaching for her food. She had stopped over grooming her tail and it had grown back in beautifully.

With her adorable face and sweet antics, she continued to become even more special to us and all of our supporters. She was a very smart cat who had a long journey both emotionally and physically.

It was bittersweet to see her emotionally heal while her body deteriorated. We continued to keep a close eye on her and stay ahead of her medical issues to ensure she was comfortable and pain-free.

We knew the time would come when her medical challenges would be increasingly closer in occurrence, and we would have to make the decision that was best for her. When that time came and before we could make such a heart-wrenching decision, we determined it was important to have the best medical diagnostics run.

We brought her to the University of Minnesota where she underwent a cat scan. At 15, she had already beaten the odds so many times. The tests confirmed our worst fears. Scarlet had little lung capacity left.

With her autoimmune issues ever increasing, Scarlet was no longer responding to antibiotic and steroid treatments. With disbelief and much sadness, we knew it was best not to wake her and let her go peacefully.

It's so hard to comprehend she's gone. I can still see her little spotted nose and long whiskers greeting us at the fence. And her beautiful long tail being the last glance as she walked into her building.

There will never be another Scarlet. She truly was special and will be deeply missed and forever in our hearts. May your journey in your new life be peaceful and pain-free.

SERVALS

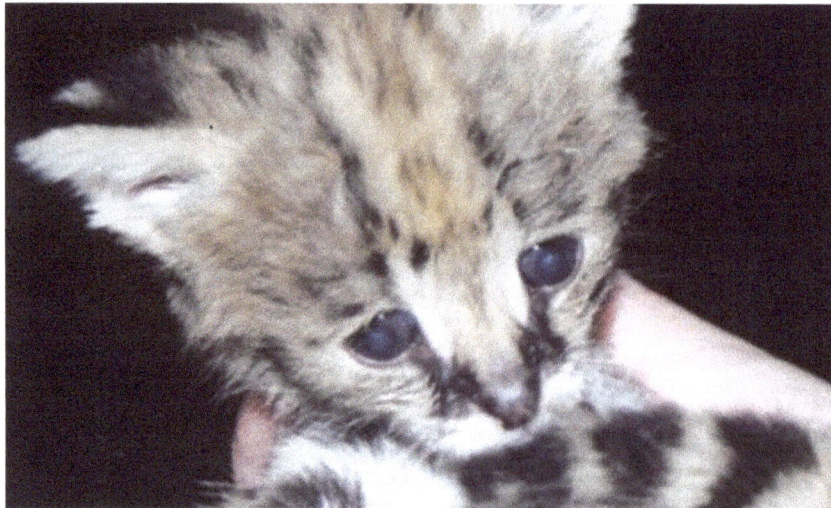

1999
SERVAL - LOUIE

Louie arrived as a 6-week-old serval kitten. His mother had been bred for several years and had become extremely ill.

The vet convinced the breeder to spay the mother after the last litter that included stillborn kittens, kittens with birth defects, and little Louie. Louie ended up being the lone survivor when he arrived at TWS.

Louie spent his week with us in the ICU. We did all we could to save him, but it was not enough.

He touched our lives deeper than any cat I had ever met, even though he was only with us for a short time. He is an example of why the over-breeding of all animals needs to stop.

With all our love, little Louie.

2008
SERVAL - KYRA

Kyra, a female African serval, and two other servals were seized by the US Fish and Game Department in Arizona. An unlicensed individual had several exotic cats confined to crates and was breeding them illegally. We don't know Kyra's age, but she seems to be the motherly one of the group. She's quite calm and doesn't seem to understand all the fuss the younger servals make over food and toys.

She shares her habitat with three other servals, Rio, Mesa, and Princess Savannah and one bobcat, Nikko. They all live in a large outdoor habitat with access to a heated indoor building.

In Memory

Our serval, Kyra, passed away last week. It was a very sad and devastating night, but Tammy was with her when she took her last breath.

Rio, a smaller serval, had attacked Kyra and we brought her into the hospital for observation. We sedated her, shaved and cleaned her wounds, and gave her antibiotics and pain meds. She had several smaller punctures on her body, but nothing that looked life threatening. Kyra purred and was the perfect patient. As the evening progressed, her breathing became abnormal and her eyes glassed over. We realized that there was nothing we could do for her, and we knew she wouldn't make it to the vet. She was not responding to the antibiotics. Kyra passed within several minutes.

For those who didn't know Kyra, she was a calming presence amongst the chaos of the servals. She was a motherly figure and very patient. It saddens us that Rio attacked her, but we know they are wild, and we cannot blame Rio for what happened.

This is such an unexpected passing and one we will continue to second guess ourselves about, thinking we may have been able to do more. But that will not overshadow our memory of her wonderful spirit, chubby tummy, and beautiful expressions. Kyra will be deeply missed.

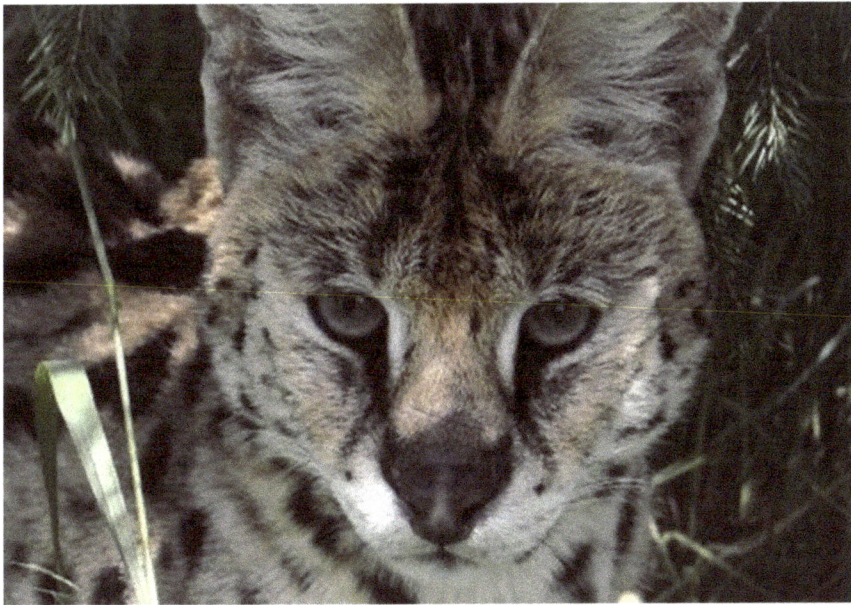

2011
SERVAL - DRAGON

Dragon, an African serval, was surrendered by a woman who had recently married and had a baby on the way. Dragon had previously attacked the woman and her husband had been threatening to shoot him. He absolutely didn't want the cat around the baby.

Dragon was being kennelled with two Bengal girls in a 14′ x 20′ kennel with an attached heated house. When he was approximately 7 months old, he had a horrible accident causing a diagonal compound break, tissue damage and possibly pelvic damage.

Words from his owner tell a story we hear very often:

Dragon used to be very easy to handle, loved to butt heads, go for walks, etc. Once sexual maturity hits though, it's gone downhill. I don't understand how to read his behavior and ended up getting bit and scratched. Sometimes he's really nice and then he starts raising his chin, making strange noises and ends up lunging at me. Luckily, I'm still able to get him crated so that I can enter the kennel to clean. I've become scared of him...which isn't a good thing.

Dragon arrived at TWS and was immediately examined and neutered. He has kidney disease, but we hope he can still live a high quality of life. He is much calmer than we anticipated and now lives with other servals in an indoor and outdoor habitat.

In Memory

We've experienced a devastating loss here at the Sanctuary. Dragon the serval has passed and left us with unanswered questions as to why. He was a happy healthy cat one day, then the next was severely ill.

Our team of vets drew blood, took x-rays, and ran tests, but nothing came back abnormal. For over a week, we tried everything we could to help Dragon. After days of giving him antibiotics, fluids, and steroids, he started responding quite well. He even started purring and rolling around. I even heard him talking a few times.

However, two days later he took a turn for the worse and his liver was shutting down. In the end, after trying everything we could, he told us it was just his time to go.

When Dragon first came to us, he was very shy and scared of his new surroundings. It took him some time to be comfortable with us and the other servals he lived with, but he eventually started to open up. I would often see him snuggling in his lockout with Princess Savannah while they waited for their food.

He loved to come in after I cleaned the building and rub on his utility brush. For some reason, the smell of soap and bleach made him drool and roll around, a common thing with servals and savannahs. Although he never really wanted to be around people, there were times when I would walk by his habitat and stop to let him sniff my hand.

One time when I was fixing his lockout, he walked right next to me, back and forth swishing his tail without a care in the world. It was great to see him so comfortable around me and other people. That tail of his was very funny. Usually during feeding, it would go wild, swishing this way and that and twirling all around, it was his signature.

He really was a sweet guy and will be missed greatly. I'm glad I got to know him while he was here but wish he could have stayed longer. I will miss that tail swishing away and that cute face poking into the building after cleaning. But I know that he is now forever free and will be chasing mice in that endless field of grass.

2012
SERVAL - PRINCESS SAVANNAH

Princess Savannah and a male serval were seized by the US Fish and Game Department in Arizona. Princess Savannah and Denali were bonded when they arrived. That is, until Denali started posturing his tough boy attitude towards the other servals. Princess Savannah had had enough so we introduced her to a mellower group, also from Arizona. She fits in quite well with her new group of friends.

In Memory

I believe that every cat at the Sanctuary is special in their own unique way and so many have left paw prints on my heart. But there are those certain cats that no matter how down you are or how bad you think you have it, just by looking into their eyes your spirit is lifted. This was Princess Savannah.

Her name was kind of silly, but it definitely suited her well. When we lose a resident as special as Savannah, it takes a toll on us and leaves us feeling sort of hollow. But when we knew it was her time, we couldn't help but think of all the fun and funny moments we had together over the years.

Savannah was a one-of-a-kind, not only in looks, but personality as well. Her absolute favorite thing to do was paint. You could barely get the canvas down before she would be drooling, moaning, and groaning and having a ball.

My favorite was during feeding time. While all the others would come up and wait patiently for their food, Savannah would race out of nowhere, jump up and down and all around grumbling the whole time, then grab the food and run off, she was such a goofball.

The other great thing about Savannah was her courage. Her kidneys were in poor condition and while we helped her with all the supplements and medications we could think of, it just wasn't enough, and so it was her time to go.

She was so accommodating to everything we did for her, going easily into a crate when she needed to be seen by the vets, moving into quarantine happily when she needed to be monitored more closely, living with other cats when she was feeling healthy.

She was still just such a happy cat no matter what. She just made life look so simple working to get through the hard times and looking forward to the fun things, like painting!

Princess Savannah you are so very, very special to us all and I think every day I will miss you but I know where you are and now there is no more pain, only endless days of fun. Goodbye P.S.

2013
SERVAL - HALIFAX

Halifax is our oldest serval. He was surrendered by an owner who loved him very much and was committed to giving him a lifetime home.

After surviving breast cancer, his owner had to move near her daughter in another city that outlawed exotic pets. There are so many reasons exotic cats shouldn't be considered pets. Whether it's their wild tendencies, life circumstances changing, new zoning laws, inability to get insurance…we've heard so many reasons why these "pets" have to be surrendered.

Halifax's owner wanted to ensure that she did not put his life in danger. So, she called our sanctuary to see if we could take him in.

Halifax has really warmed up to the staff but has plenty of wild cat friends, too. He enjoys his life here, sharing a large outdoor habitat and heated building with other servals. We're happy he can spend the rest of his days with others of his own kind.

In Memory

Sadly, we had to say goodbye to our dear friend Halifax this week. At 20 years old, he was an inspiration for my spirit.

Despite his age, Halifax was so virile and full of life. He loved any kind of enrichment, but especially had a blast chasing little rocks or pinecones when thrown in his habitat.

In the summertime, he'd even jump in the pool after them, his playful spirit was definitely contagious. He always had this sort of regal look to him, especially when he sat basking in the sun. It conjured images of him in his own native habitat watching for any prey in the savannas of Africa.

I'm very sorry that he never experienced true freedom like that in his life but know that he was a happy cat and that many people loved him dearly. He had some bumps along the way with his health, but he never let that get in the way of his fun for too long.

Twenty years is a long time to live for a cat and I believe he lived them to the fullest. I will miss seeing his handsome face every day but will always remember the fun times we had just being silly. That was one of the things I liked best about him, his ability to look so serious one second then be a total goofball the next.

I am so glad that I knew Halifax. He was, and still is, such a special boy. Goodbye, sweet boy, thank you for your wonderful spirit and may you be forever free.

CARACALS

2005
CARACAL - PHARAOH

In the fall of 2002, TWS began receiving emails regarding a caracal in Oklahoma in need of a home. The caracal, Pharaoh, had been purchased as a pet. But when the owner moved to Colorado, his city did not permit exotic cats.

After a few weeks, we heard that Pharaoh still did not have a permanent home. TWS did the only thing we could. TWS staff members Tammy, with her faithful sidekick, Kelly, made the 13-hour trip to pick him up during the Christmas holiday. Pharaoh did fabulously on the trip back and was the perfect traveler.

Pharaoh has adjusted very well to his life at the sanctuary. He chirps to all his human friends from across the sanctuary. If that does not get our attention, he'll keep himself busy by tossing his stuffed animal high into the air and swatting it down.

Pharaoh tends to be very independent and gets bored with roommates. He has shared a habitat with other servals, a caracal and even a bobcat but seems to prefer the company of his stuffed animals most of all.

In Memory

Whether a cat enters our rescue system for a matter of days or whether they become a life-long resident, each one holds a special place in our hearts. One of the challenges we face in providing a permanent safe haven for our residents is that one day, each will leave us to cross the Rainbow Bridge to finally be forever free.

One of TWS' special caracal residents, Pharaoh, recently made that journey, quite unexpectedly. Luckily, the transition for Pharaoh was quick and painless. With the swiftness of his passing, those of us who knew and loved Pharaoh were faced with coping with the grief of loss, while also celebrating his life and the knowledge that he is finally free from the captive life he knew on Earth.

Tammy, TWS' Executive Director, wrote this special message in memory of Pharaoh which so eloquently captures how all of us at TWS felt.

I almost was not able to write this. I am just devastated at the loss of dear Pharaoh. I know I should feel comfort in knowing we rescued him, provided him a wonderful sanctuary home and that we found the cancer before he was in a lot of pain. But unfortunately, I feel truly helpless and a terrible void. I know with time it will get better, but Pharaoh was uniquely Pharaoh, and he will never be replaced. Thankfully, I can find comfort in the two very special last days I spent with Pharaoh.

Pharaoh seemed a little under the weather, so I brought him in the house with me. He lay at my feet while I worked on the computer, and he rubbed against my legs when I would look down and smile. He slept on his blanket and followed me as I did my chores. Those two days I will cherish forever. On the last day, I brought him to our veterinarian's office, and they found several cancerous tumors in Pharaoh's digestive track. We did the only thing we could do and helped Pharaoh pass over the rainbow bridge.

I am told that with each passing resident it will get easier. But the truth is, I hope that it doesn't. For the loss I feel now for Pharaoh mirrors the love I had for him. And if the loss is to get easier next time, the love must be less as well. I will move on and rescue more cats, each as special as Pharaoh and I will mourn the loss of each one, as I do Pharaoh today.

Pharaoh has been cremated and his ashes will be spread across wildlife land where he will spend his first moments and the rest of forever living outside of the confinement of fences. We call this the freedom trail, and this is how he was meant to live.

I love you, Pharaoh, and thank you for blessing my life.
Tammy, Founder

2014
CARACAL - IVAN

We were contacted by the International Fund for Animal Welfare (IFAW) about a California event center using animals for exhibition. The US Fish & Game authorities declared their tiger enclosure to be non-compliant. The owner was given 60 days to upgrade it, but he claimed that it would be impossible to do.

While IFAW negotiated with the owner, trying to convince him to surrender all his exotic cats, we agreed to take them all. That included two tigers, two servals, and two caracal brothers named Nigel and Ivan. Another sanctuary offered to take in a lynx from the event center and provide transport for the cats to us, too. Everything was in place.

But then, the owner decided he would not surrender all his cats. We stood by our commitment to provide a home for Tonka, the tiger, and the two caracals he did agree to release to us. We also offered, in the spring, to pick up the two servals he still has on display there, as well as his remaining white tiger.

Tonka and the caracals made the long, two-day journey and arrived in the wee hours on a Sunday morning. At daybreak, they were more than anxious to get out of their transport carriers.

Nigel and Ivan, born in 2000, had lived at the event center their entire lives, after being purchased as kittens. They both moved into our large indoor/outdoor quarantine area when they arrived. Though Nigel adjusted right away, something was wrong with Ivan. Sadly, he passed away and we are all heartbroken by his loss.

In Memory

We were saddened that Nigel's brother Ivan passed away upon arrival at our sanctuary and could not experience the same blissful new home.

Ivan, Nigel and Tonka arrived before dawn on a Sunday morning. It was about 4:45 a.m. when his transporters pulled in. They'd driven several days from California to deliver these three new residents who would now call our sanctuary home.

Upon arrival, Ivan the caracal was weak and not walking. But he didn't appear to be critically ill. We had no information that would lead us to believe otherwise.

Supportive care was given for dehydration. Our vet was consulted, along with several exotic animal vets and sanctuary directors. He was scheduled to be seen by the University of Minnesota veterinary team that Thursday morning, but Ivan passed away shortly after arriving. We had Ivan in our care for a scant 48 hours before we lost him.

His former caretakers, the transport staff from the accredited sanctuary who provided transport, and our sanctuary all came together to try and piece together what could have happened to Ivan.

With the information we had, it was believed to be neurological (Ivan had a prior history of neurological concerns) or capture myopathy (muscle damage resulting from stress). Everyone was concerned and everyone's hearts were broken.

Conference calls took place to share as much information as possible, as we knew his necropsy report would not be back for several weeks. When it came in, the report raised more questions than answers. The results for the cause of his passing were inconclusive, but Ivan had several fractures in his pelvis which explained why he wasn't walking.

His former caretakers said his capture on their end was stressful, but no information we were given led anyone to believe he had injured himself badly. Our hearts were broken again. We may never know what happened to Ivan. Did the stress of the capture and move, mixed with a pre-existing condition, cause his passing? We would only be guessing.

But we do know that it's not the ending we wish for any animal. We are here to rescue animals in need—that is our mission. We feel strongly we made the right decisions with the little information we had available.

We go to extraordinary lengths to provide the best care possible for each and every one of the animals. Rescues are hard work, and losing Ivan was heartbreaking. We cried for his loss as we do for each and everyone we say goodbye to.

We'll continue to celebrate his life, though, and do the best we can for each and every animal we rescue. Each time we see Nigel, we know that Ivan's spirit is here with us, urging us to continue with our mission. We take comfort knowing that's what he wanted for his brother…and all those yet to be rescued.

2015
CARACAL—NIGEL

We were contacted by the International Fund for Animal Welfare (IFAW) about an event center using animals for exhibition. The US Fish & Game authorities declared their tiger enclosure to be non-compliant. The owner was given 60 days to upgrade it, but he claimed that would be impossible to do.

While IFAW negotiated with the owner, trying to convince him to surrender all his exotic cats, we agreed to take them all in—two tigers, two servals, and two caracal brothers named Nigel and Ivan. Another sanctuary offered to take in a lynx from the event center and provide transport for the cats to us, too. Everything was in place.

But then, the owner decided he would not surrender all his cats. We stood by our commitment to provide a home for Tonka, the tiger, and the two caracals he agreed to release to us. We also offered, in the spring, to pick up the two servals he still has on display there as well as his remaining white tiger.

Tonka and the caracals made the long two-day journey and arrived in the wee hours of a Sunday morning. At daybreak, they were more than anxious to get out of their transport carriers.

Nigel and Ivan, born in 2000, had lived at the event center their entire lives since being purchased as kittens. They both moved into our large indoor/outdoor quarantine area when they arrived. Nigel began exploring the outdoor habitat area rather quickly.

While Sundays mean the start of a new week for most of us, for Nigel, this particular Sunday meant the start of a new life. We're so grateful to all our supporters who helped with this happy "beginning" for them

In Memory

If love could keep an animal alive, Nigel would still be with us today. Nigel, and his brother Ivan, arrived at The Wildcat Sanctuary just this past year. Never did we think we'd have to say goodbye so soon.

Ivan left us within days of coming to The Wildcat Sanctuary, and Nigel has also had chronic medical issues since his arrival. Each of Nigel's new medical hurdles unveiled more about their previous life and gave us some insight as to why Ivan had so much trouble.

Nigel had blood sugar issues symptomatic of diabetes or an endocrine disease. He was also diagnosed with severe chronic joint degeneration due to age, being 4-paw declawed, and having lived in a small space with hard substrate for over a decade before arriving at our Sanctuary.

On top of that, he was a senior cat and suffered from renal disease with hypertension. He received expert medical care and pain medication to ensure he was comfortable each day he lived at The Wildcat Sanctuary. He always showed his appreciation whether it was strolling his outdoor area, rubbing on enrichment, or rushing indoors for a great meal with all his medications.

He was loved. So, loved. Not only by our staff, but by previous caretakers, sponsor parents, and so many TWS supporters.

Most days you would never know Nigel had so many issues. But, over the last few weeks, they became more apparent and he deserved to keep his dignity. We closely monitored his comfort level and assessed him daily.

Nigel was very confident and was always clear in communicating his feelings and expectations. He lived the days as he wanted and told us when he wanted space. He often greeted us nicely for meds and meals and then, when our service was complete, he let us know we were no longer needed and ventured back near his cat neighbors to say hello.

We began to take it day by day and let Nigel tell us when it was our role to help him pass on. One day, he was less active and alert than usual. Our vet and I watched him closely and discussed whether he was ready.

At that moment, he stood up, chirped at us and then to his friend Sampson until Sampson called back. He remained standing and began grooming. He looked over at us and then curled back in the grass. It wasn't his day to leave us.

His last few days were reminiscent of Ivan's first and only days. He was lethargic, yet comfortable. We would see him basking in the sun during the day and then napping on his indoor hammock in the evening.

This particular day was different. Nigel walked slowly into his yard to take his last nap in the sunny grass outside. He let us know today was his last with us, and we let him nap in the sun all morning. When it was time to say goodbye, we helped Nigel pass peacefully and released some of Ivan's ashes in his space. They were back together again.

Our hearts ached for his loss, for our loss, and also for the life we had wanted for both Nigel and Ivan. They deserved so much more time in open, natural space. Now they have found it, even if it is beyond the walls of our Sanctuary.

2015
CARACAL - SAMPSON

Sampson was the second cat to come to The Wildcat Sanctuary and therefore, holds a special place in our hearts. He is a very sweet little caracal. Though we've tried to introduce Sampson to other cats of his species in the past, he seems to prefer living with his little spotted friends.

Sampson lives with a group of servals who are, like caracals, another species of African wildcats. We think he just likes being the 'different' one in the group. Sampson's serval friends have accepted this 'outsider' and love him for who he is. They're very accepting of the differences between them. You'll find them all curled up together napping in the tall grass during the summer or lounging on their inside hammocks during cold winter days.
]
Animals can teach us so much about tolerance and acceptance, can't they?

In Memory

I am so sorry to let you know that dear Sampson lost his battle with geriatric renal disease. Sampson had rebounded and had a great fall season. He spent his time out in the sun, curled up with his friends or taking walks under the trees. When fall arrived, he huddled under a heat lamp in the den or inside the building on his fire hose hammock with his friends.

I know the pain I feel today mirrors the love I had for Sampson. Even though I thought I'd prepared myself for this moment, it was more difficult than I can express. As he slowed down, the treatments needed to be increased.

As devastating as it was to think of a day at the Sanctuary without him, I always promised him I would not keep him here for me. It was his life, and he deserved a great one. So, today was the day I had to honor that promise.

As one of the founding cats of The Wildcat Sanctuary, Sampson was lucky and spent 17 years only knowing love and compassion. Sampson touched the lives of so many. I think it was because his personality was so distinctly different from that of a typical caracal, and his floppy ears mirrored that.

Caracals in general may imprint on an individual caretaker, but often have a hissy demeanor. Not Sampson. Sampson would bulldoze his way into the hearts of his habitat mates and visiting humans. He wanted to be friends with everyone, and he wouldn't take no for an answer.

The only cat he never completely won over was new arrival Aurora, and I believe that was only hindered by the time he had left. During the last month, Aurora was in a den in the habitat and Sampson decided to join her. She hissed, smacked, and protested about sharing the space, but Sampson being Sampson, he went in anyway and curled up beside her. She was surprised and just sat behind him. Sampson went to sleep in the way only Sampson could.

Celebrating Sampson, you cannot help but smile. Most of his life, he was a little chubby for a caracal and his tufts were floppy. He was very animated and would call and chirp in response to a caregiver saying hello, a serval talking and even caracal Nigel talking when he was here. He was very excited to have a conversation with a cat that sounded just like him.

In the sea of servals that he lived with, he definitely stood out. He liked to initiate "the huddle" and curl up with all of his habitat mates. But Cleo the serval always had to be the closest. She was his girl. She was the first resident of TWS, and when they met at a young age, Sampson was smitten with her.

And for years, he just assumed he was a serval, too.
To Sampson, Cleo was special and the most beautiful serval in the world. They were bonded, but luckily over the years, they expanded their circle of friends to include servals Rocky and Mufasa. Cleo has been seen with them since Sampson's passing.

Sampson never had a grumpy day. The only conflict that ever arose was a small hiss and smack at feeding time to let Bosco and Rocky know, Sampson wanted his meal. How else would he maintain the rotund figure he was known for, for so many years?

Later in life, Sampson slimmed down. It was good for him since he also had degenerative joint disease in his hips. But he never lost his signature ear flops, or the twitch of the head before he let out a huge hello.

On windy days, he would walk, and his ear tufts would stand straight up like other caracals. He seemed to enjoy that very much.

His last day, he made just as special and filled with love. He talked, when spoken to, and passed peacefully. He made it as easy on us as he possibly could, because that was just how Sampson was. He never lived his life solo. It was always about those around him. And that is how he will be remembered.

Sampson, I promise you, I will stop the tears soon and remember you with a smile. Because bringing others joy was your life mission, and I know that's what you would've wanted. Cleo and you will be reunited one day. Until then, she continues to have "the huddle" and love here at the Sanctuary.

I will miss you, my dear friend.

CARAVAL

2015
CARAVAL - ZEPO

We received a call from the Humane Society regarding a wild cat who was being kept in a suburban area of Minneapolis. The humane officer had spoken with the owner and he agreed to willingly surrender the cat because he was biting his son and girlfriend. At the time of the surrender, Zepo's story was featured in City Pages.

TWS was provided very little information about Zepo the Caraval's background. A Caraval is a cross between two wild cats, a serval and a caracal.

We do know that this man was Zepo's second owner. The first owner had purchased Zepo from a breeder in northern Minnesota. The man who surrendered Zepo informed us he had no toys or "personal" items because Zepo destroyed everything.

Zepo arrived dealing with a few medical issues, including ear mites and a bacterial infection. At two-years-old, Zepo weighed a mere 13 pounds and vomited frequently. Zepo's malnourishment was caused by an intestinal blockage.

Zepo underwent emergency surgery to remove the foreign object—a large piece of plastic about 1-inch in diameter that he had ingested prior to coming to TWS. Zepo rebounded nicely from the medical conditions he came with.

The next obstacle Zepo faced came when he was introduced to the other servals at TWS. Zepo is a hybrid and looks a little different than the other servals. The other servals did not accept Zepo at first due to his differences.

Bosco, a baby serval, did not care about the differences and saw something special in Zepo. The other servals opened up to Zepo once they saw the special bond that developed between him and Bosco. We are happy to report Zepo's now a full-fledged member of the team.

This story of friendship through diversity caught the eye of a National Geographic Kids Magazine editor who put their story in the October 2003 issue.

Zepo now shares a habitat with other servals who have whole-heartedly accepted him. He has also completely overcome all the health issues he came to TWS with.

Formerly a cautious and apprehensive cat, Zepo has blossomed into a confident and inquisitive soul. We feel so fortunate to be able to provide Zepo a home where he can be wild at heart.

In Memory

Our hearts are heavy as we had to say goodbye to Zepo, the caraval.

At 15-years-old, he was geriatric. Caracals normally live between 15 to17 years in captivity, but hybrids' lives are even shorter.

Even so, Zepo did not seem old to us. We have had cats live to be in their 20's. Zepo had health issues over the years and so we were hoping this was another hurdle we could get him through.

He had good and bad days. He was calm and patient during the bad ones, and playful and full of personality on the good ones.

Zepo was different, not just because he was a hybrid between a caracal and serval, but because he was so accepting. He accepted every cat he was ever introduced to, even if they did not accept him. And in his 14 years at the Sanctuary, that was quite a few.

He had special bonds with servals Bosco and Rocky. He was calm and happy and accepted his life in captivity, living each day to the fullest. Even during his recent medical issues, he was patient and accepted the treatments we provided to try and pull him through.

Zepo touched so many during his lifetime. His rescue was featured in a local paper educating many people why exotic cats do not make good pets.

His story of friendship with Bosco was featured in National Geographic kid's magazine educating future generations about tolerance. And over the 14 years of his life, he touched every caretaker, intern, volunteer, and sponsor parent.

Even the last few months of his life, he was still making an impact on us. Due to his unique symptoms, specialists, sanctuary veterinarians and exotic veterinarians were involved in his case. Some checked in every day to see how he was doing and how he was responding.

During the last month, our own veterinarian and caregivers spent so much time with him, and we felt so connected. He was so patient and allowed each of us to do what was needed for him.

It has been a devastating loss, but he told us it was time for him to let go. He accepted it and we had to honor that for him.

We know he is stronger now without his body to hold him back. He was part of our feline family for over a decade and it will not be the same without him here.

Zepo, it was our honor and privilege to be your caregivers. You were truly special in so many ways. Enjoy your freedom and visit us often.

JUNGLE CATS

2010
JUNGLE CAT - MILO

Milo is a Jungle cat, who is very down to earth and takes everything in stride. He gets along great with everyone from domestic cats to Bengals and even people. He can also be quite vocal to the keepers, especially while playing with a feather toy. While most cats like to chase the feather end, Milo prefers the stick. He can usually be seen lounging in the grass or hiding out in the concrete cave.

In Memory

We are very saddened that Milo, a Jungle cat, has passed. Milo was a very gentle soul and very dear to our hearts. When Milo first came to TWS, he found comfort and companionship with another cat, named Tamu. After Tamu's passing, Milo decided to find a new friend and found that and more in a domestic Bengal named Zac. Milo and Zac became inseparable, often found grooming and snuggling with each other.

Milo was always very calm and took most things in stride. He loved his famous drive-by butt pats and so did his keepers. If you didn't know Milo, the noises coming from him would probably have scared you, but he was as gentle as a butterfly.

After moving to a new habitat, separate from Zac, he found yet another companion in Luna. Milo was diagnosed with Spondylosis which caused him severe pain. When pain medication no longer helped, we decided it best to help him pass to relieve his pain.

Milo was loved by all who were lucky enough to meet him and cleaning his bungalow will not be the same. Milo you will be greatly missed, and we hope you get as many butt pats as you want now that you are finally, forever free.

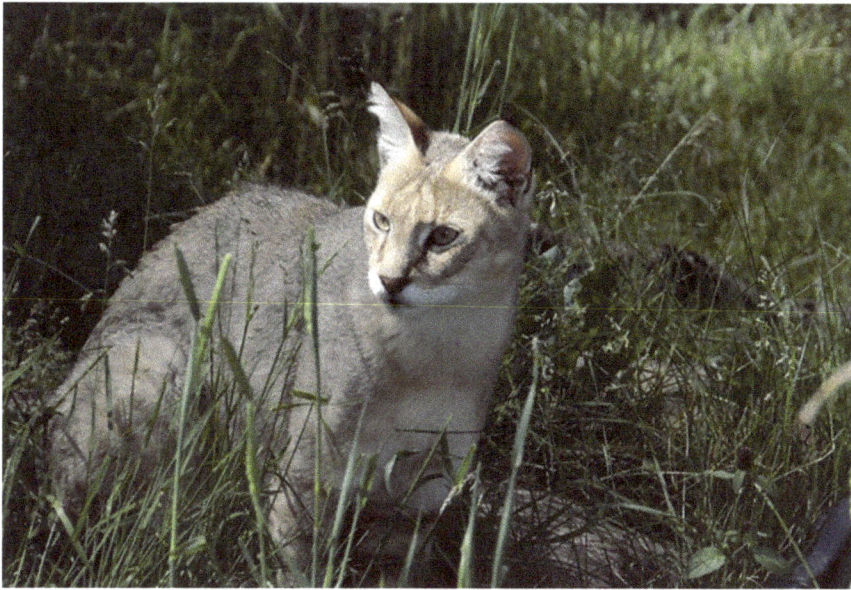

2018
JUNGLE CAT - ABBY

Abby is a female Jungle cat. This is a wild cat species native to the Middle East, South and Southeast Asia and southern China. And certainly not one that belongs in someone's house as a "pet."

Abby came to live at The Wildcat Sanctuary in 2007. She was four years old at the time. We'd received a call from a veterinarian working with a Humane Society. She had taken in Abby and soon realized Abby was not just a regular cat. Abby had tried to kill a small dog and needed to be placed in a new home.

The veterinarian decided Abby needed a special home, where she could live and be wild, as she was intended to be. We were happy we could provide that type of home for her.

Though Abby is a small cat, she's still a wild animal. She loves getting her chicken in the morning and will greet the caretakers with little grumbling noises at the gate. She also likes to lounge on her hammock or perch high in her tree, secretly watching the caretakers.

One of her favorite things to play with is a feather toy, but you'd better be quick, because she sure is!

In Memory

Abby was a little cat with a huge will to live. She had been in our comfort care program for several years due to severe arthritis of the spine and rib cage. We were able to manage her pain for quite some time, but we could see her body was slowly deteriorating.

She rebounded several times, but we knew the end of her time with us was drawing near, and we had to make the difficult decision in her best interest to let her go.

Abby had a quiet and controlled personality but could never be underestimated. She asserted herself when it was needed or when the right motivation struck. And that motivation usually came in the form of a visiting dog—which is why she was surrendered.

Abby arrived after being brought to an out of state Humane Society. One of the vets took her home, but soon realized a jungle cat, no matter how small, was too much to handle. The vet came home to find Abby had her pet dachshund pinned by the throat.

Luckily, the vet was able to save the dog, and Abby was sent to our Sanctuary. She continued to be bold through the fence with the staff's dogs—no matter the size. Her fenced yard kept both her and the visiting dogs safe.

Other than that, Abby preferred to nap in the sun in her hammock or tall grass. She would sleep soundly for hours soaking up every ray of sunshine. She lived with other cats for many years and could be found sharing a hammock with Kashmir on occasion, but otherwise she was independent.

As she aged, and her arthritis progressed, it was time for her to live on her own. She preferred the much slower pace. Our donors helped us build a wonderful new bungalow for her and other solitary cats—each with their own room and access to their very own yard. Even though she was small and aging, she meant just as much to all of us as the young, rowdy big cats.

Staff and interns built her multi-layered hammocks and perches for easy climbing. She received her very own firehose hammock—her favorite place to be the last year of her life. And she received one on one attention from her caretakers and neighbor cat Maximillian, the savannah who lived next door.

Abby will be missed very much, but we do find peace that we were able to know her and provide individualized care when she needed it most. Abby, you can be as big and bold as you want to be now. Please play nice and have fun! We love you and will miss you very much.

SAVANNAHS

2016
SAVANNAH - ESTEBAN

Esteban is an energetic 10-month-old Savannah cat. He was surrendered by his family when they could not get his chronic bloody diarrhea under control. They'd purchased Esteban from a breeder who never informed them of the common health issues of the breed. After thousands of dollars of veterinary bills, tests, and treatments, they reached out to The Wildcat Sanctuary.

Esteban tested positive for Tritrichomonas and had symptoms of inflammatory bowel disease. Both of these conditions are common in many Bengal and Savannah cats surrendered to The Wildcat Sanctuary. The owner also consulted the original breeder who would not accept Esteban back due to his health issues.

Upon arrival, Esteban received an intake exam where further tests were performed. His diet was slowly changed, and he was put on supplements and an anti-inflammatory medication to calm his GI tract. Within a few short days, he was having solid stools. Treating the symptoms of IBD is a fine balance and, for the remainder of his life, he and his diet will need to be closely monitored.

Esteban loves people and is a huge cuddler. He is very playful and does happy somersaults to have his belly rubbed. He loves watching the birds out the windows and chasing bugs. We will slowly introduce him to other cats, because that is the one thing, he is not too fond of yet.

To meet him is to love him. Esteban is the sweetest 11-month old kitten you could ever meet. He's very confident, loves everyone he meets and could have a whole life ahead of him…hopefully.

What we knew about precious 11-month old Esteban was:

- *He had a grade 2 heart murmur*
- *He had tested positive for the parasite tri-trichomonas*
- *He had chronic, bloody diarrhea from inflammatory bowel disease*
- *He had been in a cat fight a day prior and was limping on his left leg*
- *He was purchased from a Bengal/Savannah breeder who would not take him back*

Within a few days, we were able to get his IBD under control and he had formed stools. We really thought we were on the road to recovery. Within the same week, Esteban began having an increased white blood cell count and fever and had to be hospitalized.

In just a few short days, we spent over $2,700 to diagnose and hopefully treat his illness:

- *He was hospitalized with an IV catheter including fluids and antibiotics to bring down the white blood cell count and high temperature*
- *We are trying to rule out feline infectious peritonitis—FIP, lymphoma and a possible bacterial infection*
- *Blood work showed high corona titers and globulins consistent with dry FIP*
- *An ophthalmologist performed an eye exam looking for changes consistent with FIP*
- *An additional serum test has been sent out with results still pending*
- *An ultrasound was performed on his abdomen and digestive tract showing inflamed lymph nodes, but no current signs of FIP. This one procedure was donated by the talented and compassionate Dr. Ralph Weichselbaum. Thank you!*
- *Radiographs revealed a bone chip/injury (most likely due to the cat fight he had the day before his arrival at TWS) which was causing the limping and could also be causing a serious bacterial bone infection*

The money and time we've spent is all worth it trying to give Esteban a healthy life and future. If you had the chance to meet Esteban, you'd agree there was no other choice. He is absolutely worth it. Esteban responds well to antibiotics for a short time, but then his fever returns.

We're continuing to try new antibiotics, as we wait for further test results, in hopes these will help. But rest assured, Esteban is comfortable. He's enjoying the personalized attention and love we're showering upon him. We have his best interest at heart. How could we not, he already has ours?

Unfortunately, it has been confirmed that Esteban has FIP, and it is terminal. We will keep him comfortable as long as we can and hope that his story and case can contribute to more information on FIP and a cure.

In Memory

Esteban now has his wings

I knew this day would come. I even prayed that when it was time, there would be a clear sign and it would go fast. We knew he was terminal, and we didn't want him to suffer. Even though all of that came true, it still doesn't make letting him go any easier.

He was full of life, even as his body was ailing. He was the sweetest kitten and always wanted to snuggle, cuddle, and show you he loved you back. He was playful and ran relays down the hallway and especially loved his walks on the deck outdoors.

His little voice was one-of-a-kind and he liked to tell you when he was happy, but also annoyed. He was good at having conversations and always answered back.

He was more subdued the last few days but there were no other major differences. We knew there was a possibility of the disease moving to his brain, especially after it had affected his eye. We increased treatment and monitored him closely.

On his last day, he had a great morning and kept to his routine. His meow greeted me at his door, he wanted treats right away, he trotted down the hallway onto the porch. It was like all other wonderful mornings with Esteban.

But late that morning, something was different. He was walking across the desk when his legs gave out. He lay where he landed and chose not to get up. He almost looked like he was falling asleep.

A few minutes later he was up eating and drinking water. On his walk back, he became wobbly, sat down, and began to star gaze and looked as if he was falling asleep again. He was having neurological symptoms, the next stage of the disease.

Our vet came to see him. We tried a few more treatments to make sure supportive care wouldn't help. It did a little, but Esteban was still not himself. He spent the afternoon comfortable, being showered with love, and playing on the deck in between his spells, but we knew it was time. The next stage would be seizures and he deserved to get his wings while he was still comfortable.

He can now reach the birds he loved to watch. Even though this is one of the saddest days I have experienced in a long time, I still feel unbelievably lucky. The few months I spent with Esteban were some of the most special I can remember. He only arrived a few months ago, but he was as loved as if he was one of the first.

Esteban, thank you for sharing what time you had and making the world so special. FIP may have given you your wings, but we hope your story raises awareness for this awful disease and one day we can give the happy news that there is a cure.

Fly high, my little boy, and please visit often.

2019
SAVANNAH - DIEGO

Diego is a male, F3 Savannah cat who came to The Wildcat Sanctuary in 2010. He was three years old at the time.

As is typical with these hybrid cats, Diego had already been through several homes in his short life. After being surrendered to a Savannah rescue group, a family had adopted him. But Diego only bonded with one individual and was extremely shy and scared of everyone else. This is also typical behavior with hybrid cats.

After two years of living peacefully with the other family house cats, he began urinating on the couch. His owners felt it would be best to place Diego in a sanctuary where he could be with other cats of his own kind.

Diego is definitely still a shy cat who prefers to watch his caretakers from afar. He lives in a bungalow in the Hybrid Haven section of our sanctuary with other small hybrid cats. He has an indoor bungalow with perches, towers, and comfy beds he can go to whenever he likes.

Or, he can enjoy his outdoor secure habitat where he can bask in the sun on perches, hammocks, and boulders. He can even play with water in a pool we provide for him, too. It's so nice seeing Diego live the life he deserved all along.

In Memory

Another beautiful little one joined his family on the other side. Little Savannah cat Diego had been losing weight. His blood work had our vets concerned about cancer. This week, our worst fears were confirmed, and we had to help Diego pass on.

Diego arrived at the Sanctuary several years ago after being turned into a Savannah Cat rescue group by his owner for not consistently using the litter box. The rescue group adopted him out and the 2nd owner tried to make life good for little Diego.

But little Diego was shy and wouldn't allow his new owner to pet or hold him. He communicated by soiling on the couch on several occasions. That's when the second owner reached out to us.

Diego was very shy and timid his first few years at the Sanctuary. We made sure he was merged with more mellow cats since changes to his environment increased his nervous behavior. Over time, his confidence grew both with humans and his cat friends.

He began coming up for treats and taking them out of our hands, greeting us at the door along with his other cat friends, and even rubbing past our legs allowing for light pets. Watching a cat like Diego learning to trust again is the biggest reward we receive for the work we do. Ensuring they have a happy life, on their own terms, is why we do what we do.

Even though we could never pick up, snuggle or kiss Diego, we loved him just as much as the other small cats. He made his way deeply into our hearts and is a cat I'm so very proud of. We gave him the tools to heal himself, and he embraced the opportunity. There's no better thank you we could receive from a rescued resident.

Diego, we love who you were and who you became. We will miss you greatly.

BENGALS

2007
BENGAL - TAMU

Tamu came to TWS with his buddy Milo the Jungle Cat. They could often be found curled up together. But Tamu would always wake up for mustard, Lawry's seasoned salt and pepperoni—the three things he just couldn't pass up.

Tamu was a kind spirit who lost his battle with cancer. The diagnosis was sudden and Tamu passed on shortly thereafter. We didn't have much time to say goodbye, but now he has eternity to be free.

2008
BENGAL - TOPAZ

Topaz's owner contacted us after he was showing signs of aggression to other animals in the house. Topaz was also marking his territory to show his frustration of having to share his space with a dog.

The owner was very committed to doing what was best for Topaz and consulted TWS on building an enclosure and other options. After several months, she felt Topaz would get more out of life with animals of his own kind and committed to helping support Topaz and TWS.

Financial support from owners is almost non-existent, and we truly value her support for Topaz and her appreciation for what we have been able to provide him.

This year, Topaz was diagnosed with severe kidney failure. His prognosis was bleak, and he was only expected to live a few weeks to a month. Topaz is still doing very well and acting normal and happy today. We will keep him with us and his Bengal friends as long as he is pain free.

In Memory

With a very sad heart I have to tell you that we helped Topaz our F1 Bengal pass. It was very difficult, but it was the right thing to do.

He was himself right up to the end and never gave up. His BUN was off the charts and the highest reading they could get was 186, but the report said it was over 186. This is 30 points higher than when he was initially diagnosed.

I am so blessed that we had this determined, spitfire of a boy in our lives as long as we did. I have never met a cat that knew what he wanted more than Topaz and he would do what it took to make his intentions clear. He will make me smile every time I think of him. I will miss him.

2008
BENGAL - MAUGY

We were contacted by a Bengal rescue group in Colorado. A large breeder was closing down and they needed to place the cats that were not adoptable. They had several hybrid Bengals that were unable to be socialized for adoption.

With the launch of our new hybrid rescue program, we were able to take in nine of their high generation Bengals. All of them were spayed and neutered and now live together in our new hybrid haven area.

The indoor area gives them the comforts of a home environment while their doggy door access gives them an outdoor habitat where they can climb trees and perches.

Wiggy and Maugy, female F1 Bengals, are two who came from the Colorado group. One of their parents was an Asian Leopard Cat and the other was a Bengal Domestic Cat. And at least a few of the other Bengals are direct offspring of Wiggy and Maugy.

In Memory

The hardest part of ensuring we give each cat a safe home is remembering it isn't forever. Every day the cats at the sanctuary touch our hearts in some way.

It is a wonderful gift when a rescue like Maugy shows her brilliant personality to the world. Maugy, a boisterous F1 Bengal lady, passed recently from kidney disease and complications from cancer. She had a voice and personality you couldn't ignore and she will be greatly missed.

2009
BENGAL - SAMANTHA

TWS was contacted by a Bengal rescue group in Colorado. A large breeder was closing down, and they needed to place the cats that were not adoptable. They had several hybrid F3 Bengals that were unable to be socialized for adoption.

With the launch of our new hybrid rescue program, we were able to take in nine of their high generation Bengals. All of them were spayed and neutered and now live together in our new hybrid house.

The indoor area gives them the comforts of a home environment while their doggy door access gives them an enclosure outdoors where they can climb trees and perches.

In Memory

TWS is saddened to announce that Samantha, the playful Bengal, has passed away from a liver condition. Samantha was a cat who always let staff know when the seasons were changing. She'd be the first to plump up for the winter and the first to get nice and trim for the summer.

This is how she got her nickname, "Summer Sam." In the winter she could be found in her warm bungalow curled up with another Bengal in a cozy bed.

But it seemed as though her favorite time was the long summer days when she could pounce in the tall grass, roll in some catnip on her perches and take her turn at the feather toy. She also loved it when she got a treat of mice for breakfast and, like any typical cat she had so much fun playing with her food.

2009
BENGAL - SHEENA

Sheena was saved by a wonderful no-kill domestic cat rescue in California. Being an F1 Bengal and unsocialized, they determined she was unadoptable and would remain at the shelter. We were contacted by a volunteer who thought Sheena may enjoy a larger area with other F1 Bengals. We agreed.

Sheena is still very shy of people but gets along well with her roommates. She lives with several other Bengals in a bungalow that gives them access to the outdoors and a heated building.

In Memory

We're sad to share the news that Sheena, an F1 Bengal, has passed. Sheena came to TWS after a shelter realized she was unadoptable given her F1 status and feral nature. Sheena was a very shy girl, but still enjoyed the occasional romp with a feather toy. She got along well with her bungalow mates—including Mystique, Peekaboo, Wiggy and the late Maugy.

Unfortunately, one of Sheena's favorite things to do was to eat. She was a plump girl and it was affecting her hips and health. The change in diet and subsequent weight loss caused fatty liver disease, something we were cautious of, but still unable to treat in time.

Sheena will be greatly missed by us all.

2009
BENGAL - HEINEKEN

Heineken is a domestic marbled Bengal. He was sent to a shelter after a horrible breeder was shut down.

Due to Heineken's timid nature and health problems, he wasn't adoptable to a regular home. He had chronic diarrhea that was not treated. It was so bad that Heineken prolapsed several times, where his colon would fall outside his body.

Thankfully, TWS has great veterinary support and through the work of our vet and staff, Heineken has been able to thrive with no relapse.

In Memory

Heineken, a handsome Bengal, has passed away. Heineken was a part of a bad breeding situation before he was brought to a rescue group in New Mexico.

He was a very shy guy, had a prolapsed colon and was heartworm positive. That's why he couldn't be adopted out. We were fortunate enough to take in Heineken and give him a home more suitable for his personality and health issues.

Although he was shy, he still loved to play with the feather toy and wait for us by his habitat door telling us to hurry up with the treats.

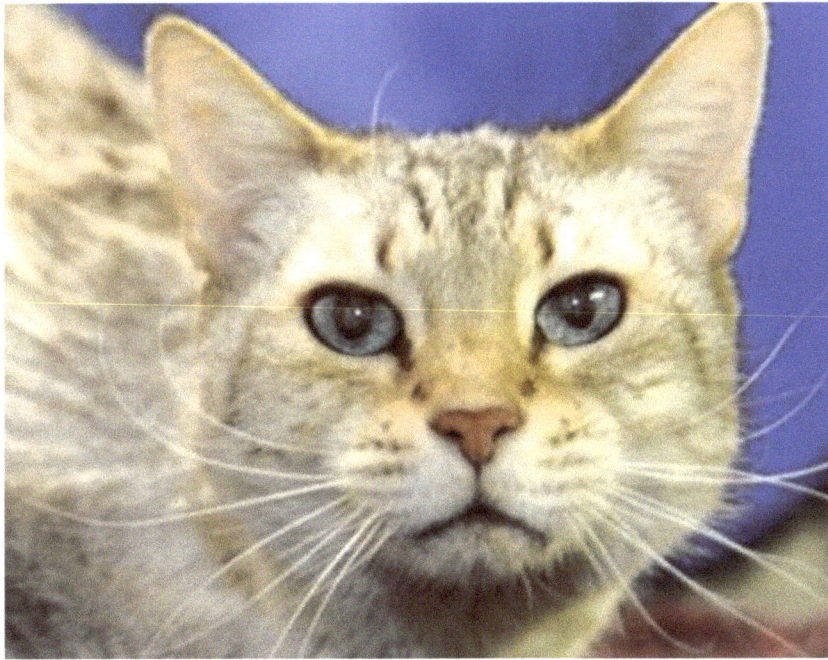

2009
BENGAL - JASMINE 2

Jazzie is a very special Bengal cat. She came into our program years ago but, given her extremely timid nature and dislike for other cats, we placed her with a special home.

Over the years, Jazzie began to urinate in the house. We agreed to take Jazzie back and provide her care for the remainder of her life.

Jazzie is 15 years old and has only one functioning kidney. Our vet also performed surgery on her to correct a defect in her bladder. We spend quite a bit of quiet time with her to help her feel more comfortable with her new surroundings.

In Memory

Sadly, we lost our beloved Jazzie this past week to cancer. She was such a special 16-year-old snow Bengal. She bonded with only a few people. But when this happened, she would be in your heart forever.

Jazzie was very timid around strangers and unfamiliar sounds. But once she knew you, she would show her boisterous side meowing for attention and love. As soon as you started petting her, she would drool in pure bliss. Becoming Jazzie's friend took time and the staff would watch "bird TV" with her and listen to music.

She made it very clear she didn't want the company of other small cats. So, she settled in as our on-site hospital cat. Even being very shy, she was never afraid of the hospital residents.

When a sick lynx or lioness was temporarily in the hospital, she welcomed their company and would go introduce herself. But as soon as a small domestic cat came in, she would voice her displeasure.

As she grew older, she knew exactly what she wanted and how to get it. Everything was on her terms and we catered to her, knowing her time was limited.

She wanted the fluffy comforters to crawl inside, she wanted every kind of cat treat we had, and she wanted to be the center of attention when the interns were trying to complete their projects. She would climb on their papers, vocalize her presence, and didn't seem to care that they were new humans she didn't know.

The timid cat we once knew was now queen of her castle and she wanted everyone to know it. We sure did…and loved her for it.

Seeing our residents grow emotionally is the most fulfilling gift. Watching them grow older is sweet sorrow. Jazzie led a long life. We just wish she had been born with the confidence she left with.

We love you, Jazzie—may there only be big cats with you now!

2010
BENGAL - JASMINE 1

Jasmine arrived at our sanctuary from a humane society. As with so many hybrids, they weren't able to adopt her out due to her poor litter box habits. It's such a shame that buyers only want the look of the wild when they pay thousands of dollars for hybrids. But, when the cats' wild tendencies come out, that's not something they'll tolerate.

So, there are few options for these cats caught between two worlds. Jasmine was one of the lucky ones, coming to live here at The Wildcat Sanctuary. She loved her caregivers and was one of the most beautiful Bengals we had ever seen. She is very social and loves humans and is friendly to other cats. When given a chance to live under the right circumstances, cats like Jasmine blossom.

In Memory

We're so sorry to share that Jasmine, our sweet Bengal, has passed. She'd come to us from a domestic animal shelter after her first two owners gave her up. She had some litter box issues and could not be adopted out. She was to be euthanized until we stepped in and opened our hearts to her. Jasmine was sweet, and very vocal. She gave many of our boisterous Bengals a run for their money.

It was a very shocking tragedy that took Jasmine's life. As a wild cat sanctuary, we know that every resident has a wild side, even our small hybrids. For an unknown reason, one of Jasmine's enclosure mates grabbed her by the throat in the middle of night. We only found one set of puncture wounds caused by one bite.

We believe that when a storm came in, Jasmine went to hide in one of the outdoor dens. She likely frightened the other cat and unfortunately, that cat responded with a fight defense. We will never know what truly happened that night, but we know it was devastating. We do not, however, hold a grudge for her attacker; it's just part of their nature.

We would never put one of our residents in harm's way knowingly; we never saw this coming and we are truly heartbroken that it happened to such a sweet girl. She got along great with all of her habitat mates. Jasmine will be missed by all.

2011
BENGAL - MYSTIQUE

Mystique, an F1 Bengal, was advertised 'free to good home' on Craig's List. A concerned citizen contacted us worried that Mystique would go to someone who couldn't properly care for a feral hybrid cat.

We contacted the poster of the ad and she agreed that TWS would be the best place for Mystique. Mystique had a rough beginning. She was underweight and already had severe ear damage when she was taken in by the woman caring for her.

Upon arrival at TWS, Mystique was diagnosed with mammary cancer. Surgery was performed to remove as much of the malignant tumors as possible. It has been a year since Mystique was diagnosed and she is currently pain free and doing very well. Lately, she has been coming out to greet the keepers in the mornings during habitat cleaning making sure they brought her chicken.

In Memory

After a long and courageous battle with mammary cancer and hypertension, it was finally time for us to say goodbye to Mystique, a beautiful F1 Bengal.

Mystique was diagnosed with mammary cancer well over three years ago. At that time, she was given six months to live. But Mystique had other plans. As the years went by, we were constantly surprised at how strong and resilient she was.

Many times, after bringing her to see the vets, we thought "this is it." But she just kept hanging in there and truly enjoyed life to the fullest. Mystique was a favorite among staff and volunteers. She had a sort of spunk to her, even through all of her health issues, that was truly inspiring. If you could sum her up it would be the old adage when life hands you lemons, make lemonade and she certainly made a lot of lemonade.

So, a toast to Mystique. Thank you for reminding me to not sweat the small stuff and live life like you mean it. Goodbye, dear friend, you will be missed.

2011
BENGAL - ZENA

Zena, a marbled Bengal, was surrendered for not accepting the owner's new cat. She has had several homes because Zena demands everything to be her way. If things get disrupted, she'll pluck her fur and even lash out at humans. Zena is a cat who becomes extremely bonded to her caregiver and does not want to share that person with spouses, children, or other animals.

She was born in 2001 and came to TWS in 2004. After three homes, TWS will be her final and forever home. Here, Zena has several caregivers so she can't get possessive over one. Today, Zena lives in a bungalow all on her own. She loves her humans but is happy not to be living with other cats.

Zena is a vocal little girl who likes to talk to her caregivers when they come into the bungalow. Her bungalow is equipped with a den, walkways, perches, a hammock, and even a scratching post.

In Memory

Zena was a very special Bengal who had a voice all of her own, literally. Her voice was the first to greet me in the morning on the way to the Sanctuary office and the last to say good night.

Zena Bean, as I called her, spoke for a reason. Some would say she was demanding, but actually she was quite patient with getting her message across.

She had been rehomed four times in five years for her boisterous behavior. When her voice wasn't heard, she would pluck her fur, bite and urinate to let her owners know how she felt. For years people heard her, but no one really listened.

Even here at her final home, she communicated daily. Especially when she was sharing a habitat with other cats. It took us some time to slow down and realize Zena wasn't just talking, she had something to say.

She was not a problem cat at all. She just needed her own space. A space away from other animals. A space where humans were her visitors. A space where she could feel confident.

When we finally heard her, we built Zena her own bungalow near all the action. She had her own perches, toys, and view of the Sanctuary. Her human caregivers visited her daily but gave her time on her own.

Zena who once bit, growled, yowled, sprayed, and plucked, now was a happy, perky, cuddly cat. Her screaming had turned into greetings.

Her fur grew in silky and beautiful. And she replaced biting with jumping up and crawling on our shoulders. All it took was for someone to listen.

Zena's eating habits had changed last week. Radiographs showed slight asthma and an enlarged spleen. She arrived back at the Sanctuary her happy self.

But a few short days later, she was breathing rapidly so we brought her into the hospital. Our vet was called and drove straight to the Sanctuary. By the time he arrived, Zena was back to normal.

Per his recommendation, an appointment was made with a specialist for two days later. The next morning, Zena's breathing increased again. We tended to her as the vet was en route to TWS. Zena passed away in my arms with all the staff present.

The radiologist confirmed that the radiographs were consistent with a malignant tumor on her spleen. Our hearts broke, not only for the loss of Zena, but also for Jazzie, Rascal, Mystique, Sydney, Sophie and Sierra who had also passed recently.

We have never been so overwhelmed by this amount of loss at once. Each had their own reason for leaving us, even if we don't understand why. We are so extremely saddened by their loss, but so blessed they came into our lives.

Zena, your voice transcends beyond The Wildcat Sanctuary. And you have taught us to listen with our hearts. Yet another devastating loss for TWS, but Zena's voice will always be heard.

2011
BENGAL - BETTE

Bette came to TWS from a Bengal rescue group in Colorado. A large breeder was closing down and they needed to place cats that were not adoptable. They had several hybrid F3 Bengals that were unable to be socialized for adoption. Beautiful Bette was one of those cats. She was born in 2002 and came to the sanctuary in 2006.

Bette is very interested in her caretakers but would rather watch them than be held. She's slowly becoming more socialized and loves being around the other Bengals. She has very unique almond-shaped, light green eyes that are captivating to look into. Bette lives in a bungalow with an indoor and outdoor enclosure area complete with perches, hammocks, logs, boulders, and an in-ground pool, not to mention several other Bengals who keep her company. She has a small genetic deformity that has given her a smaller nose and nasal passage.

In Memory

We have some sad news for everyone. Our sweet little Bengal cat Bette has passed. She was such a strong girl, right up until the end. She never let on that she was sick. We took her to the veterinarian's office last week since she was dehydrated and looked like she'd lost some weight. An X-ray showed a very large mass in her abdomen, and it was cancer.

It was such a shock because she had just been at the vet not long before, and everything looked good. We decided to help her pass and we're glad we caught it early enough that she wasn't in any pain. Bette was a very curious girl, always interested in what her caretakers were doing or what fun things they brought with them. She was caught between wanting to play and wanting to hide, never sure which she wanted to do.

The one thing she was sure about though was mice. For such a little girl, it was always funny when she would grumble at the others if they thought to even get near her mouse. We are so glad we got to know Bette and she will be greatly missed by us and her friends out in her bungalow.

2012
BENGAL - JADE

We were contacted by a Bengal cat rescue group in Colorado. A large breeder was closing down, and they needed to place the cats that were not adoptable. They had several Bengals that were unable to be socialized for adoption.

Jade was born in 2005 and came to the sanctuary in 2007. Jade is one of the shyest Bengals we've ever received. She was having seizures and getting picked on by the other Bengals. Several vet tests could not determine the reason for the seizures. But once we took her out of the stressful environment, they subsided. Jade now lives with more socialized Bengals. She is still very shy but will come around during feeding time to allow the caretakers to look at her.

In Memory

It's heartbreaking to share the news that we lost our sweet Bengal cat Jade to cancer this week. Jade had made huge strides in the past couple of years.

She arrived back in 2007, along with many other Bengals from a closure of a breeder in Colorado. She was frightened of people and not too social with other cats. She also had a few episodes of seizures and so we had to keep a close eye on her.

After about a year with no seizures, we decided to try her outside in a bungalow with a quiet group of Bengals. She soon came bounding out of her shell. Not only did she bond with the other cats, but she started to want some affection from people, always on her own terms mind you.

She had a very endearing way of showing affection by taking little nips on your arm or the other cats. Always at feeding time, she'd be waiting by the door, nipping at Issy or Max or Mark, then bound off toward her food bowl.

It warms my heart that she was able to find peace here and let others into her own heart as well. She passed too soon but I'm thankful for the years I spent getting to know her. She's now forever free to be herself. Jade, we will miss you.

2012
BENGAL - ISSY

Issy and Max, a pair of Bengal cat siblings born in 2002, were surrendered to a rescue group in Illinois. Though they were very outgoing and had terrific personalities, they were inconsistent in using the litter box. So, they'd been surrendered to the rescue group.

Like so many Bengals, they were deemed unsuitable for adoption. With few sanctuaries in the country taking these hybrid cats in, we were contacted to see if we could. We welcomed them to our Sanctuary in 2008.

Issy lives in a bungalow with her brother Max, and several other Bengals. They have full access to an indoor and outdoor area complete with perches, hammocks, an in-ground pool, and rocks to sun on.

Issy is a very talkative girl and loves to follow around the caretakers and loves getting her favorite food: tuna.

In Memory

It's so sad to share the news that our beautiful Bengal cat Issy has passed from soft tissue cancer.

This has been a very emotional month for all the staff and volunteers here. Issy's passing came so suddenly and is still a shock to us all. She gave only very small clues to her declining health and was still her spunky self, right up until the end.

As you probably know, Issy and her brother Max came to TWS from a shelter in Illinois. Like many Bengal cats, Issy and Max were deemed unsuitable for adoption due to litter box issues. Luckily for them, we don't care one bit if they can use a litter box. They found their forever home with us.

Issy was such a sweet girl, always following her caretakers around, wondering if they had her favorite snack tuna, of course. She loved to take long cat naps in the sun with her brother and their friend Mark, an F1 Bengal.

She was very curious, always coming to inspect any new enrichment and she very much liked to tell the keepers her opinion.

We feel for Max having lost his sister and their other friend Jade not too long ago. Please send Max your thoughts and love so he can get through this tough time.

It heartens us to know Jade was there to meet Issy when she passed and they can be together in their new life, free to be wild forever.

2012
BENGAL - RORI

TWS received a call from a rescue group asking if we could help a Bengal that was at animal control. Given the demeanor of the cat, they deemed her unadoptable and she was going to be put to sleep.

She came to the Sanctuary in 2007 where she found her forever home. Rori is a beautiful cat who has the appearance of a spotted Snow Bengal. She is the sweetest little girl and has a very distinct meow and loves talking to her caretakers.

She likes to nap, but then gets spurts of energy during which she'll play with anything in sight. Her favorite toys are pens that may be left out. She also likes to be petted and talked to. She loves being around the caretakers and will come out whenever one calls her. She does not enjoy the company of other cats, so she lives by herself.

In Memory

Back in 2007, we welcomed Rori the Bengal to the Sanctuary. Her tiny feet stepped out of her transport crate and into our hearts forever. She was a shy and independent little girl but loved the undivided attention of humans. Sadly, these little feet have walked on to the next journey Rori will take, her trail of freedom.

We shared many silly moments with her and would often refer to her as "Rori Borealis." She was nicknamed after a beautiful gathering of energy, Aurora Borealis or as many refer to it as "Dancing with the Spirit." A meaning that seems even more true to her to this day.

She was a healthy and curious little feline up until her last days when she was diagnosed with interstitial pneumonia. Which is why our souls were stunned when we were faced with the sudden decline of her health. The staff realized it was time to make the most heart wrenching decision those with animals can make. We decided for her well-being that it was time to help Rori pass.

While her time with us felt all too short, we are so grateful we were able to walk in each day to see those big blue-green eyes staring back at us, followed with such an innocent little mew.

From early on. Rori Borealis made it clear to us that she preferred her independence over living with the other Bengals. Needless to say, her soft-spoken charm managed to land her living quarters all to herself, in the caretakers' office and prep room.

When we first brought her in, we laid down several blankets and cat beds for her to get cozy. But being the "goofy girl" she was, she preferred that her bed consist of one large box, half full of paper towels and that it sit on one of the top shelves. We kept a couple beds out for all this time and she still preferred that box where she could look out from her little tower.

She liked to be in the hub of the human action and so for her this was a perfect fit. She even started to play practical jokes on us, like climbing in our key safe when we opened it or leaving little hairballs on the office chair. But her signature move was to mess with the pens near the logbook and desks.

She would often be resting on the logbooks when we came to sign off for our animal care duties for the day. She would play so innocent and look up at us with her soft little mew. We of course would give her some pets while signing away and then return to our work.

It was not long before we realized it wasn't just the pets she was after, but the pens that we pulled out of the cup. She loved to bat at them, while playfully twisting her head and shoulders around, knocking the pens to the floor and then sneaking up to pounce on them until they went missing.

The next person to come in would be confused as there would be no pen to write with and upon looking around, they would see Rori sound asleep in her box. Once we caught on to her little practical joke, we ended up tying the pens to the book for loss prevention.

Those little feet also loved to walk across the keyboards of our computers, creating new words and deleting important documents. But we just couldn't get mad at her as she would look up with her big eyes and that tiny mew would come out… and we would just melt.

We then welcomed her into our lap and she would spread out with her belly slightly up in the air. Upon petting her belly, she would wrap her little toes around your fingertips with all four feet and cling on while you wiggled them around. With each new day, we would be greeted in the morning by Rori Borealis, pick up as many pens as we could find and leave wondering where the pens that were not tied down would be the following day.

She may have been a small cat, with an even tinier voice, but she left such a big impact on all of those she met. She fit right in with our crew with her practical jokes. Her hushed playfulness had the ability to get us all laughing at the start of our day and this in turn had a waterfall effect for everyone, whether two or four-legged at the sanctuary.

We miss you so much Rori and wish you a safe journey sweet girl. During each Aurora Borealis we will be watching for your beautiful dance. You shall be the quiet movement that begins the amazing display of lights.

"It is (often) the quiet gesture which carries the most significance—the one which suddenly directs the symphony." ~ Mary Anne Radmacher

2012
BENGAL - ZAC

TWS received a call from an owner who needed to surrender Zac for urinating in the house. So many Bengals are surrendered for this reason, so Zac fits right in here at TWS.

He was born in 2002 and came to the sanctuary in 2007. Zac is a great addition to the hybrid family. He's a very social cat and likes to be around the caretakers when they are in the enclosure. He even likes to jump onto the shoulders of the caretakers when they're not looking. And he loves to get a little treat of chicken at the beginning of the day.

Zac went through radiation treatment due to his hyperthyroidism but is doing well since ending treatment. Zac lives in a bungalow with an indoor and outdoor area complete with perches, hammocks, trees, dens, and even an in-ground pool. The indoor area is equipped with heat for the harsh Minnesota winters and a fan for the warmest summer days. He lives with several other cats who keep him company and serve as excellent playmates.

In Memory

The Wildcat Sanctuary has unfortunately lost another one of our littlest residents this week. Zac, the Bengal hybrid, was in his late teens, but behaved like a youngster up to his last days. He came to the Sanctuary in 2007 because his owner surrendered him for urinating in the house. Luckily, we were able to give him a home for life.

We knew right away how special Zac was through his loud purrs and rubs. He immediately became best buds with Milo, a jungle cat, and the two were inseparable.

When Milo crossed over the Rainbow Bridge, Zac kept up his positive attitude and gentle demeanor. The great thing about Zac was that he would adapt to loss. Because of his ability to befriend every cat, the love he always had to bestow upon someone was always received.

Zac was quite special in that he just seemed to love everything in life. His habitat was his domain. We liked to call him the "Ambassador Cat" as he made every one of his roomies want to be his best friend. He loved them all and made them feel welcome.

He wouldn't mind if one grabbed at him when he sniffed their food, he would simply wander off in his merry way. He would even go to the shared wall to make friends with his neighbors.

He was thrilled with every enrichment, large or small, from a specially created enrichment box to play in, to the slightest sprinkle of catnip. And he would always share.

What made Zac really special to all of the humans who got to know him was how much he loved them as well. He would run to the front of the bungalow anytime someone walked by on their daily tasks and meow loudly at them. Everyone would stop and have a chit chat with Zac because he could brighten your day in any season.

When caregivers cleaned his bungalow, he would follow them around and rub and talk, as if he was sharing the Ambassador Report with you! He would always look you in the eyes intently, almost as if to ask, "How are you doing today?" and would be so happy that you took the time to share with him, too.

Zac was a very strong cat, and made it through some difficult health issues, yet always accepted the care he needed. This week, we made the difficult decision to help Zac cross the Rainbow Bridge when he succumbed to lymphoma of the intestinal tract.

He purred through to his last breath. We know Milo was there to greet him on the other side.

Sometimes the littlest paws leave the largest impression upon your heart. We will always love and miss you, Zac, but know you are making new friends wherever you go.

"The creatures that inhabit this earth–be they human beings or animals–are here to contribute, each in its own particular way, to the beauty and prosperity of the world." ~ Dalai Lama XIV

2015
BENGAL - MARK

A couple in Michigan called The Wildcat Sanctuary needing to place their F1 Bengal. Though they owned Mark for 9 years, they said they were rarely able to pet him. He was kept on a tether in the backyard.

The owners wanted to have a family and were concerned Mark was not the appropriate pet for small children. We were called and a place was made for Mark here at the sanctuary. Mark was born in 1995 and came to The Wildcat Sanctuary in 2004 to stay.

Mark is doing very well at the sanctuary. He loves to get chicken from the caretakers when they come to clean his habitat and will follow them around looking for more chicken.

Mark's large eyes are very distinctive. Late in 2012, we noticed Mark was not opening his left eye all the way and it was very runny. We monitored it very closely and it seemed to resolve itself.

A month later, the same eye was not opening all the way and it appeared there might be a scratch on that eye. Our veterinarian sutured Mark's third eyelid, the nictitating membrane, closed to help heal the scratch.

Once the stitches came out, it looked better, but the scratch then reappeared. We took Mark to an eye specialist, Dr. Connie Sillerud of The Companion Animal Eye Center, and she determined that the ulcer was very deep and would require surgery.

Though drops four times a day might have been an option, since Mark was unable to be handled, it would have caused him undue stress and, most likely, would not have healed properly.

The surgery involved using microscopic instruments for a pedicle graft in which the healthy cornea next to the ulcer is slid across to aid repair. The conjunctiva, or the pale pink tissue that covers the white of the eye, is slid across since the cornea is attached to it. Had we not treated the eye, a bacterial infection might have developed, resulting in Mark losing his eye.

We are happy to report that the surgery went very well, and Mark is back to his old self, enjoying life in Hybrid Haven with his bungalow buddies.

Though the cats may be small, their healthcare expenses can still be monumental, too.

In Memory

At 19, Mark was one of the oldest cats at the sanctuary, an almost unheard of age for an F1 Bengal (a cross between an Asian Leopard Cat and a Bengal Cat).

Saying goodbye was bittersweet. We were able to celebrate that he lived a long, good life surrounded by humans and cats that loved him. But it was still sad to see him go.

We hope all hybrids and wild cats get to live a life like Mark did, where their wild sides are appreciated vs. trying to make them a domestic cat.

Mark was born in 1995 and arrived at TWS in 2004 from a private owner. At that time, he did not want to warm up to his human caregivers, but that changed over the years.

In the morning, he and his friends Bullet and Max 2, would always be at the door of their outdoor bungalow greeting their caregivers. Eventually, he loved to rub on your pants and enjoyed cheek rubs. Mark enjoyed spending his time laying in the sun on his outdoor hammock, as well as rubbing different scents provided as enrichment.

Besides Mark's loving nature to other cats, he was also known for his big beautiful eyes. Everyone knew who Mark was. Everyone commented on his beauty and he knew it. He also had a curious nature and would be one of the first to explore anything new put in his outdoor habitat or indoor building.

Bullet and Max will miss cuddling with Mark, and we are grateful they still have each other. We will miss Mark's morning greetings. Mark may there be plenty of sunshine, hammocks and cats to cuddle over the Rainbow Bridge now that you're finally, forever free.

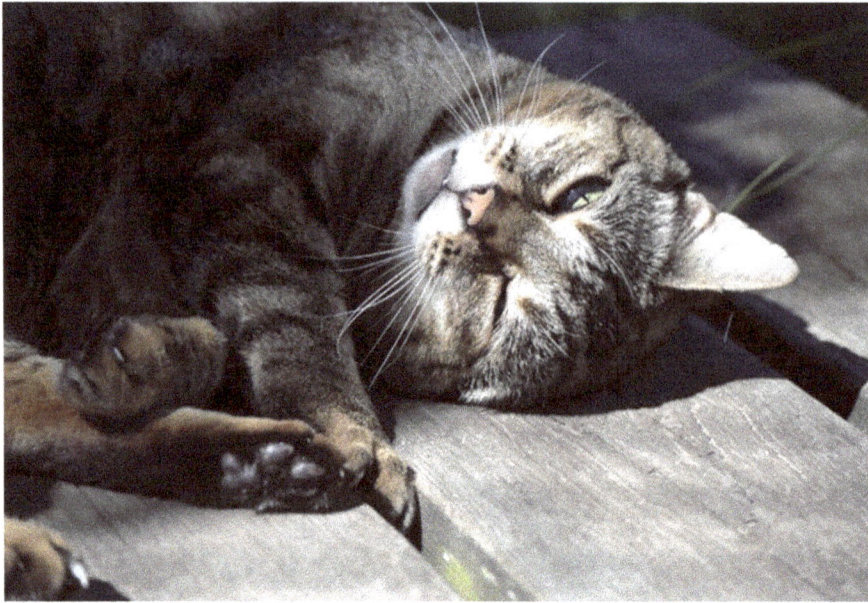

2015
BENGAL - SUMATRA

TWS was contacted by a Bengal rescue group in Colorado, where a large breeder was closing down and needed to place the cats that were not adoptable. They had several hybrid F3 Bengals that were unable to be socialized for adoption.

TWS was able to take nine of these cats and give them a forever home. Sumatra was born in 2003 and came here to TWS in 2006.

Sumatra is one of the more socialized Bengals of the group and will jump in her caretakers' laps to be petted. She is usually at the gate when the caretakers come into the enclosure and is always ready for affection.

She is very vocal and lets us know each time she wants to eat or get a treat. She lives in a bungalow with an indoor and outdoor area, along with several other cats to keep her company. The outdoor area is complete with perches, hammocks, boulders to perch on, and an in-ground pool.

In Memory

At the time, we had 106 residents, 47 were senior or geriatric with 27 of those being over 15 years old. The hardest part about rescuing so many cats is that they will one day leave us.

It never gets easier and it tends to come in waves. It can feel like too much to bear sometimes. But we know we must continue, we have so many animals that count on us.

Even with all the heartache, we know we are giving them a life of dignity and our job is to say goodbye while keeping that dignity intact. I feel so blessed to have the caretakers, managers, and veterinarians that we do. They are so empathetic towards each animal and there is always love and appreciation for every individual cat, even as we say goodbye.

Sumatra the Bengal cat had come from a cattery that was shut down and was the mother to several other cats we took in from the same rescue. She was not only a mother hen to her roommates, but also to her caretakers.

She would peck other cats in the head when they rushed into the food bowl too quickly. She loved to be held by caretakers and then would give love nips to them—often on the nose. She did this the day we helped her pass. She was a lady you just had to love.

Sumatra was diagnosed with cancer of the mouth that was in her soft tissue and moved to the jawbone. She continued to be loving right up until the moment we helped her pass.

During her last days, she was comfortable and cuddled up with her daughter Willow. She also received many loves and hugs from her caretakers. We were not ready to let her go, but we helped her go peacefully and before she was in too much pain.

Sumatra's little wobble and love kisses will never be forgotten, and we feel true joy every time we think of her and the love she brought to the sanctuary.

2015
BENGAL - MAX 2

Max and Issy were a pair of Bengal cat siblings who were surrendered to a rescue group in Illinois. Though they were very outgoing with terrific personalities, they were inconsistent in using the litter box. That's why they were given up to the rescue group. They were deemed unsuitable for adoption and came to live with us here at The Wildcat Sanctuary.

Max was born in 2002 and came to his forever home here at the sanctuary in 2008. We were glad we were able to accept both Max and his sister Issy into our Bengal program at that time.

They both greeted the caretakers each time their habitat was entered, and they would sit next to anyone, just waiting for attention. Max was always a little more vocal than Issy and would talk to the caretakers whenever they were cleaning his habitat.

Sadly, and unexpectedly, Issy passed away in 2012 from soft tissue cancer. Thankfully, Max has the comfort of living happily with other Bengal cats—Mark, Bullet, and Jewel. They all live together in a bungalow with indoor and outdoor areas, complete with perches, hammocks, an in-ground pool, and plenty of room to play. They also have an indoor area where they can escape from the harsh Minnesota winters and warm summer days.

In Memory

Sadly, I am writing to tell you that we helped Max cross over the rainbow bridge. We knew today was coming and we prepared for it the best we could, but it didn't stop the tears from flowing when it was time to say goodbye to our beloved Bengal, Max.

Max was diagnosed with squamous cell carcinoma of the jawbone (cancer) about six weeks ago. It was very difficult knowing his time was limited, but also a blessing because it gave us the opportunity to make every day special.

His last weeks were filled spending time in his bungalow with friends Bullet and Jewel. The weather was great, so he had dozens of sunny days to nap outside.

As we saw him declining, we knew we would make the decision to ensure he never had a bad day. The night before he passed on, we gave him a rug filled with piles of catnip. He rolled and rolled and rolled even more. He was covered from head to toe with the catnip he loved and had a wonderful time.

He spent his last day surrounded by animals and caretakers who loved him. He napped in the sun most of the day, happily lapping up two cans of tuna. It was the best way we could say goodbye, but it still wasn't easy.

Max had such a sweet demeanor and let Bullet be the bossy cat in the bungalow. He loved to be petted and doted upon, but not to be picked up. He was such a happy and calm boy and was able to leave that way, too.

He will be forever loved and forever missed. Losing a resident is the most difficult part of what we do. It's something that never gets easier, no matter how many times we go through it—even knowing we gave them the best years possible.

"There are souls in this world which have the gift of finding joy everywhere and of leaving it behind them when they go." ~ Frederick Faber

2015
BENGAL - BULLET

Bullet came to TWS from a Bengal rescue group in Colorado. A large breeder was closing down, and they needed to place the cats that were not adoptable. They had several hybrid F3 Bengals that were unable to be socialized for adoption. He was born in 2004 and came here to his forever home in 2006.

Bullet is a very shy cat who enjoys the company of his fellow Bengals more than the company of humans. Luckily, he has several other Bengals to play with in his bungalow that includes an indoor and outdoor area. These areas have perches, logs, boulders, trees, hammocks, and an in-ground pool. The cats seem to really enjoy all the different surfaces to sleep and perch up high on.

In Memory

We always say how hard it is to say goodbye. When the time comes, the goodbye words can struggle to come out, and saying them just doesn't seem like enough. Today, we had to say that heartfelt and painful goodbye to one of our TWS residents, Bullet, our silver Bengal.

Bullet always greeted caretakers and staff at his bungalow door, ready for his morning meal. Then he'd promptly lead the way to his appropriate feeding place on or below his favorite perch.

But this morning was different. When he came up, it was clear something was wrong. He didn't show his normal enthusiasm and was far more subdued than normal. A warning sign that we knew to act on right away.

Bullet's breathing was off, and his signature soft meow wasn't the same. We called the vet right away, arranging to have Bullet taken in to receive medical attention. Showing a bit of his normal spunky attitude, he hopped into his crate to go and even gave an indignant 'meow' about being asked to do so. It was easy to see he was declining fast though.

He arrived at the vet and the exam showed Bullet was in the advanced stages of cancer. A mass had grown and put pressure on his lungs, reducing his ability to breathe with fluid building up in his chest cavity. With heavy hearts, we made the decision to let Bullet go peacefully.

Always with a spunky attitude and the heart of a big cat, Bullet routinely greeted staff and caretakers at his bungalow door with a distinctive soft and repetitive meow that will be missed.

Over the past few years, Bullet had increasing health issues that he took on with a fighting spirit. He showed that, no matter how small you are, you can surmount any odds. In true Bullet fashion, he showed his spirit by choosing to let us know the time had finally come for goodbye.

Thinking back to when Bullet first arrived here at the Sanctuary, he didn't have trust for his caretakers and was standoffish. He made friends with his bungalow Bengal mates Max 2 and Jewel, before accepting our newer arrival Dante.

What made Bullet even more special was that, even with the treatments for his illnesses, he still came around to trust those that were patient and let him come to them for a few scratches and well-placed rubs. He knew we were here to help and only wanted to give him the best possible life.

So, it's with tear filled eyes that we let Bullet go, with his head held high, to meet his friend Max 2 once again over the rainbow bridge. Knowing they can have all the space and freedom they should always have had, with no walls to hinder them, is a comfort.

We strive every day to give our residents the best possible life, and when we have to help them cross over, we hope their next life is the one they always deserved. Bullet, you have a special place in our hearts and minds. We are thankful you came to TWS and truly lived wild at heart.

2015
BENGAL - GRACE

We were contacted by a Bengal rescue group in Colorado. A large breeder was closing down, and they needed to place the cats that were not adoptable. They had several hybrid F3 Bengals that were unable to be socialized for adoption. Grace was born in 2004 and came to the sanctuary in 2006 with her brother Max.

They now live in a bungalow together with several other Bengal cats, including Grace's love Tiger. Grace is very shy around people but can be seen following Tiger around the enclosure and even lying out together on perches on a sunny day. It's definitely true to say opposites attract when talking about these two because Tiger is one of the most outgoing cats we have.

They all live in a large bungalow that has both an indoor and outdoor area, perches, hammocks, logs, boulders, and an in-ground pool. The bungalow also has enough room to run around and just be normal cats.

In Memory

Our little Bengal cat Grace was just eleven years old when we had to say goodbye to her. She was too young when she left, but every day was a good day for Grace. For that, we are very thankful.

Grace was known for her love of Tiger, another Bengal cat in her bungalow. If you saw Tiger, Grace wasn't far behind. She was smitten. Her brother Max would also compete for her attention. But if she had a choice, her attention would be focused on handsome Tiger.

She and her brother Max arrived as very shy cats from a rescue group and always bonded with other cats over their caretakers. But they were active cats, running around their habitat, climbing their logs, and playing with their bungalow mates.

Grace was one of the most beautiful Bengals with a shimmery coat and golden eyes. Her demeanor mirrored her outside beauty.

She had been treated for chronic respiratory issues for over a year. She was picky about her meds, but her caretakers always found the right treat to make sure she ate them all. She was monitored weekly by our vet and was actually doing pretty well, compared to some bad spells she had had previously. So, we were stunned we would be saying goodbye so soon.

Grace went peacefully in her sleep, but we needed answers. Diagnostic tests were completed, and we found her lungs were compromised and the cause of her passing. A mass was also found on her liver.

Having the answers won't bring her back, but it will bring us some peace. Every time we say goodbye to a resident, they take a piece of our heart with them. Grace was no different. She was small in stature, but still filled our hearts.

Grace—Tiger, Max and the others will miss you. They will find comfort in each other. We will miss you, too! May you watch over your friends from your new, forever life.

2015
BENGAL - DANTE

Dante is an F1 Bengal who was privately owned and surrendered by his owner when life circumstances changed. Caring for him had become too much of a challenge for the family. It's sad that we hear this story over and over again. Luckily for Dante, we were able to accept him into our program.

When he arrived in 2014, it was estimated he was approximately 5 years old. He had a history of chewing cords and material, a problem that a lot of hybrids have.

When caring for cats like Dante, caretakers must assure there's nothing dangerous for him to ingest since it can lead to intestinal blockages. We've seen this happen with many of the wild cats people try to keep as pets in their home—something they, of course, are never meant to be.

Dante's one of the most vocal of the hybrid cats here and is always the first outside to greet his caretakers in the morning. He's always seeking attention, but physical interaction is not what he wants.

He's adapted well to life in the Hybrid Haven section of our sanctuary, enjoying the freedom to go inside his bungalow to enjoy climbing and napping opportunities there, or to explore his outdoor habitat that's safely roofed.

Though we tried introducing him to another Bengal named Kasha, it wasn't a good match. So, we'll try to introduce him to another friend in the springtime.

For now, Dante likes having neighbors on both sides that he can interact with and learn from. We're pleased that we're able to offer him the opportunity to live among others of his species, thanks to our wonderful sponsors and supporters.

In Memory

With so much energy, it's hard to believe he was so sick. What a strong, little guy who made huge paw prints on our hearts. Sometimes you have years, sometimes days, sometimes minutes to say goodbye. The worst part is many times you never know.

What happened this week was completely unexpected and we're still numb having lost Dante, our F1 Bengal. Though it's been an emotional time saying goodbye to several of our older residents lately, we seem to have been better prepared for those—if there is such a thing? But we weren't ready to lose our spunky little Dante.

He came to live with us in 2014 and immediately took such a special place in our hearts. It had taken a lot to arrange his rescue. He'd been given up, along with another wild hybrid, by a family whose life circumstances had changed.

Then, the person who took them in also found these two cats were too much to handle. She looked for alternatives and we agreed to take them both in.

We set about finding a suitable group for him to live with. After many introductions, he was very happy living with Bullet and Jewel. Dante settled in and was always zipping around his enclosure, eager to eat and a ball of energy.

But when his buddy Bullet passed away recently from chronic cancer, we noticed Dante wasn't acting normally. We thought it might be due to the loss of his friend, but we scheduled a veterinary exam to assure everything was okay with him.

Never would we have expected what we found. During his exam, a large mass was detected in his abdominal area. Emergency surgery was performed to remove what appeared to be a very aggressive lymphoma. Sadly, Dante passed away after a long surgical procedure to remove the mass and a section of his intestine.

Going in, we thought this would be a routine physical exam. How is it he's gone now? Like you, we can't help but question the fairness when we lose our loved ones, too. There's not a person here who isn't walking around choking back tears. He may have been a little one, but our love for him was huge.

We know we provided the best life Dante would have wished for. We know there's nothing that could've prevented the health issues that took him from us so suddenly. Yes, we know all of this in our heads.

But, in our hearts, we know only sorrow and grief right now. His future was so bright. We have many cats around us, thankful to be here and for the wonderful lives we've given them. We know Dante would want us to dry our tears and carry on. And to treat each and every day with them as the special gift it is.

That's Dante's legacy to all of us—and we'll continue to honor him this way, making every day count.

2016
BENGAL - PEEKABOO

We received calls from a few people reporting that someone needed to place their jaguar or leopard who was living in a basement. We've heard a lot of stories, but this was a first.

After further investigation, the cat in question was a Bengal, an Asian Leopard cat/Domestic cat mix, not a Leopard or Jaguar. He was born in 1997 and came to the sanctuary in 2003.

Peekaboo was extremely feral and very overweight. He has lost a lot of the weight, but he still loves a snack of turkey or chicken in the morning. He even comes to the door to meet the caretakers to be given chicken, which shows he has warmed up to them.

Peekaboo lives with several other Bengals in a bungalow with an indoor and outdoor area complete with trees, perches, hammocks, dens, and even an in-ground pool. And the bungalow has an indoor area to escape the harsh Minnesota winters and warmest summer days.

In Memory

At 19 years old, it was his time to say goodbye.

Peekaboo was very much the strong silent type. He lived here at the Sanctuary as a member of our family for the past 14 years. Saying goodbye is never easy, but knowing he had a long, good life surrounded by those who loved him does ease our sorrow.

I've told his story many times, but it's worth telling again. Years ago, I was out of state inspecting another Sanctuary when I received a call from a volunteer and employee of Petco. A customer had mentioned needing to find a home for his son's big cat that was living in the basement—a jaguar to be exact.

It may sound crazy, but not to us since we've removed bobcats, lynx and even tigers from homes in Minnesota. So, in the next few days, we went to the house with equipment in hand. They told us he was running free in the basement.

When we went into the basement, you could only see a few feet at a time. There were stacks of boxes, books, and tables. It was great for a cat, but very unsettling for us. Finally, we saw an object swiftly run by. We caught just a glimpse. But enough to realize this was no 150 pound jaguar, this was a 25 pound cat—a feral one at that! After several attempts through the piles of books, around tables and into the crawl space, Peekaboo was safely crated.

He was a very obese Bengal cat. So big that he couldn't groom himself and had a mat of fur that ran from his shoulder blades to his rear end—it looked like a separate animal.

We spoke with the owner, who began to show us paperwork of his Leopard Cat lineage all the way back to an accredited zoo on the east coast. Somewhere through the line of communication with the Petco staff, Leopard Cat and zoo got transformed into jaguar.

For us, it didn't matter. We were there to provide a cat in need of a home and that's exactly what our donors have helped us do for the last 14 years. Peekaboo remained feral throughout the years. He responded very well to our male volunteers but shied away from our female staff. He was very kind and gentle to the other cats at the Sanctuary and became good friends with former resident Zac, who also lived to a ripe old age.

During the last few years, his health began to decline, and he was diagnosed with hypertension and he lost his eyesight. As arthritis set in, he lived quietly, but happily. We knew his time was coming near and the caretakers and sponsors provided him with all the beds and treats he could desire.

As his health continued to decline, we had to make the decision that was best for him. And that was to let him go meet Zac and many former residents living over the Rainbow Bridge.

Peekaboo, you may have been the strong silent type, but today we voice our love for you. You will be remembered always!

2016
BENGAL - LUNA

Luna is a domestic Bengal cat. A nice couple had adopted Luna, but their existing cat was very aggressive towards her. Luna would hide and no longer wanted to come out.

Her owners knew this wasn't the way they had ever wanted her to live. They wanted to find a home for Luna where she didn't have to hide. They found The Wildcat Sanctuary and, luckily, we had the space to take Luna in.

Luna was born in 2000 and came here to the sanctuary in 2005. When she wants food, she is one of our most vocal cats, and that's why she's earned the nickname "Luna Tunes" from the Sanctuary staff.

She lives in a fantastic enclosure for Bengal cats. Luna has an indoor and outdoor area that has everything from trees, perches, caves, and dens to an in-ground pool. There is also a temperature-controlled, indoor building that provides shelter during the harsh Minnesota winters and the warmest summer days. She enjoys the company of several other cats in her enclosure, too.

Luna's days of hiding are far behind her. It's a wonderful feeling knowing you've made such a difference in the quality of life for a rescued wild cat.

In Memory

"Luna Tunes" was her nickname. As one of the most vocal Bengal cats, Luna's voice could be heard across Hybrid Haven. At 17, it was a little raspier than when she first arrived at the Sanctuary 11 years ago. It was her signature song and one we will now deeply miss.

Luna, like many of our Bengal cats, was loved by her original family but surrendered for territorial urination and also being picked on by their other cat. Specifically, Luna was urinating on the bed and her family while they slept. Over the years, they stayed in touch and even sponsored Luna, not something we often see.

Luna was sweet from the day she arrived until the day she left. She loved people and her caregivers loved her back. She was showered with kisses and hugs, not only from her human friends but also from her bungalow buddies Ty, a Chausie cat, and Ledger, a Savannah cat.

These big boys towered over Luna but loved and protected her. It was a drastic difference from earlier years. Since she'd been picked on at her former house, we tried having Luna live with blind Bengal cat Ciega. But Luna's big voice became a little annoying to Ciega, and she would chase Luna up on top of the refrigerator. She couldn't hurt her since Luna could get out of her way pretty easily.

Luna would call from the refrigerator even louder down to Ciega, which just made Ciega swat her tail back and forth harder. Given Luna's gentle nature, we thought she would do well with Spartacus who is handicapped from a birth defect. But he too got tired of Luna's vocal antics and would chase her.

That's when Luna met big boy Ty. Ty is an FI Chausie cat and four times her size. Ty fell in love with Luna instantly and followed her everywhere. He didn't seem to mind her loud demeanor and it didn't deter him from loving on her one bit—whether she wanted it or not.

Ledger, a very large F1 Savannah cat, also formed a quick crush on Luna. Soon, the three were inseparable and Luna was the center of their world. It remained that way until her departing day. Ty and Ledger are doing well and are staying close to each other since her passing.

Luna had more than a good life, she had a great life and was loved by so many. She is luckier than most hybrid cats who move from home to home and then to a shelter only to be put down for territorial urination. Luna continued to mark her humans, claim her territory and sing her demands. But that was Luna and we loved all of her.

Sing as loud as you want now, Luna Tunes, the heavens welcome your song. We will love you always!

2017
BENGAL - RAVEN

TWS was contacted by a Bengal rescue group in Colorado, where a large breeder was closing down and needed to place the cats that were considered not adoptable. They had several hybrid F3 Bengals that were unable to be socialized for adoption.

TWS was able to take in nine of the cats needing homes. Raven is an F2 Bengal who was born in 2006 and came to the sanctuary that same year. Raven has gorgeous blue eyes. He is very timid with humans and hid for a long time after his arrival. Now he comes out for treats or a feather toy as long as the caretaker sits down to play.

Raven had luxated patellas on both hind legs that made it a little hard for him to get around. Luckily, generous veterinarians donated this little guy a corrective knee surgery and he is now doing well. He lives with the other cats from Colorado in a bungalow with the comforts of indoor and outdoor areas.

2017
BENGAL - SAFARI

Safari is a domestic Bengal who was turned into a rescue group for not using the litter box consistently. Because of this, Safari was not put up for adoption and TWS was asked to take her in. She was born in 2005 and came to the sanctuary in 2008.

Safari is very loving, social, and vocal. She lives in a bungalow with an indoor and outdoor area equipped with perches, dens, hammocks, and logs.

In Memory

Saying goodbye to little Safari and her sparkling personality wasn't easy, especially since it happened so suddenly.

Safari began to lose weight and became dehydrated. Several vet visits and supportive care weren't having an effect. Just a short week later, Safari was diagnosed with abdominal cancer and a fast-growing mass. At 12 years old, it felt too early to say goodbye, but we knew it was the right decision.

Safari always had a pep in her step and was the first to greet caretakers at the gate. She was never quiet about her excitement to see her human friends. She would trot up to the door, then find the first log she could scratch and show off, while she waited for you to pet her. And if by chance you walked past her to say hi to another cat, she was sure to skip on over and butt right in for her pets.

Her sparkle in her coat matched her personality and for many years of her life she also had a chubby belly that matched her jolly spirit.

I can't remember a time when Safari wasn't a happy girl. She was also quite social to her feline roommates and took shy Savannah Diego under her wing. Under her friendship, he came out of his shell and now enjoys human contact. Her only vice was not using a litter box, which is why she came to the sanctuary in the first place.

When Safari started being quieter in her final days, we knew she was communicating in her own way. She still wanted to be loved on good days, she rallied and called out to her human friends, but her voice was different.

It was now time for her voice to join the angels. A voice we will miss every day. We love you Safari!

2018
BENGAL - CIEGA

Ciega is a marbled domestic Bengal cat. She was born in 2004 and arrived at the sanctuary in 2006. As far as phone calls go, the one I received years ago didn't seem all that strange at the time. Another rescue group had been contacted by a private owner. He was having trouble with his Bengal cat not using the litter box consistently.

We get these calls all the time since it's such a common complaint about hybrid cats. He wanted to surrender her. And one more thing. There seemed to be a problem with her eyesight, too.

I drove to pick up the cat, agreeing that we'd take her in. On the way, I called our vet to give a heads up that this cat might have some eye issues that would have to be addressed. What I found when I arrived was rather shocking. This cat didn't have poor eyesight. This cat appeared to have no eyes at all!

From the minute I brought Ciega back to The Wildcat Sanctuary, she showed what a force she'd be. When I opened her crate, she began mapping her new world, venturing out a set distance, and returning to her crate. Then, she'd go a bit farther and return. She did this over and over again, learning her way around so quickly.

It turns out Ciega was born with a birth defect known as microphthalmia. In this condition, one or both eyeballs are abnormally small. In some affected individuals like Ciega, the eyeball is so small it can't be seen. But, even in these cases, some remaining eye tissue is generally present.

Ciega had surgery to close the open sockets where her eyes should have been. This eased the discomfort she experienced from having weeping eye sockets and lessened the chance for bacterial infections. Being the trooper that she is, Ciega recovered well from her surgery.

Today in 2018, Ciega's 13 and continues to astound anyone who sees her. Watching her play, it's hard to remember that this cat has no eyes!

You'll find her on the highest perch in her bungalow, jumping up to nap on high platforms in her outside habitat, playing on top of caves, interacting with her other bungalow mates—just about anything a sighted cat would be doing.

Ciega may mean blind in Spanish, but don't tell her that. She won't know what you're talking about!

In Memory

We never thought we'd have to say goodbye to Ciega when just a short week ago, we were sedating her for a possible abscess. But our vets quickly discovered the lump was consistent with cancer and the biopsy confirmed this.

The mass had metastasized and spread to her lymph nodes and one lung, causing a respiratory issue. As the days passed, it was clear it was time to let Ciega go.

I want to be strong the way Ciega was. She was a girl that confronted life with confidence and had beaten all the odds, except this last one. But the reality is that I'm a sobbing mess right now. Anyone who knows Ciega knows why.

She was so special in every way. Though we never want to see any of our residents move on to their new wild and free life, when it's time, some you just have a harder time letting go.

I know you know the feeling. I know you've lost an animal you loved and adored, too. So, you understand the hours you replay every moment in your head, hoping and wishing the news and outcome were different. Wondering why this had to happen to her. If it could've been avoided and beating yourself up for not knowing sooner.

You pray the more you hug and kiss her, the longer she'll stay. The more you research, you hope you'll be the one to find the answer to save her. Because you can't imagine a day without seeing this beautiful girl who makes everyone smile. A girl who never complained, not even when cancer had taken over her body.

Ciega spent every day inspiring those around her. Though she was blind from birth, you'd never know it. She chased butterflies, climbed perches, and had a sixth sense. She never pitied herself or saw herself different from her bungalow friends. Well, maybe a little—she always acted as though she was better than other cats. But she sure loved her humans—all of them.

Ciega has been with me since she was a kitten and surrendered for not using a litter box. She is as close to me as my founding cats.

But I know she's just as close to those who've known her for only a few years, or only a few months. Ciega made sure she filled everyone's heart she met.

That's why her loss is not only devastating to me, but to all who know her. And on top of our other losses, it can feel like we're under a cloud we'll never get out of. I know I can move forward without her—I have to, and my head knows that. But my heart doesn't want to—my heart just wants her back with us.

When I feel this way, I need to turn my focus not on how many ways I will miss Ciega, but how many days she filled with joy and resilience. How would Ceiga approach today and the next?

She'd take every moment as it came, appreciate every pet and hug. And then, when she'd had enough, take the personal space she needed away from her bungalow mates.

She didn't pine for certain humans. She opened her heart to the next volunteer, intern and staff member.

She wouldn't want any of us to close our hearts or stay in a state of despair. Instead, she'd celebrate and feel joy about how much she was loved. She'd want us to share that love with other cats in need, just like her.

She inspired us all each day she was here, and she'll continue to do that for days and years in the future.

Ciega, the loss we feel now mirrors the love we had for you. We promise to ensure we share that love with others—the way you would want us to.

Being blind, you made us learn to see not with our eyes, but with our heart and soul. Thank you! We'll hold you in our hearts forever.

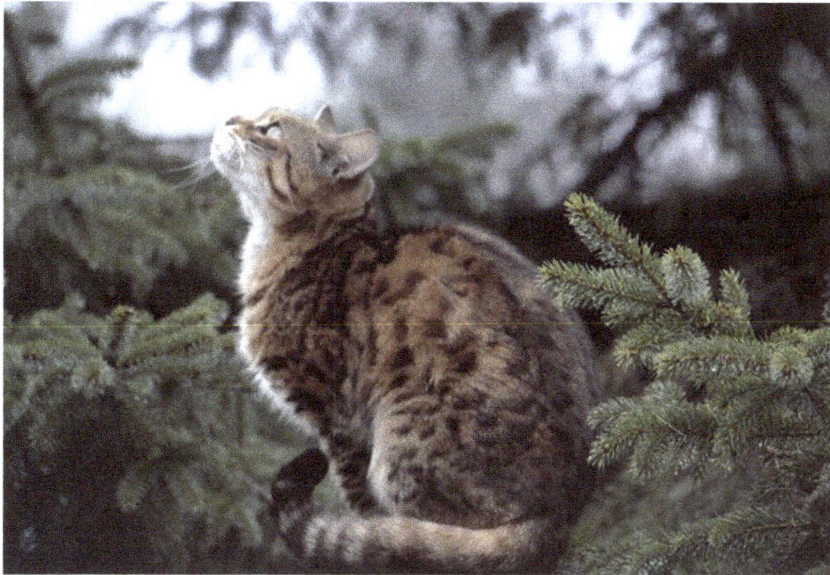

2018
BENGAL - WILLOW

We were contacted by a Bengal rescue group in Colorado, where a large breeder was closing down and needed to place the cats that were not adoptable. They had several hybrid F3 Bengals that were unable to be socialized for adoption. They called TWS and we accepted nine of the cats into our hybrid program. Willow was born in 2004 and came to stay at the sanctuary in 2006.

Willow is by far the smallest cat at the sanctuary. She is very shy but can be found lying out in the indoor bungalow area on the perches or even perching on top of the fan. She lives with several other cats that keep her company.

Willow lives in a bungalow with both an indoor and outdoor area complete with rocks, perches, hammocks, logs, and even an in-ground pool. The indoor area is temperature controlled for the harshest Minnesota winters and the warmest summer days.

In Memory

Small, but oh so mighty

We're so saddened that it was time to say goodbye to Bengal cat Willow. Her chronic health issues became too much for this little girl and it was time to leave her sick body behind.

Willow arrived in 2006 with 8 other Bengal cats from Colorado. A Bengal breeder was finally going out of business and our sanctuary agreed to take in all the unadoptable and unsocialized cats.

When Willow arrived, she weighed only 4.2 lbs. We thought she was a kitten, but her records showed she was 2 years old. She suffered from inflammatory bowel disease, common in Bengal cats, and soon after arrival needed emergency surgery for a prolapsed colon due to chronic diarrhea.

No wonder she was so small. She wasn't absorbing any of the nutrients she was eating. Over the years, it took a specialized diet, supplements, and close monitoring to keep her on the right track. At her largest, she was a little over 6 lbs. It was a never-ending balancing act with several setbacks, but many good years too.

This little girl had a strong voice and loved to call to the birds. She enjoyed playing in her pool and always joined her friends when treats were handed out. Climbing logs and the cave in her outdoor yard was a favorite pastime.

She loved to sleep on cat condos in her bungalow, and often would be found curled with her sister Tahiti—also a very small Bengal with chronic health issues.

For being such a small peanut, she made a huge impression on all of us. She will be deeply missed by her human and cat friends.

Willow, you now get to join your family on the other side. You were small only in stature. Your sweetness and personality filled the sanctuary.

2019
BENGAL - BRONX

Bronx is a first generation (F1) Bengal hybrid, meaning one of his parents was an Asian Leopard Cat and the other was a Bengal domestic cat. Bronx and his brother Phoenix were imported from Malaysia to New York. Bronx was born in 2001.

Within the first year, authorities seized the pair. The owner said he'd imported them to breed and make money selling small exotic cats. Little did he know, he'd been sent two male cats. The authorities contacted TWS to take in the two brothers in 2004.

Both cats are absolutely gorgeous but very unsocialized to humans. They live together with other hybrids and domestic Bengals and get along wonderfully. They choose not to want human contact but will accept our presence as long as we have a feather toy in hand.

In Memory

We had to let magnificent Bronx, our F1 Bengal, go this week. He was being treated for hyperthyroid disease, and we were concerned that he still wasn't gaining weight and was being picky with food.

We're so thankful our caretakers were alert and knew he wasn't acting like himself. That's often hard to tell since Bronx was an unsocialized cat, rarely allowing himself to interact with people.

His vet exam showed his thyroid was in normal range. But we also found a large mass surrounding his esophagus. We had no choice but to help him move on to his new forever wild, life.

Arriving at TWS almost 17 years ago, Bronx and his brother Phoenix had many years of being showered with treats, toys, heated and comfy areas to sleep and plenty of outdoor space to stretch their wild side. But life could've ended very differently for them.

They were imported from Malaysia to New York to be used for breeding Bengals—what a shock when the buyer found out they were both males! They were seized by authorities and were supposed to come to TWS at that time.

Instead, they knew a veterinarian in Arizona who wanted to try to socialize them and they were flown there. After several months, we were again contacted asking if we could still accommodate them. They weren't using a litter box and they wanted no human contact at all.

We of course said yes and welcomed them to their forever home. Because of their travels to New York and Arizona, we named them Phoenix and Bronx.

Both brothers remained very feral for several years. Bronx was the shy bombshell beauty with aqua eyes. He was often found following his brother's lead. Phoenix was the more outgoing of the two, but also very shy.

It was difficult to capture their beauty in photos because, when humans appeared, they'd run back into a cat condo or under a perch. But, as they got used to their human caregivers, they eventually would stay out on their platforms when breakfast arrived. Even sometimes taking treats from our hands.

Bronx was dependent on Phoenix. So, if one of the two brothers had to leave us this way, it happened in the right order. It would've been difficult for Bronx if it had been Phoenix passing first.

Bronx will be met by our pride on the other side and he'll have plenty of the support he needs. And Phoenix will accept other friends. But knowing their special bond, it was important for us to put Bronx back in with Phoenix after his passing. We wanted Phoenix to understand, in his own way, what happened.

But in my heart, I know Phoenix already knew. Animals are far more intuitive and open minded than we are. And the ones who are closer to their wild cousins tend to be even more sensitive.

It can be challenging spending 17 years with a cat that prefers the company of their own kind, especially the small ones. Our hearts want to hug, cuddle, and wrap ourselves around them. But that's us, not them.

Instead, we spent 17 years respecting the needs and desires of Bronx. Sometimes that had to be from afar. But that's what we do here. It's about them. It's always about them.

Bronx, you are loved by your brother Phoenix, and by so many more than you'll ever know. We respected your space and who you were. May you enjoy your wild side—it's who you are. We love you.

2019
BENGAL - SPARTACUS

This little boy arrived at TWS as a 12-week-old Bengal kitten with a walking disability. One of our supporters contacted us after seeing that the owner was looking for just the right forever home. We contacted the owner who had Spartacus' mother and both of us agreed that the sanctuary would be a good place for him to grow up.

He was born in 2008 and came to the sanctuary the same year to spend his life at his forever home. He is affectionately called Sparty by many of the caretakers.

Due to a genetic spine deformity on his vertebrae, his back legs do not work properly. He can prop himself up on both legs but cannot walk on them. He hops around the enclosure or he drags his back feet.

He gets around very well in his non-traditional way and is the boss in his bungalow. He likes for his caretakers to come in and hang out in the habitat with him, rubbing his head and talking to him.

In Memory

Sparty, our hearts are breaking. You lived 11 years, 10 years longer than any vet said you would. But to us, that's still too short of time. Spartacus' loss was sudden and unexpected. Knowing all his birth defects and medical challenges, you might wonder how it could be such a shock to us all?

But, if you knew Sparty and how resilient he was, you'd definitely understand. He was the strongest of cats in such a broken body. But that never stopped him.

Spartacus came to TWS as a kitten. A donor had seen him for sale for a discounted price due to his birth defects and incontinence and asked if we could help. I contacted the seller and she agreed to place Spartacus with us at no charge.

He was just like every other kitten—playful, full of life and friendly. But once we saw him move, we knew he was very different. He would drag his back legs and couldn't control his bladder.

Vet exams showed extreme and critical birth defects, including a deformed spine where vertebrae were on top of each other, compressing his spinal cord. The vertebrae were so frail that we were told, if he tried to climb or even fell once, he'd be paralyzed from the chest down and need to be put down. He also had deformities in his back legs and feet.

We confirmed he wasn't in pain, since the compression of the cord made him numb on his hind end. We took him home to give him the best life possible, no matter how much time he had left. And he was a project.

Trying to keep Sparty down and off furniture, cat condos, etc. seemed like the biggest feat ever. He was determined. Cleaning up after Sparty's leaking bladder and defecation was a labor of love.

Eventually, summer came, and we thought we'd try putting him in a bungalow. There, we could remove all climbing structures for his safety. He always had heated beds on the floor and friends to live with.

When donors met Sparty, you could see their face drop the first few seconds. He didn't move normally. He scooted instead of walked. But Sparty didn't pity himself. And he would scoot over with his bold voice and win that person over.

Then, he'd bounce himself up and trot away to play with a cat or grab a treat. Sparty was a much better runner than walker, even though he did it non-traditionally.

He lived with other special needs cats like blind Bengal Ciega, who left us last year. Both preferred to be called just special, because they were more resilient than any other cat at TWS.

Follow-up visits amazed the vets. Spartacus' spine had fused itself in a humplike position, which stabilized it. His tail was dying due to the compression, so we removed it for his comfort. He was incontinent and couldn't fully express his bladder on his own. We assisted by simply giving him a hug around his belly.

But over time, his organs were being compromised by the shape of his spine and size of his bladder. Medically, he was one-of-a-kind. And so was his personality.

Spartacus was always vocal and eagerly wanted treats. He had days where he wanted love, and other days his favorite pastime was to chase other cats to be just like them. He was always happy and amazed us. From climbing on rocks and hammocks—something we're told he could never and should never do—to being the biggest and one of the loudest loves around.

This past week, a caretaker noticed his abdomen was distended. The next day, he was seen by our vet. We were given the sad news that his bladder had torn, and toxins were filling his body.

He began passing on his own under anesthesia from being so compromised. We had no choice but to help him. It was such a shock to us all. Spartacus had received a lot of exams and always came out stronger. But I know he went the way he would've wanted to go—with his family around him, suddenly and boldly. He wouldn't want to have slowed down and been sick for days or weeks.

Sparty, you are free from your body now, and nothing can hold you back. You are an inspiration to us all. Eleven years with you was a privilege, my dear boy!

2019
BENGAL - TAHITI

TWS was contacted by a Bengal rescue group in Colorado, where a large breeder was closing down and needed to place the cats that were not adoptable. They had several hybrid F3 Bengals that were unable to be socialized for adoption.

Tahiti was born in 2004 and came to TWS in 2006 to spend life in her forever home.

Tahiti is called melanistic in reference to the dark pigmentation of her skin. Any black cat can be called melanistic and actually this genetic mutation can happen to any number of animals such as leopards and jaguars.

She is a very shy small cat but is intrigued by the enrichment the caretakers put out. She can be found watching the pool fill up with water or playing with a new paper bag in the habitat.

In Memory

So little, but oh so mighty

This week, we had to say goodbye to our tiny—but mighty—little black Bengal cat, Tahiti. After a lifetime of chronic health issues and a mass growing in her throat, she lost her courageous fight.

Weighing in at only 6 lbs. and having lost all of her teeth from dental disease, it would've been easy to underestimate her. Tahiti may have been small and sleek, but her larger than life meow is what really brought out her strong spirit. She loved chatting back and forth with her sister Willow, especially when they could see birds perched along the tree line.

Arriving with a dozen other Bengal Cats from a closed breeding cattery, she and her family found peace here at the Sanctuary. She was the last survivor of her original family, but she definitely found kinship with her bungalow mates Tiger and Max.

She also loved scents and often would rub on volunteers' and caretakers' shirts or hats they left on the ground for her to play with. She loved the grass and basking in the sun. But also liked to spend evenings curled up in a cat condo or blanket.

To her former breeder, she may not have been worth a lot of value. She was melanistic, giving her a black coat. But to us, she was worth her weight in gold—our tiny leopard and just as special and spirited as Shadow or Shazam.

Everyone grew so close to Miss Tahiti because, due to her chronic issues over the past 14 years, she needed ongoing vet exams, daily medication. With her congestion and lack of teeth, it could take a lot of patience to wait for her to finish an entire meal, while protecting it from her habitat mates. But to her caregivers, this was no burden. It was a privilege and a very special time spent with our special girl.

Tahiti, you get to join your family once again. As we shed our tears, I know they are happy to see you. We will see you one day again, too. Until then, stay strong—stay mighty. You are free now. We love you so much.

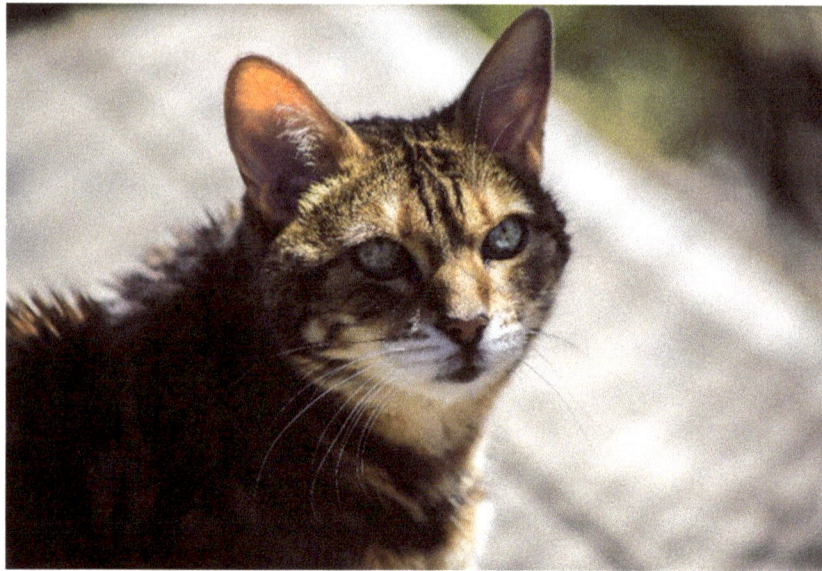

2020
BENGAL - GABBY

Gabby is a female Bengal cat who came to The Wildcat Sanctuary in 2018. She was ten years old at the time. We were in the middle of rescuing seven lions from Argentina when the call came in about little Gabby.

We've heard this story countless times before. Gabby had been returned twice to an out-of-state, domestic animal shelter after coming to them from another overcrowded shelter. She'd been bounced from place to place, home to home. And they wanted better for her.

Why was she returned so many times? Because Gabby is like so many Bengals. She doesn't use a litter box. People buy Bengals for their wild looks but can't tolerate their wild instincts. But to us, these cats are just as important as the big cats we rescue. They deserve a home for life, too.

We're one of the few sanctuaries in the country that will take in these cats stuck between two worlds. Breeders sell them as domestic cats. But so often, their wild behaviors lead them to being surrendered—just like Gabby.

But, as we knew she would, she blossomed when she was given the chance to live wild at heart with others of her own kind in the Hybrid Haven section of our sanctuary. Today, she shares a habitat with other hybrids and loves being able to spend her days outside or even snuggled up inside in her bungalow. We hate to think what might've happened had we not stepped up to provide another chance at life for Gabby.

In Memory

We had to say goodbye to our very vocal girl, 12-year-old Gabby. She was being treated for a very severe urinary tract infection and our vets found that it had caused irreversible damage to her kidneys and bladder wall. Her unexpected loss came just hours after saying goodbye to Nikita.

We didn't know if our hearts could take anymore. We find peace in knowing Gabby spent the last week inside the Animal Care Office getting so much love and attention from all her caretakers. We know that is how she would have requested her last days.

Gabby arrived in 2018 after being returned twice to an out-of-state, domestic animal shelter after coming to them from another overcrowded shelter. She'd been bounced from place to place, home to home because she urinated outside the litter box.

She came with her name which we found to be quite fitting giving she loved to talk, talk and talk. Because she had a big voice, in a small, sweet body, we knew just the perfect bungalow for her, with Ty our big Chausie. Ty had lost his love interest years earlier. Her name was Luna Tunes and she was just as vocal as Gabby and just as small. It was a match made in heaven.

We know both Luna and Gabby are looking over Ty. And we are so thankful that Gabby allowed us to look over her. She was a gentle girl that loved human affection. She preferred that one of her caretaker's sit with her during mealtime. That was the only time Gabby was quiet.

Volunteers working onsite remember Gabby fondly because she would greet them with her voice as soon as she could see them, even if they were 100 feet away. Gabby might have been small, but her voice and personality filled our hearts. Gabby, you will be missed. You are now at a place your voice will always be heard.

2020
BENGAL - TARA

Tara is a female, marbled Snow Bengal, who arrived at the sanctuary in 2007 when she was five years old. As with so many Bengal cats, she was surrendered by her owners because of her destructive behavior in the house and excessive vocalizations. People buy these cats because of their wildness yet refuse to tolerate their wild tendencies when they're in their home.

Tara has become a real love bug and loves to be petted by caretakers and staff. She'll roll over on her back for her caretakers to rub her belly. She definitely makes an impression with everyone she meets.

Over the years, Tara's lived with several different cats here at the sanctuary. She shares the Animal Care Office with caretakers as well as Bengal cat Cooper. They both make sure everyone's doing their jobs the way they like! She loves cuddling up for a cat nap on the huge plush tiger toy in the office. After all, she thinks she's in charge of the big cats, too.

In Memory

Tara just turned 20 years old a few days ago. Our hearts are saddened as we said goodbye to her due to congestive heart failure.

The best words to describe Tara are a "bundle of joy." She lived in the Animal Care office and was the biggest cuddler ever. Her perfectly round belly, soft silky fur, bright blue eyes, and adorable disposition will be deeply missed by all.

Tara arrived in 2007 after a dog was welcomed into her owner's house. Tara protested by slamming cupboards, refusing to have any door closed that prevented her from being queen of the castle. The owners reached out to our sanctuary to see if Tara would be happier here. We sure hope she was, because we know she made TWS a much happier place for us all!

She was a cat who would've been adoptable. But the moment she came to the sanctuary, we knew she was home. She tolerated all the different cats (and dogs) that passed through the office, though she made sure she was the steadfast cat who remained.

She greeted so many staff, interns, and volunteers over the years. She'd sleep through 25 people in her space for lunch or breaks, that's how comfortable she was. Tara was like a living soft plush squeaky toy. As you picked her up and hugged her, she'd make a Buddha belly exhale with her signature Siamese-like sound.

She loved to be curled up in a ball, whether it be on a bed, a cat condo, on your lap, or even inside your sweatshirt while you worked at the computer. She also had chronic eye issues due to the herpes virus she arrived with. But she was a patient little girl with all the treatment and cleanings she got.

Tara, we're so thankful you had a long, fulfilling life. But when you're loved like you were, we still wish for a few more days. May you find every soft spot for your daily naps now!

We will love you always.

2020
BENGAL - BURTON

Burton's beautiful boyish cheeks sure left an impression in our mind and hearts. His unexpected loss leaves our hearts heavy, but also full of love.

Diagnosed with aortic thrombosis, we knew it was sudden. But we also knew there wasn't anything else we could do but help him be pain-free in his new wild life.

This wasn't Burton's first time with a medical emergency. Found as an emaciated and dehydrated outdoor cat, animal control picked him up and rushed him to emergency for medical attention. Once stable, they reached out to rescues knowing he needed more medical care.

Arriving at our vet, we sure learned a lot about Burton and how tomboyish he truly was. Un-neutered, his signature cheeks took up most of his beautiful face. Ulcers on his eyes from cat fights left scarring and permanent squinting. Fractured and abscessed teeth made it hard for him to eat or drink. Parasites and ear mites made everything uncomfortable.

But, despite it all, he was a true charmer. He won over every single one of us, all of you, and eventually his bungalow mates, Dream and Keesa.

He was tough and gentle at the same time and a natural Casanova.

To see him nurtured back to health and living his best life was the greatest gift of all. We're just so saddened his sanctuary life was as short as it was. But we are so thankful he passed amongst those he loved, and who loved him.

There will never be another Burton, but then again—our Burton was enough to fill our hearts for a lifetime.

2020
BENGAL—ADRIAN

Adrian is a female F3 Bengal hybrid cat who came to the sanctuary in 2012. She was five years old at the time of her surrender. Like countless others, she was being surrendered by her owners due to the soiling and marking traits this breed is well known for.

Since she's a cross between a wild Asian leopard cat and a domestic cat, Adrian is caught between two worlds. Domestic cat shelters won't take her in because they consider her wild and unadoptable. Most wild cat sanctuaries won't take her in because they consider her domestic.

And even the Bengal Rescue group contacted recommended having her put to sleep. This is exactly why so many hybrid cats are euthanized. Once owners choose they can't keep the cat in the house anymore, it's too late and there aren't many options.

Adrian, who was nicknamed "AP," is one of the lucky ones. Even though we had no open space, we felt we owed her a home since she is a Minnesota cat.

From the moment she arrived, she's been very curious, vocal and fits right in. But, as much as she acts like she'd like living with other hybrids, she doesn't. That's why she has her own private suite in a bungalow we built especially for her and two other hybrids who also preferred their own space.

But, with this bungalow set up, they have the best of both worlds. They're in their own private habitat, but the shared walls allow them company of others.

In Memory

Adrian, our 13-year-old F3 Bengal (also known as AP), was diagnosed with cancer of the jaw just a short time ago. This aggressive cancer took over most of her lower jaw in such a short amount of time, making it uncomfortable for her to eat.

Saying goodbye to such a sweet little girl was so difficult for all of us, but the only thing we could do.

AP was the best combination of soft and strong. She arrived at the sanctuary after soiling in her owner's house. At the sanctuary, this was still AP's favorite way of communicating. Well, that along with the morning choir cries for her boneless chicken heard all the way from Hybrid Haven.

Adrian loved people and loved to cuddle. But she never wanted to share her humans with other cats. There were several attempts to merge her with others, even in our office, but AP wouldn't have it. She would curl up with the overnight staff, settle in and then mark all over the bed as soon as Cooper would try to join in.

As petite and sweet as she was to us, she made sure we heard her displeasure each time we tried to introduce her to others of her own kind. She'd chase after them and, even though she was a little girl, she could sometimes be a bruiser to other cats twice her size.

All of us loved her just as much as she loved people. So of course, we did what she asked. We built her a private suite with a very special yard and bungalow, just for her alone. The staff and interns would spend one-on-one time with her in her very own space—and that was when and where she was happiest.

We loved to hold her and talk with her. She had the softest coat ever, like chinchilla fur. And she had the most adorable pink toe pads set in dark fur. It was hard to resist wanting to kiss her forehead and feet each time you saw her.

Our hearts are filled with sadness today, but as soon as we remember our petite girl, we are overwhelmed with warmth in our hearts. She was loved and cherished by all who knew her and will be missed each and every day.

2020
BENGAL - KASHA

Kasha is a female F1 Bengal cat who came to live at The Wildcat Sanctuary in 2014. She was estimated to be about five years old at the time.

For those of us involved in rescue work, there's no resting on holidays and this particular July 4th was no exception. That's when Kasha arrived, after a small non-profit cat rescue contacted us.

The rescue group had been called about a cat that had shown up in a couple's barn. It took several months of feeding the cat before they were able to trap her. Once they did, they realized this wasn't an ordinary domestic cat.

Kasha was confirmed to be an F1 Bengal—a hybrid crossbred between an Asian Leopard Cat and a Domestic Cat. Kasha does not enjoy attention from humans and paced rapidly in front of her window all day in her foster room.

Learn more about hybrids and why we do NOT support breeding them.

The rescue group vetted and spayed Kasha and took their personal time to fly with her all the way to the Sanctuary. They spend their time saving feral cats and helping Kasha was extremely important to them. Like us, they do not believe hybrids make good pets.

Life at the Sanctuary

Though we tried merging Kasha with other hybrids living in the Hybrid Haven section of the sanctuary, she made it clear she preferred her own "private suite." When we rescue a cat, we are committed to doing whatever's needed to make them happy.

So Kasha has her own habitat featuring shared walls with other habitats. This way, she has company of her own kind—but on her own terms. We're happy we were able to provide her this chance for a wild at heart life.

How You Can Help

Caring for a wild cat for life—even a small hybrid like Kasha—can be quite expensive. Hybrids usually come to us with special needs, genetic and/or medical issues due to their breeding.

Our sponsorship program helps support the cats' care costs and allows you to form a special bond with them.

Thank you for caring about the little wild ones, too!

In Memory

What's worse than having to say goodbye to a furry family member, is saying goodbye to multiple loved ones in a short amount of time.

It hurts deeper when we have waves like this. And it happens every few years. Just as your heart is grieving from one, another leaves us.

Each cat is so special and individual and Kasha, the 11-year-old F1 Bengal, was no different.
Her loss was unexpected. This petite independent lady was eating her food, following her same routine, and wanting drive-by pets from her caretakers. It was the small nuance of her side being wet from grooming that initiated a wellness check. The morning it was scheduled, she had groomed down to her skin the night before.

We were devastated at what we found during her exam. Kasha had oral squamous cell carcinoma of the tongue. It had advanced to the point that we had no choice but to help her pass.

Even though Kasha was small, she left a huge imprint on our hearts. Being loose in Michigan for several months during the winter, a feral cat rescuer was finally able to trap her.

They realized she was not a domestic cat. They drove Kasha all the way to the sanctuary to live out her life.

During her time here, Kasha made it clear she was an independent female. At only 6 pounds, she ensured any territory was hers and wouldn't share it with another cat. So, she lived in her own bungalow with plenty of trees, platforms, fun enrichment, and her own heated building.

She was absolutely stunning, but her bold independence was just as apparent as her beauty.

She liked her caretakers, but on her own terms. Before feeding, she'd zoom by quickly for a quick pet, before she circled back several more times for more affection.

Losing the small cats can be extra difficult because so many come in with health issues due to the hybridization or behavioral issues.

We give them each extra attention. The hybrids seem to leave us earlier than any domestic cat or 100% wild cat. It's just one more reason hybrids should not be bred.

We will keep Kasha's story alive to help others. She will be in our hearts always.

CHAUSIE

2006
CHAUSIE - SASHA

Sasha arrived at TWS a little shy, but soon warmed up to her favorite two caregivers. Upon her intake exam, lesions and gingivitis were found in her mouth and we had to pull a few of her teeth.

As time passed, the lesions increasingly got worse. Sasha tried so hard to be well. She would play with her feather toy and lay on top of the cat condo. But as the bacteria grew in her mouth, it made the rest of her body sick.

In Memory

It became apparent that Sasha could not win the battle no matter how hard she tried. Sasha passed away and we are saddened by her loss, but so happy she is now pain free.

SAFARI CAT

2019
SAFARI CAT - ELLA

Ella is a Safari cat who came to The Wildcat Sanctuary in 2017. She was nine years-old at the time. We often receive calls for common hybrids such as Bengals, Savannahs, and Chausies. But this was our first hybrid surrender call for a Safari Cat.

What is a Safari Cat? It's a cross between a Geoffroy's cat and a domestic cat. The Geoffroy's cat is a small feline species from South America. Geoffroy's cats are the size of small domestic cats. The fur that makes the Geoffroy's coat so sought-after is marked by small black spots of equal size, spaced evenly over the body. These spots merge into striped markings around the neck, chest, and face.

As we've heard countless times before about other hybrids, Ella was soiling and destroying her owner's house. The owner didn't make the decision lightly but did choose to surrender her to our sanctuary in hopes she could live wild at heart.

Ella is a melanistic Safari, which means she has a black coat. The breeder bred a Bengal cat with a Geoffroy's cat, so her coat is more striped than the typical Safari Cat. Ella quickly settled in and loves living in the Hybrid Haven section of our sanctuary. We were so happy to be able to merge her with two other hybrids, so they could all have companionship of their own kind.

In Memory

Whether they've been in our lives two years or 20, it's always painful to say goodbye. We unexpectedly had to say goodbye to our little Safari cat, Ella.

The weather had been in the 90's and all the cats were pretty lazy. But when Ella was quiet, it was different. She usually always came up to greet her caretakers. We thought she may be a little dehydrated from the heat. So, we scheduled a vet exam just to be sure.

We were shocked and saddened to find a fast-growing cancerous mass in her abdomen. Our hearts broke. We called all the staff and interns in and made sure she was surrounded by all those who loved her as we helped her pass on. Our hearts hurt that Ella's life was cut short at 10 years old. But we were blessed to have her in our lives these last two wonderful years.

Ella had been surrendered for territory urination in the house. Not only did she ruin the carpets, but she also ruined the bed—using it as her litter box. Her owner tried many things to curb the behavior and was devastated when he made the choice to surrender her.

At the sanctuary, she had indoor and outdoor areas and never had any more soiling problems. She was so social and loved to be petted by anyone who had a free moment to do so.

Even though she was a black cat, her charcoal two-toned coat was just as spectacular as her spotted hybrid friends. Her big gold eyes always carried so much cheer, and you couldn't pass her by when she gave you that look. Treats and pets were soon to follow.

She had a very cute meow and raised her voice to call for attention. She liked the outdoors just as much as the inside, and always climbed her perches, then dropped and rolled asking for pets.

We will miss you so much Ella. Our hearts are filled with sadness now at your sudden loss, but we can't help but smile when we remember all the joy you brought to us and the Sanctuary.

Enjoy your newfound freedom and visit us often.

GEOFFROY'S CAT

2006
GEOFFROY'S CAT - RINGO

Ringo, a Geoffroy's cat, was surrendered to the Humane Society with three other exotic hybrids. The owner stated that the cats were soiling his house and wanted them euthanized.

After putting one cat down, the Humane Society realized that these cats were not domestic and contacted TWS. We were so sad to hear one cat had already lost his life, but we were happy we could save the other three.

Ringo was truly one of a kind. He bonded to only a few caregivers and his love for them was all consuming. He would bring his feather toy to them over and over and would throw a tantrum if he was not given attention.

But many did not know Ringo. He made it quite clear that he had no time for any other humans than the few he loved. He was the same with other cats.

In Memory

If there was ever a tiger in a small cat's body—that was Ringo. He was 6 pounds of spitfire with all the confidence in the world.

Being purchased from a breeder as a pet, it soon didn't work out and he and three other hybrids were surrendered for euthanasia at a shelter.

When I received the call, I found little Ringo hanging upside down on his wire kennel. This is something Geoffrey cats are awesome at since they're South American tree cats who love to climb and run.

At the sanctuary, he imprinted on me quickly but would spit, hiss and stomp at every other caretaker. He knew how to make me feel special, even if it was at the expense of the other humans.

Vet care for Ringo was just as difficult. He was small in stature, so every vet thought they could handle him. But Ringo proved them wrong—evading everyone that tried until they would sedate him like the big cat he thought he was.

At the sanctuary, he liked to hide his treasures—from cat toys, to food bowls and material. He would sneak, steal and stash it where it was hard to find.

Being so smart, elusive and mysterious, he won my heart. But it also made it hard to tell when he was sick. So when Ringo slowed down, I knew something was very wrong.

The vet exam showed an increased white blood count, so high that it was amazing he was still with us. After oral and IV antibiotics, Ringo stopped eating. He began to lose weight and decline. More vet exams, but a clear diagnosis could not be found. During one exam Ringo didn't wake up. I was devastated that he was gone and gone without an answer.

But I know Ringo never wanted to live halfway nor compromised. He wanted to live full throttle and that's why it was time for him to move on to his new wild life.

Some are harder to comprehend that they are gone more than others—especially those full of life. Ringo continues to hold a piece of my heart and always will.

2011
GEOFFROY'S CAT - RASCAL

The British Columbia SPCA Animal Protection Office contacted TWS regarding a Geoffroy's Cat in need of placement. The Vancouver Police Department seized a capsizing boat with cats aboard. The cats included three Bengal hybrids and a male Geoffroy's Cat.

The Bengals were socialized and able to be adopted. But the Geoffroy's Cat needed to be placed into a sanctuary and TWS was happy to accept Rascal into our program. Rascal is a feisty little guy and will do pretty much anything to get chicken. He loves the carpeted scratch post with perches that was donated and can often be found happily sleeping in the circular compartment.

In Memory

We have very suddenly lost our little Geoffroy's cat, Rascal. Aptly named, Rascal touched each of our hearts with his wild personality and crazy antics during feeding time. In the sea of boisterous Bengal cats, Rascal stood out not with his voice but with his curious nature and the ability to make everyone who saw him absolutely melt.

For such a little guy, he had the appetite of a lion and would make it known that it was time to eat.

We have had many ups and downs with Rascal over the last three years with his health. When he first arrived, he was diagnosed with heartworm and had to be given a steroid to help his breathing.

Earlier this week, Rascal refused to eat and was vomiting and given his usual voracious hunger we knew something was wrong. After tests at the vet showed kidney failure, it was decided to help Rascal pass with as much peace and dignity as we could provide him.

Given his previous diagnosis of heartworm, kidney failure came as a shock. It all happened so fast and still doesn't feel real. Cleaning his enclosure tomorrow will surely not be the same.

Rascal, thank you for sharing these past few years with us, you will be missed every day. Wherever you are now, may your plate always be full, and your curiosity be satisfied.

DOMESTIC CAT

2017
DOMESTIC CAT - HOMER

Homer, a long haired domestic cat, was a stray at our first property and we couldn't bear to leave him behind. He was born in 1998 and showed up a year later to stay with TWS. His life now is drastically different, and this little guy loves every minute of it.

Homer lives in the office and is definitely the boss of the office cats and demands attention from the interns and the staff. He likes to peruse the table during any mealtime and with luck may even sneak a snack if someone looks away.

He likes to spend his days sleeping with occasional bouts of play wrestling with friends. Being an older cat, Homer has arthritis. He receives several rounds of laser therapy a month which keeps him active and pain-free.

In Memory

I was wondering how I put over 18 years onto one page. I guess I'll just let my mind turn the pages of each year Homer was part of our lives and share with you the moments that made him Homer.

Homer's first days

In 1999, I'd just purchased a house, five acres, erected the first habitats and was beginning the sanctuary. I always knew I wouldn't have to search for animals in need, they'd find us.

But I was surprised that one of the first arrivals was a gray and white, long hair domestic cat that appeared in the yard just days after we moved in. We named him Homer, since he came with our home.

It was obvious Homer was an outdoor cat. He was an avid hunter and gatherer. We often found him up in a tree and, just a few days out of the week, at the front door with a prize for us. He never wanted to come in, but insisted we bring him food and a bed on the front porch.

The five acres was located at a dead end. And the road coming in was known as the "bad side of town." That's probably why I could afford it. It was intimidating on the nights I was alone.

One night, the alarm went off, but I couldn't figure out what triggered it. Alone, I was scared and locked all the doors. And of course, that was at the exact same time Homer appeared at the front door demanding a meal. You never said no to Homer. So, I opened the door as quickly as possible and pulled him inside, locking the door again.

From that moment forward, Homer was an indoor cat. And it was my turn to demand something from him—the job of being my security blanket and sleeping with me that night to ease my fear.

Moving to Minnesota

A few years later, I made the decision to move myself and the sanctuary's 10 wild cats to Minnesota to be near my family. I rented a cargo airplane named the Kitty Hawk to move the cats.

Massive transport crates housing lynx, cougars and servals lined the airplane. And in the middle, was a tiny crate for Homer. True to form, he was brave and didn't mind sharing space with his intimidating neighbors for the trip.

Over the years, Homer was a daily part of the sanctuary. He saw new cats come and beloved cats pass. He lived in bungalows with Bengals when he wanted to be outdoors. He lived in the overnight quarters inside, cuddling up to staff.

Homer was popular with the volunteers, too. I think he had more fans than any big cat here at the Sanctuary! Homer was a friend to all.

Life with Homer

The only way to describe Homer is that he was Homer. He was easy going, went with the flow, but was never a push over. He got exactly what he wanted and was a pretty good manipulator making us believe it was our idea.

He could even turn his biggest critics, like ShyBear the Bengal, into a fan. It took over six months, but ShyBear finally realized she loved Homer.

I don't know how old Homer was, the first time he chose us, but he wasn't a kitten. He had thick, angora fur and, over the years, he became as plump and fluffy as Remoh.

Later in his life, Homer's coat thinned, he lost weight and marched in small steps due to his arthritis. But as soon as you looked in his eyes, it was still Homer. He had no idea his body had aged, and he still demanded the same respect. He'd walk across the keyboard, sit and put his paws on your hand, preventing you from further work. This meant it was mealtime.

And when it was time for the staff to eat lunch, Homer made sure he was always in the center of the table. If he didn't get a treat, he'd swipe as you brought your sandwich to your mouth—and would always come out the winner. If that didn't work, he'd pull your plate towards him. He was always very determined.

Homer's last days

So, near the end, when he was picky with food, we knew his body was failing. He was given so many kinds of food and treats. Whatever his heart desired. That worked for a while, but then he lost his appetite, even for that.

On his last day, he was surrounded by staff and longtime volunteers and true to Homer, he rallied. He got up and did his power walk around the office. He ate every treat handed to him. He relished the hugs and kisses. But we knew he wouldn't be able to rally again.

And after over 18 years of hard work at the sanctuary welcoming new residents, assisting office staff, being a confidant to staff and volunteers, it was time to let Homer be free and able to rest. He'd done such a good job being there for all of us. Now, it was time to be there for him and set him free.

Homer, you weren't just my cat, you were everyone's cat. You had the amazing gift and determination to be a friend to all. You did it without ever losing sight of yourself.

Thank you, my friend, for being you. You will be deeply missed.

DOGS

2011
DOGS - SOPHIE & SIERRA

Sierra and her sister Sophie, the husky girls, came from a large puppy mill rescue effort in Iowa. The girls were born in 1998 and came to the sanctuary in 2000. They are still shy with most humans but love all their toys and treats. They also love to have the keepers' dogs visit them and play with them for the day.

Barb, a volunteer, spends a lot of one-on-one time with the huskies to help socialize them to people. Sierra has also developed arthritis in two legs.

They live in their own area with lots of room to play and run, complete with an indoor area with heating and air conditioning. The outdoor area has trees, perches, logs, dens, a lean-to, and even an in-ground pool to play in.

In Memory

It's been just over a decade since we rescued the two huskies, Sophie and Sierra. Coming from a puppy mill, they had an understandable distrust of humans. This adversity brought them closer together and they were to embark on their new journey at TWS as an unbreakable team.

While Sierra was strong, she was very dependent on Sophie. Sophie was silently the braver of the two, always approaching new circumstances first. She led the way to ensure it was safe and trusting her every move, Sierra would be sure to follow.

In the late winter, we knew Sierra's time was quickly approaching as she began showing signs of her age. As mid-summer approached her arthritis worsened and her pain medications were increased for her well-being. What we were not ready for was Sophie's abrupt change in health.

She seemed younger and, more full of life than ever, until a couple days before her passing. Getting up from her morning rest was difficult and walking seemed uncomfortable. Her physical symptoms worsened rapidly, and pain medications were ineffective.

Staff and veterinarians knew her quality of life was compromised and recognized it was her time. Her unfortunate turn in health was symbolic of their relationship. Sophie was to lead the way, ensuring the next adventure after this life was safe for Sierra to follow.

The heartbreaking moment of helping these beautiful girls pass was bittersweet. We always dreaded the thought of one leaving before the other. However, we are happy they were able to pass together, side by side, the way they would have wanted to go.

Sophie and Sierra may have been of old age upon their passing, but thankfully they experienced some positive changes late in life. They were introduced to some new canine friends and met an amazing volunteer, Barb.

They quickly bonded with the keeper's dogs, hanging out with them on a daily basis. They enjoyed their moments of playing with toys, howling as a pack, and snuggling in their air-conditioned building on hot summer days. Their new four-legged friends brought out a youthful side of them.

Barb's amazing patience and dedication built their trust in humans to an unbelievable height. We're very grateful for these new additions into the girls' lives, as it allowed Sophie and Sierra to finally be the confident dogs they were meant to be.

We may be a feline rescue organization, but these furry little gals each have a huge paw print in all of our hearts. How we will miss sliding open the entrance gate each morning as we come to work, and seeing them run up to greet us with their husky howls.

We love you Sophie and Sierra and you will forever be missed and cherished.

Volunteer Barb's tribute to the girls

It was nearly three years ago when I asked The Wildcat Sanctuary staff if I could work with Sophie and Sierra. The goal seemed easy enough—get them comfortable with people so they would go on leash or crate for vet visits with less fear.

I remember the staff telling me to give it a year. After all, these girls had no reason to trust anyone. In short, they came from a puppy mill in Iowa. They spent their time in a small trailer without windows, hungry and flea infested. She was right. Trust can take a very long time to return, if it does at all.

During the first nine months, it was Sierra who was most curious about me and she would approach slowly and nuzzle or even lick me as long as I was perfectly quiet and still. Sophie followed her lead.

I was always greeted at the door with the husky howl before they quickly moved to a safe distance. With patience, persistence and help from the staff, interns and other volunteers, by August of 2009, Sophie started asking to go for walks outside the compound. She walked next to the fence to start so Sierra could be with her.

Her favorite path was to see the lions and Donoma when he lived near the trailer. She even visited the trailer and had a fascination with Remoh, the domestic cat, who did not mind her sniffing and nosing him. She began to enjoy petting and playing with the staff dogs.

Her favorite game with me was playing fetch even though the other dogs got to the ball first. In time, she was known to jump up and place her front paws on an intern's shoulder, follow the staff dogs into the double door so she could go with them and occasionally ask staff and interns for a walk.

Sierra was more cautious than Sophie. It took a year for Sierra to make eye contact. She walked inside the enclosure with me and Sophie. She allowed an occasional pet and was so brave as to walk into the double doors when invited. On a warm summer night or a cool winter evening, they often just lay next to each other and enjoyed the quiet.

That simple act was a difficult decision for Sierra. Often, we walked in the compound together for exercise, Sophie and Sierra nudging my hands and knees gently with their noses.

Through our time together, Sophie and Sierra taught me the true meaning of patience, respect, and the ability to trust in spite of past disappointments and hardships. I found them to be smart and very much in love with play time, especially with the other dogs.

I will miss their gate greeting, the insistent attention seeking nose bops and their gentle spirits. Thank you for the gift of time with these two very special girls. Thank you to the other volunteers/DACs for enriching Sophie and Sierra's life. They will be missed but not forgotten.

Barb Rein—TWS Volunteer

2019
DOG—COOKIE

The phone rang while I was in a staff meeting today. A good samaritan was trying to catch a stray dog that was in really bad shape. Would we be able to help?

Yes, even though we're a sanctuary for wild cats, I can't tell you the number of phone calls I get about all sorts of animals in need. Of course, we'll do everything we can to help any animal suffering.

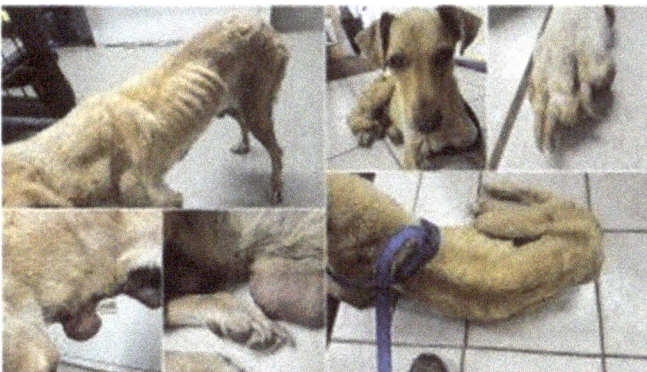

That's how this sweet little girl ended up at our gate. Though she should weigh 70 lbs., she's so emaciated she weighs only 38 lbs. She has mammary tumors, as you can see in the photos. She's partially blind with cataracts.

As hard as the photos are to look at, you can imagine how heartbreaking it is to see a stray like her in person. And yet, she's so sweet and trusting, despite how she must've suffered.

The plan for helping her

I had one of our caretakers rush her over to our local vet to be examined. She's approximately 9 years old and is heartworm negative, but positive for Lyme disease. The vet X-rayed her tumors and I'm thankful they haven't metastasized. Once we can get some weight on her to improve her health, they can be surgically removed.

Her vision could be fine if she has cataract surgery. She's staying at the vet overnight to receive hydration before returning to the sanctuary.

We've reached out to a special rescue group to see if they can accept her into their program. We will hear this weekend. We will continue to care for her until she finds the perfect rescue group or home.

I know you'd do the same thing we did, taking in a stray dog in need. You'd also want to give her a chance to finally know compassion, too.

Thank you for caring about others, as much as we do for the cats in our care, too.

October 11, 2017

We were sorry to find out that Cookie has been diagnosed with diabetes, too. Her glucose levels came back very high and may be a reason why she is afflicted with cataracts.

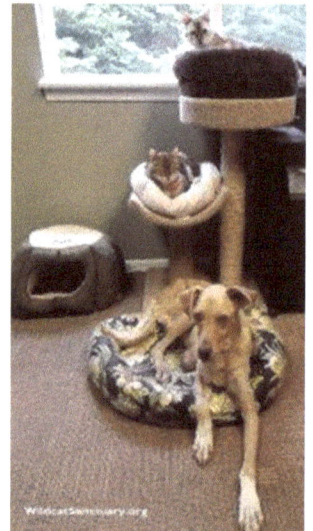

We'll be administering daily insulin and monitoring her levels. We're hoping to stabilize it so she can begin to put on the weight she needs for future surgery.

October 17, 2017

The first few days, Cookie wasn't responding to the insulin injections we were giving her. Our vet increased the dosage and the last 48 hours, her glucose numbers are coming down. She'll be seen again this week by the vet to check-in on her.

Her other surgeries are being postponed until we can get her glucose a little more regulated. Every time she wags her tail whenever we're around, we know it's a thank you straight from her heart to us—and to all of YOU—for going the extra mile to save her.

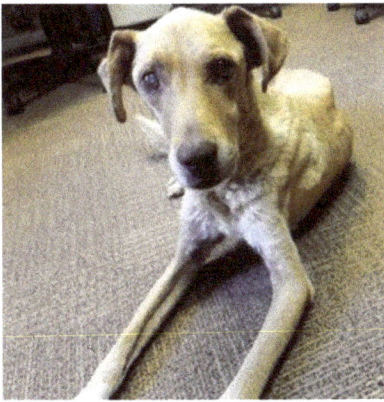

We're so thankful to share that Cookie had her first surgical procedure. The vet said she was recuperating well and she's now back at the sanctuary!

Cookie was healthy enough that they were able to spay her while they also removed six of her largest mammary tumors. They left some of the smaller tumors because the surgery was quite extensive.

Cookie has seven total incisions. They've sent the tumors out for testing and we're hoping to have results back in 7-10 days. Cookie will be on medication for 7-14 days. They reported she was stable during surgery and woke up well afterwards.

Cookie enjoyed staying at a staff member's home before and after her surgery, but she's back at the sanctuary today.

We're so thankful for the outpouring of love and support you've sent Cookie's way. She's made so much progress in the six short weeks since she showed up here!

Remember how emaciated she was then? Look at her now:

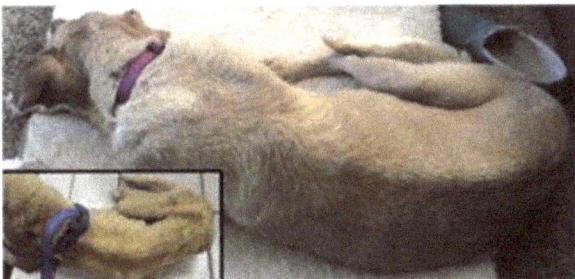

While we've been treating her diabetes, she's gained weight steadily and is beginning to look and act like the adorably sweet dog we hoped she could be.

After she recuperates, we'll begin to look into the cataract surgery she'll also be needing. For her to be able to see again and be healthy is our greatest wish—and we thank you so much for helping make that wish come true for her!

November 28, 2017

We had fun letting everyone guess what breed Cookie actually is. We sent in a DNA test on her and these were the results….

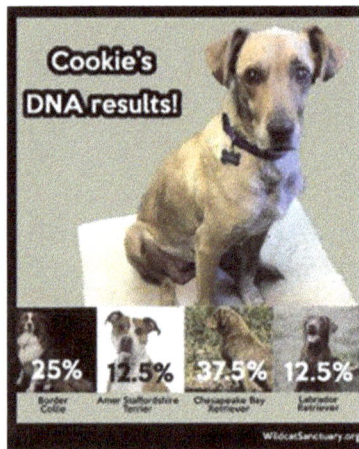

Cookie's
DNA results!

25% 12.5% 37.5% 12.5%

Border Collie Amer Staffordshire Terrier Chesapeake Bay Retriever Labrador Retriever

WildcatSanctuary.org

January 4, 2018

We're starting off the New Year with the best news!

After undergoing another examination by Dr. Robert Larocca at Animal Eye Specialty Center in Andover, MN, our rescue dog Cookie was cleared for surgery to remove the cataracts causing her blindness.

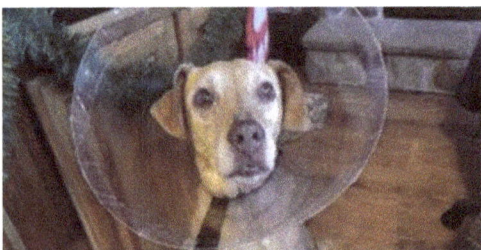

It's been a long three month uphill journey for this little girl—and you've been there for her every step of the way!

Found as a starving stray, she was so emaciated. The first step was letting her gain weight back slowly and carefully. Since she had diabetes and out-of-control glucose levels, we had to manage that safely, too.

Then, she had surgery to remove her mammary tumors and was spayed. After recuperating from that, she was finally ready for this last step. Could we save her eyesight?

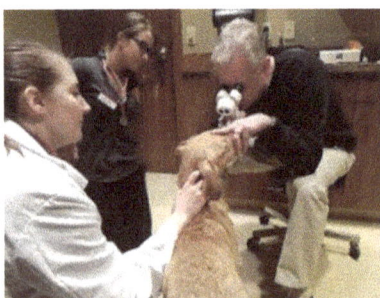

Dr. Larocca was able to remove the cataracts in both eyes and replace them with an artificial replacement lens. As always, Cookie was a very good patient but woke up from the general anesthesia very groggy.

She spent the night at the home of one of our staff members and returned to the sanctuary the next morning. What would her reaction be?

YES, she can definitely see!!

Being rescued was one thing. But being able to see again—that's truly been life changing for her! Cooper, the Bengal cat she's been friends with in the animal care building, is suddenly far more interesting. Cookie's been trotting after him now as he wanders across the room.

She spends so much time looking out the window, watching all the activity outside. In the past, caretakers would take Cookie for a walk. Now, she takes them!

Cookie will be recuperating for several weeks. She'll wear a cone for two weeks to prevent self-trauma to the eyes. She'll get three different eye drops four times a day during that time, too. We'll be taking her for several follow-up appointments with the ophthalmologist over the next weeks and months.

All while continuing with the daily management of her diabetes. Caring for Cookie is time consuming, but so worth it with every wag of her tail she gives in thanks.

This procedure alone cost $3500. But it's hopefully the last major hurdle Cookie faced on her journey to becoming one of the most loved cat sanctuary mascot dogs ever!

She's one of a kind, that's for sure, and we thank you so much for all the love, good wishes, and support you've given to get her to this amazing point in her life!

In Memory

Do you believe in miracles? I do, because I met one. And her name was Cookie.

We're heartbroken to share that Cookie lost her final battle with cancer. It just doesn't seem real. Even though she rallied for a few days, she again quickly became very tired.

Even her routine tasks became more difficult as her breathing became more pronounced. She began leaving food, which wasn't like our girl at all. And even though she still loved seeing all her friends and family, we could all see her time was drawing near.

Cookie had done so much for all of us—including all of you. We promised her we'd be there for her, too—when she needed us most, no matter how difficult it would be.

Goodbye is only for now. The impact Cookie has had on us all will live forever. Because that's just how special she was.

She arrived diabetic, emaciated, blind and tumor-ridden, barely able to survive another day on her own. But even that didn't break her spirit. Several surgeries later to remove the tumors and give her back her sight, she wasn't recognizable as the same dog. But that wasn't why she was a miracle.

Cookie was a dog living in a cat's world—literally. Just like a cat, she had 9 lives and used every one of those lives to the fullest. She adapted so quickly to sanctuary life among the tigers, lions, and other big cats. She enjoyed long walks past each habitat and never even gave a second thought to the big cat just a few feet away. But that still wasn't why she was a miracle.

While this sweet, quiet and calm girl was healing herself, she was also connecting and healing the world. That's what made her a miracle! She wasn't just our special dog, she was yours, too.

People from around the world rallied to support Cookie and embrace her and her story. She embodied hope, forgiveness, resilience, and happiness. And she did so until her last breath.

She inspired cat fanatics to love dogs, she helped an autistic boy share his first words, she taught us how working together can provide a second chance to live and love.

Amazing! This lost, blind dog could have found her way into the woods, curled up and passed away. But Cookie had more love to give and work to do. She made our lives better and I know she did the same for you.

We'll shed our tears of sadness and grieve together for the loss of our special friend. But we must also honor Cookie. She'd remind us to be resilient, move forward and love again. We still have important work to do. And we'll always remember Cookie's walking beside us each and every day, helping us.

Cookie, you were truly a gift. We were honored you found your way to us, so we could share you with the world. Everyone deserves to know you. And our lives are better for having you in it.

Sleep peacefully now so you can enjoy your walks with all your family of fans around the world. I know they will welcome you with open arms.

Say No to Cub Petting

As an animal lover, if someone were to make you this offer, would you accept?

You can pet, play with and bottle feed this cub and we'll take a picture of you so you can share it with your friends—BUT, it means one of the following will happen to this cub once he/she is too big for this anymore:

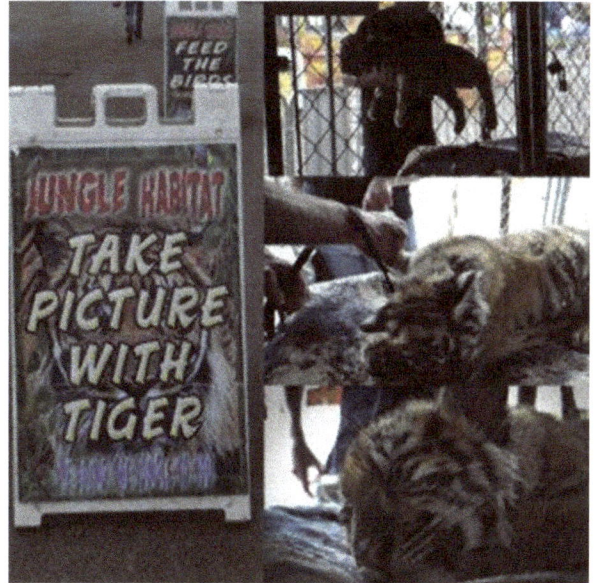

- This cub will suffer the rest of his/her life in a cage without proper food or care
- This cub will be slaughtered for the exotic meat market
- This cub will be sold off at auction to the highest bidder, fate unknown
- This cub will be killed for parts and bones for the medicinal market
- This cub will be lost in the illegal black market trade of exotic animals

We know you'd never say "yes" to any of these. You love animals. That's why you want this experience. But that's exactly what you agree to when you say "yes" to this thrill-of-a-lifetime offer. It doesn't matter if we're talking about tourist attractions in South Africa, Mexico, or the United States. Sadly, this is the fate for so many cubs bred for money-making ventures like these.

A former exhibitor of our white tigress Nikita said her owner could make $5000 each week offering animal interactions like this. It's obvious, **money is what drives the industry—and the breeding.**

But someone is surely regulating this, right?

In the United States, the USDA feels there should be no contact with cubs under the age of 8 weeks, since that's when they receive their first disease-preventing injections.

They also feel there should be no contact with cubs over 12 weeks old, since they can be dangerous even at that young age.

But these are just guidelines, not regulations. If breeders/exhibitors were to follow these guidelines, it means **a cub used for public contact would have a "shelf life" of only 4 weeks!**

What does this encourage? Rampant breeding. Knowing they won't get caught, breeders/exhibitors don't follow these guidelines.

So, where do all these cubs go when they're too old and can no longer be used for public contact?

Their fate is often tragic. They're killed, their bones and parts sold off. They're auctioned to the highest bidder, often becoming a caged backyard "pet." They become part of the illegal black-market trade of exotics.

Don't inspectors make sure everything's ok for these cubs?

In 2018 in the United States, there were only 110 USDA inspectors to monitor almost 10,000 facilities, ranging from slaughterhouses, pet stores, pet breeders and dealers, farms, laboratories and other animal-related businesses. That's nearly **1 inspector for every 90 facilities!**

When traveling exhibitors often move these cubs all over the country to fairs, festivals, and malls, relying on inspectors to ensure quality of care for them is unrealistic.

And even when cubs are being exhibited when they're too young or too old, violators aren't cited unless an inspector is there to personally see serious harm to the cub—screaming and squirming isn't enough.

Doesn't touching a tiger or lion help promote conservation since we're losing them in the wild?

As more and more of these cub petting attractions spring up everywhere, guess what? Tigers and lions in the wild are still endangered and nearly extinct.

Touching a cub does nothing to conserve their cousins in the wild, though exhibitors claim you're helping conservation efforts.

Tragically, it may be doing the opposite. If you can visit a facility to pet a tiger cub, then why protect them half a world away where you may never see them?

Studies have shown that public interaction with captive wild animals has done very little to cause the public to donate to conservation in the wild. And no, there's been no successful release of a captive born tiger or lion to date.

When a cub needs to be with its mother for at least two years to learn survival skills, this simply isn't something humans can duplicate. So, the answer is "no," touching a lion or tiger cub in no way helps save them in the wild.

What Can You Do?

- **Contact the USDA by emailing them at: aceast@aphis.usda.gov** Let them know you want to see an end to physical contact with big cats, to prohibit public handling of young or immature big cats, and to stop the separation of cubs from their mothers before the species-typical age of weaning.

- **Never, ever give in to the temptation of public contact with a wild cat.** It's dangerous for you and sentences these big cats to life in a cage—or far worse.
- **Educate friends, family, and media about the reality of this cruel practice.** So few know this is an insidious form of animal abuse—but now you do. Share it through social media channels, too.
- The next time you see a cub in your town or at some of the tourist attractions you visit while on vacation, we hope you'll **remember the truth** and you'll **help raise awareness.** When the demand ends, so will those who profit by supplying these experiences.
- **Contact your local, state and national representatives** to let them know you do NOT support these exhibits. They often need to be educated, too.

Together, let's be their voice and put an end to cub interaction exhibits.

Say No to White Tigers

What is a white tiger—really?

Though you may have heard differently, white tigers are simply Bengal tigers. They're not albino or their own separate species. White tigers occur when two Bengal tigers that carry a recessive gene controlling coat color are bred **together**.

It's been said the entire captive white tiger population originated from one single white tiger and has been inbred ever since. In order to retain this recessive gene, zoos and breeders must continually inbreed father to daughter, father to granddaughter and so on.

This inbreeding has caused many genetic problems with tigers. Many of the cubs that are born either in zoos or by breeders have to be 'disposed' of because they are malformed at birth.

White Bengal tigers have also been crossed with Siberian tigers to produce a larger specimen. This causes even more genetic problems.

For years, breeders and exhibitors have been using the excuse that white tigers are an endangered species, so they need to keep breeding them. This is completely false. Breeders of white tigers do not contribute to any **species survival plan;** they are breeding for money.

In reality, the breeding of white tigers has also caused a giant surplus of normal golden-colored tigers in the private sector worldwide since most litters have several unwanted golden tigers, too. Out of a litter of cubs, the breeders will pick the white cubs that bring in a lot more money on the market and euthanize, inhumanely destroy or neglect the cubs that do not meet the white color requirement.

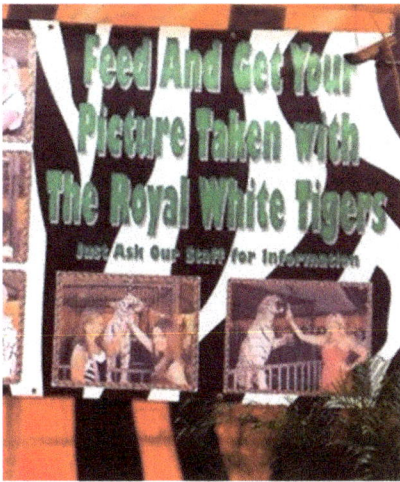

Google to read the June 2011 AZA White Paper declaring the practice of breeding white tigers as "not in adherence with AZA's Board-approved Policy on the Presentation of Animals."

"Step right up and come see the rare, endangered Royal White Bengal tiger!"

If you've been to a fair or local festival, chances are you've probably seen or heard this from exhibitors. Whether they're baby white tiger cubs for you to hold and play with. Whether they're full-grown tigers they offer you the opportunity to take a photo with—make no mistake, **it's a for-profit business.**

And if white tigers really are so rare, why has The Wildcat Sanctuary been contacted to rescue so many of them?

Because, the truth is, **they aren't rare anymore.** Years ago, a breeder might sell a white tiger for tens of thousands of dollars. Now, since the market's been glutted with them, they're sold for a fraction of that. But, it's still a lucrative business.

How are white tigers created?

White tigers are simply Bengal tigers with white fur. They're not a separate subspecies of tiger. They're the result of a mutant gene that's been artificially selected through massive inbreeding to essentially produce man-made tigers for entertainment.

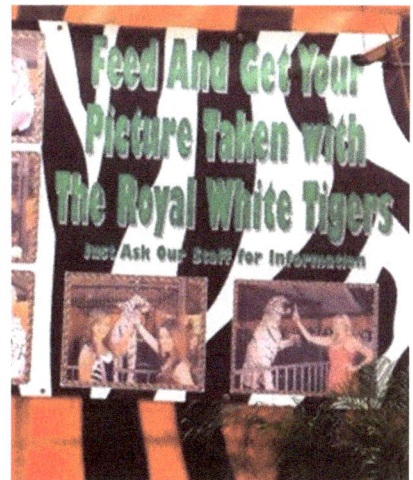

You'll still find famous magicians and entertainers trying to promote them as a rare separate species. Only a minority of the general public knows the truth about this business of breeding for birth defects. So, it's easy to manipulate many who'll pay to see them.

Do we need to conserve white tigers in the wild?

And let's dispel the myth that, if you pay to see or play with one, this is somehow helping conserve white tigers in the wild. **White tigers are simply a novelty with no conservation value at all.** They're very rare in the wild for a reason, possibly as few as 1 in 10,000 wild tiger births. They're a bad genetic mutation that Mother Nature eliminates.

Odds are against them being able to survive infancy to adulthood in order to reproduce and pass on this mutant gene. White is, quite obviously, terrible camouflage for a predator that has to hunt to survive.

It's estimated there are perhaps less than 5,000 orange tigers left in the wild. There are currently no known white tigers alive in the wild. But that doesn't mean the genes aren't carried by orange tigers living in captivity who are exploited for carrying that mutation.

How does paying to see one hurt other tigers?

When you pay to see a white tiger, you encourage the irresponsible inbreeding needed to supply this abusive industry. It's been reported that the neonatal mortality rate exceeds 80% for white tigers! To put that in perspective, it's typically only 30% for orange-colored tigers in AZA zoos.

What does that tell us? That a lot of tigers must be bred in order to get that one "perfect" white tiger everyone wants to see. And a lot of surplus orange tigers and imperfect white tigers born in the process are unwanted and disposed of any way possible.

This white tiger mania is also a big reason why we have more orange tigers in cages in the US today than tigers left roaming in the wild.

Do white tigers have other health issues?

What happens to the captive-born white tigers who survive but also carry, in addition to the white gene mutation, numerous life-altering complications thought to accompany this gene?

These tigers tend to have difficulty processing visual stimulation, problems with the way their brains control their eyes, trouble understanding spatial relationships when young since so many are cross-eyed in one or both eyes. Kidney problems, cleft palates, club feet, spinal deformities, and shortened tendons are also common disorders that may afflict them.

Do AZA zoos still breed white tigers?

As William Conway, former director of the New York Zoological Association put it many years ago, **"White tigers are freaks. It's not the role of a zoo to show two-headed calves and white tigers."**

In 2011, the Association of Zoos and Aquariums (AZA) took a huge step in banning member zoos from breeding white tigers, lions, and cheetahs. But it doesn't stop these zoos, roadside attractions, and traveling exhibits from displaying them. They're also not prohibited from obtaining them from other sources.

Jeremy, Callie, Mohan, Nikita, Simon, Callie—all rescued by TWS

What can you do?

So, it's up to all of us to stop supporting the cruelty involved in displaying this mythical, non-existent species. The white tigers being dumped after they're no longer earning their keep in the exhibition world didn't ask to be in this situation.

As Jackson Landers said, **"Humanity has a collective responsibility to care for the two-headed calves and white tigers that we create for our own entertainment, but do we really need to be creating more of the genetic disasters that pull resources away from truly endangered species?"**

We hope you'll join us in clearly answering that question—"NO!"

Say No to Hybrid Cats
Domestic Bengal Cat Policy

NOTE: *The Wildcat Sanctuary can no longer accommodate domestic Bengal cats into our program. We cannot keep up with the overwhelming number of calls we receive for hybrid surrender. Our mission is to help wild cats in need, and we will accommodate F1 hybrids only if there is room at our Sanctuary.*

Imagine receiving more than 20 calls every month from owners begging you to take in their little Bengal cat. Their cat has become too much to handle or he/she urinates throughout the house. How would you feel when time and time again, you had to say "no"—you had to explain the reality of the situation? This is what we deal with on a regular basis at The Wildcat Sanctuary.

The breeders don't have to answer these calls, though they've caused the problem. But we, and countless other shelters, have to. **This is why we advocate No More Wild Pets as an important part of our mission, and we want to end hybrid breeding.**

Our mission is to rescue wild cats, i.e. lions, tigers, leopards, cougars, etc. We can barely keep up with the demand of big cats that need sanctuary. Now, the calls for Bengal cat rescues have become overwhelming and therefore, we can no longer accept Bengal cats for placement at the Sanctuary.

What's life like with a hybrid cat like a Bengal?

There are millions and millions of perfectly wonderful domestic cats at shelters waiting to be adopted, so it's frustrating to find people opting to pay thousands and thousands of dollars for exotic hybrids like Bengal cats. Why do this?

These cats end up behaving just as they're genetically programmed to—"wild!" Owners are led to believe they'll bring these little wild ones home, give them a litter box and they'll live peacefully with others in their homes. That's not the case at all, as you'll see when you read all the information, we have below about hybrid cat species.

How to create a home for your hybrid cat

So many of these desperate callers love the setups we have for our hybrids and Bengals here at the Sanctuary. It's easy to duplicate these in your backyard or attach to your garage for your Bengal cats.

Your cat doesn't need to be given away. And, more importantly, they don't need to be euthanized for behavior that was easily predictable. You spent so much money to acquire them. Don't they deserve a bit more so they can enjoy life?

Giving up your Bengal cat is traumatic for you, your family, and for your cat. By investing a bit more time and money, you can give them a suitable environment that meets their needs, just like we do here at The Wildcat Sanctuary.

As the pictures show, our hybrid cats live in temperature-controlled sheds/bungalows that we've adapted for their enjoyment. You'll see perches, beds, washable walls, litter boxes, and food inside the buildings and a cat door that allows them access to an outdoor area.

These outdoor areas are securely fenced, with a roof. Ramps, hanging toys, landscaping, water features, and hammocks allow the cats to fill their days with endless enjoyment. Some of our volunteers' favorite times are spent playing with the Bengals and hybrid cats.

The bottom line is you made the decision to acquire something with a wild personality. They're active, vocal, mischievous, and they love water. Why, then, give up your cat for the things that originally drew you to them?

Please make the commitment to give them what they deserve—a safe, enjoyable home that meets *their* needs.

You won't change their wildness, but you can learn to live with it and enjoy many years of happiness together. You purchased a hybrid cat in hopes of a life-long companion. Do the right thing now and provide them the life you promised, right in your own backyard.

How's a domestic Bengal different from an F1 Bengal?

The Bengal cat breed resulted from cross breeding an Asian Leopard Cat (ALC-Felis bengalensis) with the domestic cat (Felis catus). The first three filial generations (F1—F3) of these hybrid animals are referred to as the "foundation" generations.

A Bengal cat with an ALC parent is called an F1 Bengal, short for first filial. They eat raw meat and will almost never use a litter box once they reach maturity. These hybrids are often prohibited and regulated by state, city and township laws such as in MN, IA, etc.

An F1 then bred with a domestic male produces an F2, or second filial. Kittens from an F2 female and another domestic cat are then termed F3.

Kittens from a subsequent F3 mating with a domestic are F4s. The F4 and later generations are considered domestic cats, but still have many behavioral and health issues due to the hybridization.

Can breeders control wild tendencies through breeding?

Breeders market hybrid cats as 'lap leopards' and say they have the look of the wild and personality of the domestic. However, genetics do NOT work this way. Breeders cannot choose which elements you get of the wild or domestic cat.

The Wildcat Sanctuary receives more calls from owners wanting to surrender Bengal domestic cats than all other wildcats and hybrids combined. The most common reason is not using the litter box, especially when housed with other animals.

We love the Bengals and hybrids we care for and we accept the soiling and behavioral problems that most people deem inappropriate pet behavior.

Other common hybrid cats that are being surrendered at an alarming rate are:

- Bengals (Asian Leopard Cat—Domestic Cat)
- Savannahs (<u>Serval</u>—Domestic Cat)
- Chausies (<u>Jungle cat</u>—Domestic Cat)
- Safari (Geoffroy's cat—Domestic Cat)

Hybrid health issues

Hybrids, whether early generation or domestic, often have the following common health issues, which can be expensive and leave the owner feeling helpless:

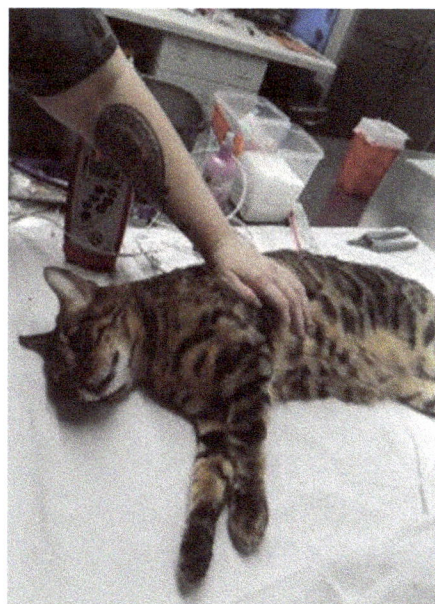

- Painful irritable bowel disease (IBD) that causes chronic diarrhea
- Hypertrophic Cardiomyopathy
- Progressive Retinal Atrophy
- Tri-Trichamonas Foetus
- Luxating patella
- Often high corona titers and the only known test for FIP—Feline Infectious Peritonitis (but not always reliable)
- Gingivitis and mouth lesions (most common in Chausie's)

Our Bengals and hybrids at the Sanctuary accumulate our highest veterinary costs because of these common health issues. They also take the most time for our keepers due to the clean-up of their indoor areas due to spraying and soiling.

Adopting a hybrid cat

The Wildcat Sanctuary is against hybridization, but we understand Bengal domestic cats are legal in most states and many are displaced and in need of a home.

We recommend any prospective owner adopt from a rescue group as well as research breed information from sanctuaries and many other resources versus just breeder sites. Adopting a Bengal from a rescue group will be valuable since the social and litter box behaviors have already been assessed.

If you choose to bring a Bengal cat into your family, you must be committed to the breed and the behavior of the breed. Even the small handful of Bengals that don't have litter box issues are active, vocal, love to play in water and mischievous. It takes a unique owner, willing to provide a lifetime of care to an animal that will run the household.

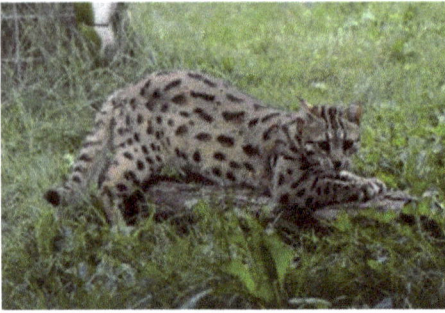

TWS does not agree with any purchase or adoption of hybrid generations (F1-F3s) given the wild nature, behavior and health issues associated with these cats.

Domestication happens over 4,000 years. Not just with a few generations of breeding hybrids**.**

Wildcats are solitary by nature except for the African lion. At maturity, they lose all alliance to their wild parents in order to survive. They'll even challenge parents and siblings for territory and dominance.

This also happens in captivity. Once the wild or hybrid cat reaches maturity it will 'turn' on its owner or other animals it lives with. It will want to mark territory by spraying and urinating, even if it's neutered or spayed.

What if I need to surrender a Bengal or hybrid cat?

The Wildcat Sanctuary is a sanctuary for wild and hybrid cats. Due to the overwhelming number of calls we receive we can no longer accommodate domestic Bengals. Only F1 foundation cats will be considered for permanent sanctuary.

Domestic shelters will not accept hybrids into their programs and most wildcat sanctuaries do not accept hybrids either. This leaves little alternative for these cats.

If you plan on contacting TWS regarding surrendering a cat, please review the following information. All requests will be considered on a case by case basis.

- Owner will pay for transport costs to TWS
- Health certificate within 10 days of transport is needed
- The cat must be spayed/neutered at the cost of the owner
- Blood profile including a corona titer must be performed
- Surrender form must be completed and signed
- Annual sponsorship or intake fee will be requested

What other options do I have?

When TWS takes in rescues, the animal's behavior and habits do not change. If the cat urinated in your house, he/she will continue to do so at TWS. The difference is we are committed to providing lifetime care for the animal and adjust the environment around them.

If you have purchased a Bengal or hybrid cat and own it legally, you should do the same. **The best thing is for you to provide a fully-enclosed, outdoor area with access to a heated den like a garage or insulated shed**.

Yes, this may cost a few thousand dollars, but it is amazing that owners pay upwards of $4,000-$8,000 for these cats but won't put that into the cost of caring for the animal nor provide the same amount of funding for a sanctuary to care for the cat.

Euthanasia should not be an option for a behavior that is common to the breed and easily researched. For example, take the Siberian husky. When a person adopts a Siberian husky, they shouldn't be surprised that the dog barks, jumps fences, digs and runs away off leash when this is typical breed behavior. There are exceptions to the rule, but anyone adopting this breed should expect and be prepared for the typical behavior.

Other hybrid owners have tried to resell the cat to recoup costs. Buyers should beware that if someone is trying to sell a cat, it is probably unwanted due to soiling or behavioral problems that they're not disclosing. This only means the problems will get worse with you.

Remember, there are millions of wonderful domestic dogs and cats in shelters that are waiting to become a lifelong companion to you. You can save a life by adopting one of these.

You will be much happier that you kept the wild in your heart, not your home, because the idea of owning a wildcat or hybrid is much more glamorous than the reality.

Breeding hybrids—the dark side

If you're familiar with all the controversy surrounding puppy/kitten mills, you won't be surprised to learn those same issues are linked with the breeding of hybrids, too. The following is a snapshot of the dark side of hybrid breeding:

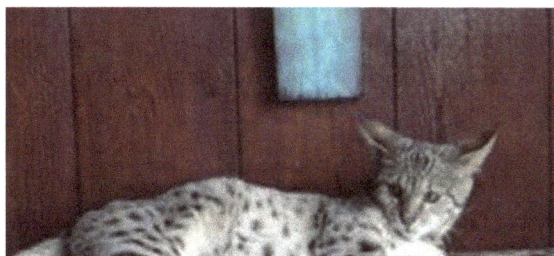

To give away F1 Wildcat Hybrid -

Neutered, 4 way declawed, he needs to go to a one cat family. He looks spotted like a Bengal, but taller. He is a very unique cat. We paid $2,000.00 for him last winter. Must see him to appreciate what he actually looks like. Google a African Wildcat. Pictures available upon request. He has not been around dogs, he would be best off on his own in the home.

Breeding Issues

During the breeding process, domestic cats forced to breed with wild cats can often be killed. Many pregnancies are aborted or absorbed by the mother cat's body when nature determines there is something wrong.

Kittens are often born prematurely due to the variance of gestation periods between the wild cats and domestic cats that have been interbred. Many of the first generation are sterile, especially the males. In some cases, breeders may kill kittens born with an undesirable appearance, or just drop them off at a shelter.

Breeding Conditions

Quite like the controversial issues faced with puppy mills, hybrid cats used for breeding can face the same poor quality of life. Forced to live in a cage the majority of their lives, they are not socialized.

The cats can suffer from illnesses and live in filthy conditions that are rarely detected since they're not the subject of inspections.

Breeding for Profit

There is no doubt that breeding a hybrid cat that will bring in thousands of dollars tends to naturally attract many whose sole motive is profit. Why breed a "normal" domestic purebred cat that may fetch only $200 when you can breed a hybrid cat that can bring in as much as $22,000?

This quest for high profits leads many breeders to house too many cats under poor conditions and leads to poor genetics as more and more are interbred.

Permits or Bans

Thankfully, many municipalities have been educated about the danger of having hybrid cats in their communities. When complete bans aren't in place, many towns are requiring special permits in order to own these exotic cats.

Servals, for instance, are extremely efficient hunters and killers in Africa. Raising them in captivity in the US and cross breeding them doesn't change this innate characteristic. This is why many areas see them as a threat or concern for the community and why they want to know where they live and who owns them.

The Wild Side

You can NOT breed the "wild" behaviors out of servals, Asian leopard cats, jungle cats, or Geoffrey's cats by interbreeding them with domestic cats for a couple of generations. When a buyer spends thousands of dollars for a wild looking cat, they get exactly what they're paying for—a cat with wild tendencies!

Hybrid cats are known for being extremely destructive. Common complaints are of ruined furniture, clothing, and personal items.

A hybrid marking territory is instinctive, whether it's a male or female, and most owners are unprepared for the reality of living with the smell of the wild constantly surrounding them.

Hybrids don't always get along with other pets and have been known to hunt them down, even causing injury to neighborhood cats and dogs. The elderly and small children are seen as weak and vulnerable to attack, just as any prey in the wild would be to these cats.

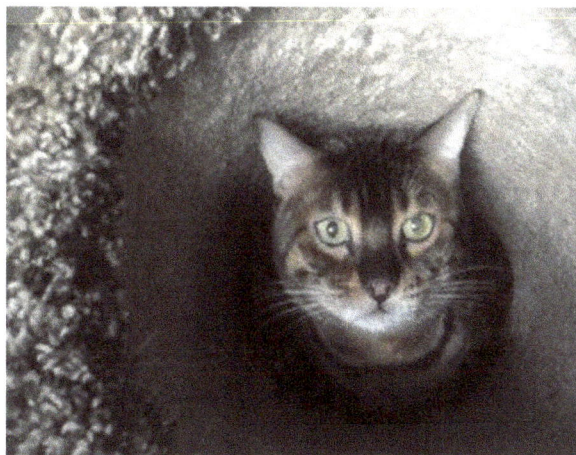

When frustration overcomes the owners, all too often, they look for an easy way out. They'll have the cats euthanized when they can't find a rescue or shelter to take them in. Some have been known to simply set them loose, forcing them to survive on their own. It's a sad, cruel fate for these cats—through no fault of their own.

Health Concerns

Finding a veterinarian to care for an exotic animal is not easy and, when you do, it's expensive! Hybrid cats have health concerns that aren't normal to domestic cats, including respiratory issues, irritable bowel disorder, and other digestive issues.

Vaccinations have not been approved for hybrid animals since it's not known if regular vaccines will protect them. Many medications don't work on these wild cats either.

Pet Overpopulation

With estimates of over 4 million pets being killed each year in shelters, there is no need to breed hybrid cats. These cats rarely work out as pets. It simply adds to the overpopulation issue in all shelters. If there is a home available for a pet, it should be for an appropriate domestic pet—not a wild animal.

To declaw or not to declaw…
that is the question.

I remember walking into the shelter to adopt my very first pet. I had looked at rescue groups, ads in the paper and had visited several shelters looking for the right cat—the one looking for me.

When I saw her, I knew. She was not exotic looking, nor a fancy breed. But she was just as beautiful. She was a black little kitten with blues eyes, amongst a sea of other black kittens in her litter.

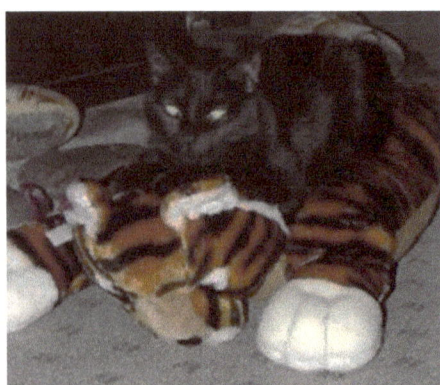

When she approached the wire door and let out one "meow," that was it! My feline family had begun, and her name was Kaya.

I had done everything to make sure we were a perfect match and that I could give her the best home possible. I researched cats and breeds. I looked into purchasing from a breeder or adopting from a shelter. I learned what costs would be involved in having a pet and I adapted my apartment to create a cat amusement park.

I know they say dogs are man's best friend. But for me, it was Kaya. I couldn't imagine life without her.

It was our first visit to the vet for her to be spayed and being away from her for a day seemed unbearable. Upon check in, the front desk asked if I would like her declawed, too? I was told this was a common practice and would even receive a discount for performing both surgeries at once. I wanted to be the best cat owner, and if that was recommended by the vet, then that is what I was going to do.

Oh, how little I knew!

Even after treating Kaya for several paw infections later, I still believed this was just part of having a cat as a member of the family.

Over my life, I have declawed 3 cats, including a wild cat, something I am not proud of at all. But, also something I am not ashamed to admit because I can educate others in hopes of changing the future.

It took being invited to see a surgery first-hand when I realized this is not declawing at all. They were surgically removing the first digits of my cat's toes with a surgical knife—it was an amputation!

That was the last cat I ever declawed. Was this really necessary I thought to myself? Why was I doing it? To make the cat safe? To protect my furniture? I didn't have a clear answer except, that's what pet owners did.

Oh, how far I've come! I can't judge others for something I've done, but I hope to offer more information so that people can make better decisions.

Our Sanctuary is home to over 100 residents. 70% of the cats come to us four-paw declawed and we see the devastating effects.

People tend to agree that declawing big cats is cruel and causes permanent damage, but it can be difficult to convince them that declawing small cats can cause the same damage. Even if your cat isn't showing the signs.

We often have to say goodbye to cats earlier than we should due to debilitating arthritis and lameness. Pain medications only help for so long. But the cats, who are genetically designed to bear weight on their toes, are now putting all their weight on scar tissue and exposed bone. No pain medications or soft substrate can compensate for that.

Halifax, the serval had several surgeries to remove bone and claw fragments, well into his teens. The regrowth would cause abscesses that had to be surgically corrected.

Even small cats like Bullet, a Bengal cat, have chronic issues. Bullet has had several radiographs on his feet. His toes have fused at a 90-degree angle because of his arthritis. His bone is right at the skin and he often shifts his weight from foot to foot.

We are hoping that through education, pet owners will stop, think and ask more questions before they make the decision to declaw. That is why we support the work of **THE PAW PROJECT.**

They are educating thousands of people and trying to make a cultural shift on how America views declawing.

We also know that we cannot change everyone's mind. That's why we encourage people who will only open their home to a declawed cat, to adopt one from a shelter vs. putting another cat through this surgery.

We know this is a controversial topic and will ruffle some feathers. Whenever you try and make change, it often does. But, we hope it will start a conversation about what is best for our feline friends.

For those who love cats enough to have one (or more) in your home, please love them for what they truly are—claws and all.

Even the best dogs will chew your shoes and put wear and tear on the house. Kids color on walls, break precious items while playing. Cats are not any different. They shouldn't be penalized for doing what comes naturally.

Instead, love their wild side and give them more options that are acceptable. Your little tiger will be happy that you love her for ALL of her! I wish I had done that for Kaya.

Tammy Thies
The Wildcat Sanctuary Founder and Executive Director

No More Wild Pets

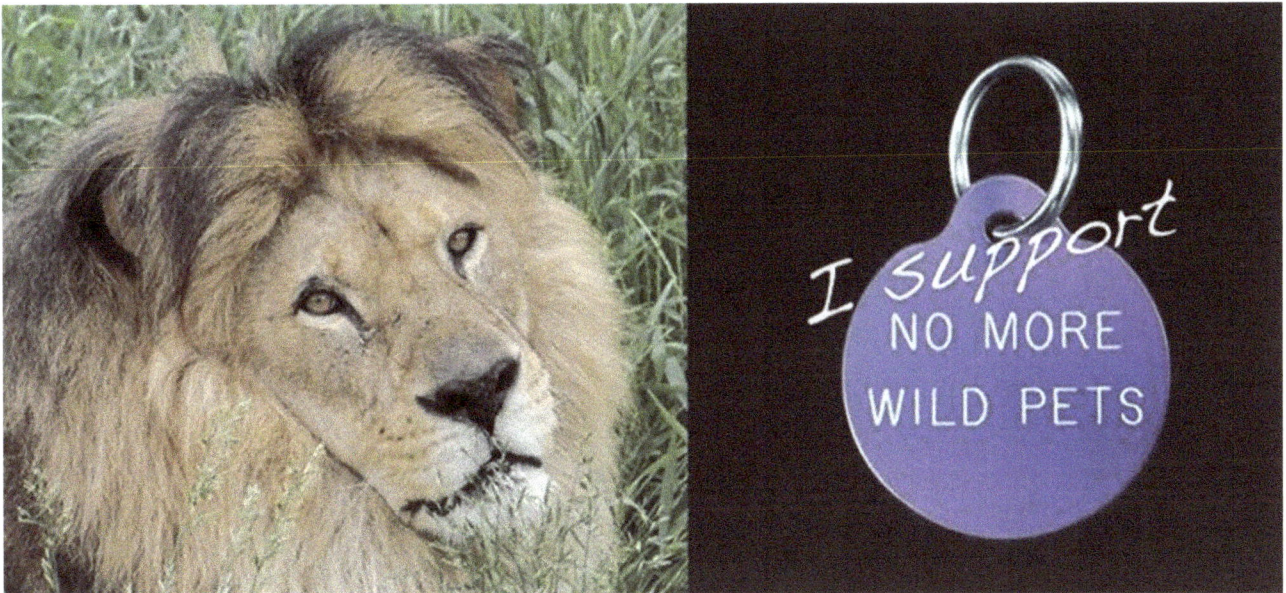

We created our No More Wild Pets© campaign to increase public awareness about the captive wildlife crisis and decrease the number of wild animals being kept as pets. We strive to inspire people to keep the wild in their heart, not their home, and advocate for adopting appropriate pets instead.

Why is education so important?

A significant factor in making the wildlife trade possible is the general public's lack of awareness of the captive wildlife crisis and the dangers involved with private ownership of wild animals.

Every year, thousands of big cats are sold as pets. What happens to these animals is criminal. Some are abused or neglected, others are simply abandoned. All are denied their right to be wild.

Because there's little regulation, exotic ownership has turned into a multi-billion dollar industry.

When a baby tiger cub can be purchased for less than the cost of a purebred dog, we have a serious problem on our hands. At first cute and cuddly, they soon grow into dangerous carnivores that are, all too often, destined to life in a backyard cage under deplorable conditions.

Unlike domestic pets, there are few re-homing options for unwanted exotics. There can never be enough sanctuaries to take in all these unwanted animals.

Why are wild pets so available?

As of 2012, there are estimated to be 10,000-20,000 big cats in private hands—and they just keep breeding. These aren't in zoos and accredited facilities, as you might think. Surprisingly, 95% of all tigers in the US are privately owned.

Wild animals can be bought at auctions, from backyard breeders, on the illegal black market, via internet brokers, stolen from their natural wild habitats, or picked up as discarded surplus from zoos, roadside attractions, game ranches, etc.

Even though big cats can be deadly, 4 states have no laws on keeping dangerous wild animals as pets. 6 states do not ban or regulate keeping big cats as pets. 21 states ban all dangerous exotic pets, while the rest allow certain species or require permits. 35 states ban keeping big cats as pets, with varying exemptions, requirements, and levels of enforcement.

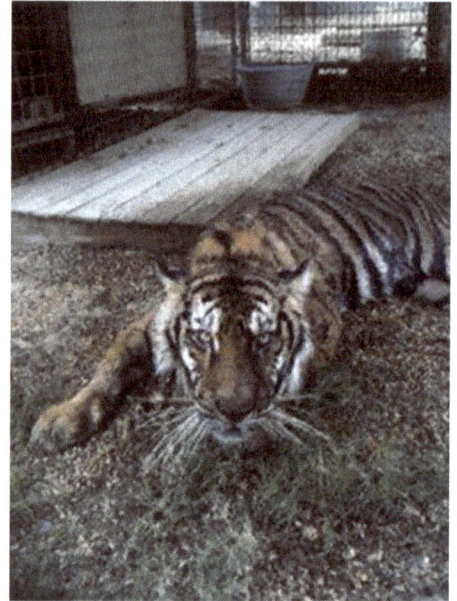

In the US, 21 people have died and 246 have been mauled by exotic cats since 2000. Captive tigers alone have killed at least 12 people in the US and mauled about 75 more. There have been 253 escapes, 143 big cat deaths and 131 confiscations.

The U.S. Department of Agriculture employs around 110 relevant inspectors for 10,000 locations countrywide. There are around 2,400 zoos in the U.S., the vast majority of which are considered "roadside zoos." Their conditions are poor even to untrained eyes. Just because a facility has a USDA license, it doesn't assure the animals are well cared for. Only minimal standards are required for a license.

It can take 5-10 years for authorities to shut down a substandard USDA licensed facility with multiple violations, injuries, and/or escapes. The legal process drags on while the animals continue to suffer, and the public is at risk.

As much needed legislation is passed and greater control is brought to the largely unregulated practice of importing, breeding, buying, and selling wild animals as pets, there are likely to be confiscated or abandoned exotic animals in increasing numbers.

Critical to this will be the provision of accredited and secure facilities like The Wildcat Sanctuary and other wild animal sanctuaries to provide big cat rescue services and appropriate life-long care for all these animals.

320

No home, no cage, no backyard will ever replace a wild animals' natural habitat. A ban on breeding and private ownership, as well as educating the public about the problems of trying to keep wild animals as pets, is our only hope for solving this captive crisis.

Why adopting an appropriate pet is so important.

Animal welfare programs have made huge strides in reducing the number of unwanted animals killed in shelters each year. But the numbers are still staggering.

With approximately 5-7 million companion animals entering animal shelters nationwide every year, 3-4 million still end up being euthanized (60% of dogs and 70% of cats).

With so many wonderful domestic animals in desperate need of homes, there is simply no excuse for purchasing or breeding dangerous exotics as pets.

5,000 independent community animal shelters nationwide offer a continuous, affordable supply of wonderful companion animals to choose from. 25% of dogs who enter local shelters are purebred.

If a family has their heart set on a specific breed, a simple internet search will lead to rescue groups for that particular breed in almost all states.

An adorable dog or cat can be adopted from the comfort of your home. Online adoptions are available through www.Petfinder.com, virtual home of 314,319 adoptable pets from 13,763 adoption groups. Other reputable online adoption agencies can be found at

www.adoptapet.com and www.pets911.com

Despite all the shelter dogs in need of homes, there are still 6,000 federally licensed puppy mills breeding and supplying pet stores with a constant stream of puppies.

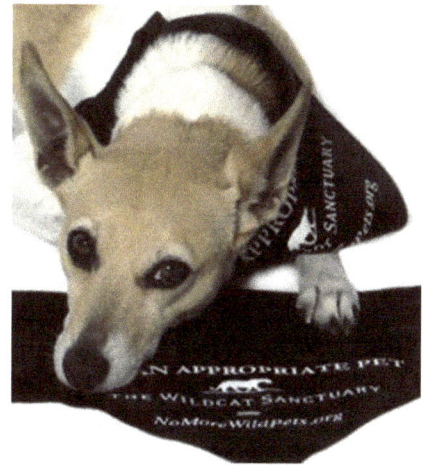

Credit respectyourdog.com

About 4 million dogs are bred in puppy mills each year, while nearly the same numbers are being euthanized in shelters each year.

It's cruel and doesn't make sense. By adopting, rather than shopping for appropriate pets, the abusive puppy mill industry can also be shut down.

What happens when a wild animal is forced to be a pet?

Liberty, a cougar rescued by The Wildcat Sanctuary, is a prime example of what too many captive exotic animals endure.

Most who buy an exotic pet have no idea about the animal's special needs, nor the lifelong debilitating effects caused when they ignore them.

We arrived at a rural farm to pick up Liberty, a cougar being surrendered by her owner. What we found was astonishing—this cougar was no larger than a lynx!

She was emaciated and dehydrated. No one could believe how small she was. Her owner explained Liberty had only gotten milk her first year of life. Liberty had fractured both of her back legs, which had gone untreated. Liberty couldn't extend her back legs fully, and she suffered from a severe curvature of the spine and pelvis.

The tops of her ears were dangling by a small amount of flesh and were about to fall off. She had urine burns on both sides of her tail.

It's hard to imagine an owner would let an animal suffer like this, but it's all too common.

The owner said Liberty wasn't eating or drinking very well either. This was hard to believe since Liberty ate 4 times the first night she arrived at the Sanctuary and 8 additional meals the next day.

She continued to love her food—in fact, she was the first to cry out in excitement when she heard keepers at mealtime—and put on weight each day receiving proper care.

Liberty weighed only 45 lbs. when she was rescued. That's what a 6-month-old cougar should weigh, yet she was 6 years old.

The initial fecal exam showed Liberty also had roundworms and coccidia, a type of bacterial infection.

Good veterinary care is often a luxury for exotic pets since it's so expensive and hard to find. Sadly, in the long run, the animals end up paying the ultimate price.

Baby Jenga, a bobcat, came to The Wildcat Sanctuary when he was just 6 weeks old. Someone in Iowa purchased him from the internet as a household pet, but found out it was illegal in the Des Moines area and surrendered him.

Soon after Baby Jenga arrived, it was obvious something was wrong. His motor skills were impaired and he wouldn't eat on his own.

After several visits to the vet, we found he had brain damage and was touch-and-go for quite some time. It was assumed he was probably dropped during the shipping process from Montana to Iowa when he was just weeks old.

But, after receiving many other surrendered bobcats and lynx purchased from the same breeder in Montana, it became clear that many had similar neurological issues. Unfortunately, the breeder is still selling wildcats via the internet.

So often, people buying exotic pets have no idea what they'll be getting and have no option for returning or re-homing the animal. That's why so many end up in backyard cages, in deplorable conditions, just waiting to die.

WHAT CAN YOU DO TO HELP?

Adopt, don't shop. Don't purchase a pet—domestic or exotic. Always adopt a homeless pet from a shelter or rescue organization and remember to spay/neuter to prevent overpopulation.

Never have your picture taken with an exotic animal or pay to play with one. These are money-making schemes that just encourage rampant breeding of more and more baby exotics. Think about where all these animals will end up when they grow up.

Don't attend traveling exhibitions or roadside attractions featuring exotic wild animals. It's a case of supply and demand. If we can stop the demand for wild animals, we can stop the breeding by suppliers.

Contact fair organizers, malls, or venues exhibiting exotic animals to let them know you will not patronize them. Also, be sure to contact your local news media with letters to the editors or phone calls about the captive wildlife crisis. Like most people, many reporters know little about what's behind these exhibits.

Educate your children, your schools and civic organizations about the inherent abuse of life on the road for circus animals and other exotics on display. You'll be surprised how few people have ever thought about it. The more who know, the more we save.

The Wildcat Sanctuary
PO Box 314
Sandstone, MN 55072

320-245-6871

info@wildcatsanctuary.org
Tax ID: 22-3857401

A Note From the Author

People say I've built a legacy, but it is the animals' legacy. If I only make a fraction of the impact the cats have made on me, then I'm very blessed. Because their legacy inspires change and only in their legacy can we end the captive wildlife crisis. It is the best way we can honor each and every one of them.

Biographies

Executive Director - Tammy Thies

Tammy Thies is the founder of the Wildcat Sanctuary, a 501(c) (3) nonprofit that provides a safe home to felid species including, cougar, tiger, lynx and other wild cats in need of shelter.

Thies has a marketing and journalism degree from the University of St. Thomas. After graduation, she developed and managed advertising campaigns for clients such as Coca-Cola, BMW, Holiday Inn and Timberland.

She is a native Minnesotan and during her advertising career became aware of the need for a sanctuary through her exposure to big cats during photo shoots. She learned that, throughout the United States, tens of thousands of these animals are privately owned as pets and used as performers or for-profit breeding. Too often, the cats outlive their usefulness and have nowhere to go.

Thies made a mid-life career change to become a voice for these animals. She began The Wildcat Sanctuary on 10-acres in Isanti, MN. Now, years later, the Sanctuary houses over 100 residents on 40 acres in Sandstone, MN. Animals are not bought, sold, bred or traded. Each resident is given every opportunity to behave naturally in a wonderful free-roaming environment and receive the best vet care at the on-site animal hospital.

The Wildcat Sanctuary provides educational outreach seminars to educate the public about the captive wildlife crisis across the United States, as well as supporting legislative efforts banning these practices. Thies was very instrumental in testifying on behalf of the Minnesota Exotic Animal Law that bans the ownership of dangerous exotic animals as pets.

Thies has appeared as an expert on the captive wildlife crisis across national media outlets such as the History Channel, Animal Planet and the CNN iReport.

The sanctuary is accredited by The American Sanctuary Association, Global Federation of Animal Sanctuaries, recognized as a top sanctuary by Tigers in America, a member of the Big Cat Sanctuary Alliance, and awarded a 4-star rating by Charity Navigator. The Wildcat Sanctuary is the only big cat sanctuary in the upper Midwest. Tammy has also served on the board of the American Sanctuary Association, as well as steering committees for the Big Cat Sanctuary Alliance.

Editor - Verena Rose

Verena Rose loves animals and has a particular passion for cats. She shares her home with four felines: Jasper and Alice, Ragdoll siblings; and Matty and Missy, rescue siblings. So it can be no surprise that once she discovered The Wildcat Sanctuary, she became an avid follower and ultimately a sponsor for eight of the cats that call TWS their forever home.

She is one of the owners of Level Best Books and functions as the chief financial officer and acquisitions editor. As their representative, Verena is a member of the American Booksellers Association (ABA), the Independent Book Publishers Association (IBPA), the Crime Writers Association (CWA), and the Crime Writers of Canada (CWC).

Verena is the Anthony award-winning co-editor of *Malice Domestic 14: Mystery Most Edible*, the Agatha Award-nominated co-editor of *Not Everyone's Cup of Tea, An Interesting and Entertaining History of Malice Domestic's First 25 Years*, and the Managing Editor of the Malice Domestic anthology series. In addition to serving as Chair of Malice Domestic, Verena is a member of Mystery Writers of America (MWA), a lifetime member of Sisters in Crime-National, a member of Sisters in Crime-Chesapeake, a member of the Historical Novel Society, and a lifetime member of the Jane Austen Society of North America.

Acknowledgements

Thank you to Julie Hanan who worked hard to ensure this book came together to honor those who are now forever free.

The Wildcat Sanctuary wishes to thank all the staff, interns, volunteers and supporters who make the cats care possible.

Our gratitude is extended to the staff of Level Best Books who made this book come to fruition: Verena Rose, Shawn Reilly Simmons, and Rita Owen.

www.ingramcontent.com/pod-product-compliance
Lightning Source LLC
Chambersburg PA
CBHW042337030426

42335CB00030B/3381